The Second Book of
a Devout Pop Picker

Peter Sulley

The Second Book of a Devout Pop Picker
ISBN 978-1-5272-7551-5
First published 2021 in Great Britain

Hot Tub Publishing Limited
27 Old Gloucester Street
London WC1N 3AX
info@hottubpublishingltd.co.uk

For Siobhan and Madeline

Introduction

We are the first generation to enter middle age with pop still fully available and acceptable. Our world of music mirrors that of our children: we have our own radio stations, our own digital TV channels, our own magazines, podcasts, club nights and even weekend festivals – all with their own scenes, all full of acts whose main purpose is to serve us old 'uns - and keep us buying the T-shirts.

Our parents and grandparents didn't have this. In the pre-digital world, many young mums as mine did, would have done the chores with the radio on, listening to Jimmy Young or Tony Blackburn and absorbing the hits for a few more years; but there was stigma attached to hanging on to your youth. "She's a bit past it for all that palaver, ain't she?" was a sneer typical of the 60s and 70s. Men would have been judged no less bluntly.

Having procreated, your means of participation were limited. There was the oldies variety circuit. There were compilation albums of big hits from the old days. Now and then a new release by an old-time artist would soar to the top of the charts. Occasionally tickets for a headline tour by popular veterans would sell out. Eventually there would be BBC Radio 2. But there was nothing close to what our generation has enjoyed. When it came to it, we never actually had to *stop*.

As a schoolboy, I didn't imagine for a second that my peer group would still be doing all this in their mid-50s. I remember a few of my friends' parents jiving at parties, sometimes waxing lyrical about original rock 'n' rollers or sharing exciting memories of the Beatles. But most of them had moved irrevocably on.

I thought there had to be a point where it all simply came to a halt. Such a moment must, I imagined, be lying in wait for me: a natural detachment; a painless un-coupling anaesthetised by age; one that spares you the trauma of being scorned by your fellow adults. You wake up one bright morning and – *pff* – that's it. Seven-inch singles go into a box and the box goes into the attic.

This book recounts the experience of that not happening, along with its attendant anxieties, visions and frustrations. And of course, joys. It is concerned only with events that relate to the music that surrounds one un-named pop picker. It includes the business of buying and owning vinyl and CDs as those formats slipped in and out of fashion. It includes the mental and emotional re-adjustments involved in continuing to seek participation while leaving your youth behind. It also includes bits of social and political background, because that always helps.

An anonymous memoir is a specific kind of device. Firstly, it allows music history to be delivered as a continuous narrative, which is how we experience it. Secondly, although it has its particular context, the attitudes and responses described can more easily represent types, or if you prefer, depict the bloody typical. It was typical of some of us to believe that the 90s was going to see the ultimate triumph of the 60s counterculture. It was typical of some of us to believe that the new popular R&B landgrab of the early 00s meant a final victory for multiculturalism. I assume that music historians care less about who I am and more about having a good original source.

Importantly, it also allows for the celebration of records that snobbery has long considered unworthy, an adjustment increasingly normalised in recent years, due in no small part to the range of media available. The modern world has infinite potential for serving niches. Whether in print, on screen or online, there are safe places for Dooleys fans to hang out, just as there are for Bowie or Prince admirers.

In the noughties, if you found yourself enjoying anything a bit cheesy or shamelessly poppy, you would reveal it with caution - perhaps in a flurry of defiance. Ten years before that, you might not have revealed it at all. But a good record is a good record no matter who makes it. That still feels right, despite the various challenges to the principle - and I'm not alone in that view. This book has plenty of references to that, too.

As before, my style is shaped by consideration of my children. They have a healthy interest in the subject and, if I can deliver it all in a voice they recognise, I can share my knowledge and experience with them in appreciated terms which will remain available after I'm gone. If you find yourself raising an eyebrow over phrasing, there's your explanation.

The Book of a Devout Pop Picker was originally meant to be a single volume, but there was too much to say. I'm glad about that now: it belongs in two parts. The first has the cute, early-childhood stuff; the second has the curious, ageing-fan stuff – and pop's vaunted age bracket of 16-24 is split between the two. It feels neat.

One

Marijuana was the only reasonable response to the 1980s.

I was given my first spliff in late 1982 by a mate on a quiet night in the Sun and Doves pub at the Camberwell end of Coldharbour Lane. We sat in armchairs by the open fire, disguised by the levels of smoke already in the bar. He coached me: I had to hold it down, gently breathe a little out, take it back down, hold it... I did exactly as I was told. It was amazing. It spread in waves. I felt heavily peaceful.

This kind of event is potentially the start of a very slippery slope, but we weren't idiots. None of us ever wanted our minds altered that much, just enough to get a buzz, to make it all different, to make it pleasingly stupid. Experienced and responsible drug users are fully-functioning members of civilised society with a track record of balanced appreciation and fun. Their experience and responsibility is such that, eventually, they stop doing it.

You could smoke anywhere then. People complained about the smell and the fag-ends, but it was all-pervasive. Some introduced "no-smoking areas" but the smoke was free to drift. Pubs were full of smoke. So were restaurants. You could fag it on buses if you went upstairs. You could fag it on the Underground, on the platforms and in designated carriages. It was rare for anyone not to let a smoker light up in their house; non-smokers would scrabble around to find a saucer or something for them to use as an ashtray.

That first Sun and Doves spliff was my entry to a secret underworld. The wider population were not yet experts on the smell. We, on the other hand, became experts on its whole range: the oily odour of dark hash and lighter tones of slate, the rich plumes of weed, the sweet wafts of moist young grass. It was an affordable alternative to being a wine buff; getting mash-up was cheaper than getting drunk. We smoked because the herb was a way to emulate culturally significant figures. But it was also being in the know, an underground nobility, a decision not to join the dickheads.

I was confident about not being a dickhead, but my precise identity was yet to properly congeal. Some of the components were obvious - I had strong football loyalties; I had a clear sense of where I came from. But, more than anything else, I existed in a world of records. By 1982 I had somewhere in the region of twelve hundred seven-inch singles, a solid stack of twelve-inches and a small cupboard full of albums, all lovingly stored and protected. They were my home base. My earliest memories were to do with records; of me, pre-school, sitting on the carpet, staring agape at the speaker on the front of the portable record player as all these powerful, gripping, mind-expanding sounds emerged. I had been lucky with my date of birth – I had formed relationships with new records by the Beatles, the Supremes and other giants from a time now revered as a kind of genesis for our culture.

Pop music was more important than anything else. Records were what spending-money was for. They were what the radio was for. They were what parties were for. They were what a spare ten minutes were for. They were where I came to recharge, to lick my wounds, to be comforted and reassured. They sustained me. At any given point, the soundtrack - that general swirl of current noise on the radio, in shops, coming from open windows and from people humming at bus-stops - had something to contribute. It might have been doing one of a hundred different jobs. But it was doing something.

There had been rapid recent change. In the space of four years, the soundtrack had become almost entirely keyboard-based, a wall of synthetic sounds. Fashion had veered towards the shiny, exclusive and upmarket, leaving earnest downbeats behind. The hippy ethic was on life support. Expectations were raised. Everything was being scrubbed up and it was stressful.

As I got stoned in that pub armchair, 'Buffalo Gals' by Malcolm McLaren and the World's Famous Supreme Team was on the soundtrack. It was an extraordinary record rather than a likeable one. Its beat seemed to stagger, as if it were walking clownishly, bow-legged, balancing on the outsides of its feet. But it was a shop-front. It used an Appalachian square dance as a frame for the emerging street music genres that McLaren had introduced himself to in New York.

There, young DJs were entertaining their neighbourhoods with funky rhythms taken from the drum sections – the "breaks" - of old records, skilfully flicking the disc so as to repeatedly play that precise passage without dropping a beat; a phenomenon which concerned me, both for the sake of the turntable and the record, especially since this technique was called "scratching". If you could "scratch" with distinction, all sorts of tricks were possible, from building long sections of hip-slippin' drums to creating effects with isolated syllables of vocal. 'Buffalo Gals' showcased these and more.

There were dances that went with these genres: robotic dances where kids moved their entire upper body, just like robots; smooth and unearthly. It wasn't long before you were hearing "watch me do my robotics" every few yards. I never knew what the distinction was between robotics and body-popping. Perhaps it was the same thing. Perhaps body-popping was a sub-division of robotics.

The Moonwalk certainly was. This was the oiled, mechanical action of walking forwards whilst actually moving backwards. Those who were good at it had high status. Michael Jackson, now the world's biggest pop star, was good at it. He wore a sequined white glove – just the one - to add to the effect. He made the Moonwalk his own.

Then there was break dancing, which was like no dancing we were used to. On a piece of linoleum, which you carried to the street party yourself, you span. Fast. On your back, like a startled turtle in a cartoon, or on your head, or on your knees. Tabloids reported twisted testicles in a bid to lampoon it on behalf of the uncomfortable. But the uncomfortable were gazing on a flourishing scene full of fresh invention.

It is the autumn of 1983, and three of us are in my step-dad's Mini heading north on the motorway to visit my longest-standing mate (LSM) in his second year of university. There is a C90 cassette of new music in the tape player, an eclectic mix of singles compiled by me on my JVC stack system. My companions are more impatient with the constant switching of genres than they are letting on. There is a lot of rewinding taking place. Much of this is back to the start of '(Hey You) Rock Steady Crew' by the Rock Steady Crew, a female voice chanting the praises of the eponymous gang over tinny synthesised percussion and echoey keyboard. There was something in the lyrics about an electrical canoe - or maybe it was an electrical gnu.

It was catchy and fun, but its backdrop was the scene: street parties, street art, and the synchronised street fashions of the b-boys - those who did the break dancing. On the picture cover, figures from the Crew were depicted as cartoons; on the back, there were tiny photos of them in basketball-kit uniform. It was a window on their landscape. Black neighbourhoods were denied a voice and squeezed by economic measures so they claimed the city and built an alternative world.

Nothing flavoured this urban scenery as much as tags. Tags were the spray-can signatures of gangs, individuals and ideas, ranging from little squiggles to huge, elaborate, metallic splurges that covered walls, street furniture and city trains with shape and colour. I mean, *completely* covered. Here was the black voice; a distinctive, ever-visible presence. When the music was hushed and the clothes tucked away, the tags remained. It swelled from the ground - a look, a fashion, a sound, an Art. Or, gibberish, vandalism and unspeakable racket. Depends how red your neck was. The UK was getting its first taste.

'(Hey You) Rock Steady Crew' was bright, up-tempo, electronic and urban. It certainly boosted morale in that Mini – we didn't care how many times we heard it. Levels of identification with its sound varied among people I spent time with, but nobody was hostile. The first label I heard for this genre was electro-funk.

You had funk. You had electronic music. Calling it "electro" gave it a bit of thrust and sizzle – it's the sort of language attached to powerful consumer goods and super-hero narratives. Adding "electro" to "funk" suggested the re-energising of a long-established genre.

Let's linger on the super-hero narrative aspect. My black friends loved science fiction. Stories about societies in outer space where the righteous gathered to battle injustice - often within their midst - pressed buttons in a way that similar storylines in westerns didn't. I understood this. Westerns where certain cowboys were the real baddies and much nastier than the Indians were refreshing. We were used to being shown redskins and fuzzy-wuzzies as unsophisticated, athletic and creeping towards us in large numbers; a tribe with a single, malicious mind, like a colony of soldier ants. These were not adventure stories for black youngsters to identify with. Those in distant galaxies had more potential.

Space had been part of the funk scenery for years. US group Funkadelic, led by George Clinton, specialised in colourful stage shows featuring a craft called the Mothership, upon which funk was imported from parts of the universe superior to ours. Theirs was a conventional 70s funk band sound, but you couldn't have space travel without cool electronics. Space ships bleeped, blooped and blurped. Put a beat under this and you were in business. It was a great idea. And, as we know, the trouble with having a great idea is that some other buggers have already had it. In this case, it was a group from Düsseldorf in Germany called Kraftwerk.

The influence of Kraftwerk is hard to overstate. Their music was pure electronic gadgetry accompanied by deadpan voices expounding on themes of industry and technology. They themselves were presented as machines, peering into the future and relaying what they saw to us. For black audiences, there was no baggage. Neither was there reliance on conventional studio set-ups. It was a good fit for the breaks scene and Kraftwerk records were extensively copied and sampled.

At the end of the 1980s, it would be said that any piece of modern music was a direct descendant of either James Brown or Kraftwerk. James Brown had made soul funky; his intensely percussive records had been a rallying-point for black awareness and now provided many of the most popular breaks, particularly the drum sections. Kraftwerk had given music-making an open-ended accessibility and a purely electronic base. The breaks scene, with its do-it-yourself ethic, was both vindicated by it and inspired by it.

It was in this scene that James Brown and Kraftwerk became linked. As I write, I am still discovering tracks by both, amazed to hear riffs, melodies and beats familiar from records in my collection that I now realise had copied them. Back at the end of 1983, I knew virtually nothing. I had heard, then ignored, Kraftwerk's 'Autobahn' single while at primary school. I had bought, then hardly played, their single 'The Model', at the start of the previous year; which had got to number one despite being as dull as a soggy Sunday. But I knew nothing more about Kraftwerk. What I knew was electro-funk.

One year previously, while 'Buffalo Gals' was current, I had been doting on 'E.T. Boogie' by the Extra T's, a bubbling morass of bloops and blurps inspired by the family movie *E.T. The Extra-Terrestrial* and only available as an import single. This had been electro-funk. So too had 'Planet Rock' by Afrika Bambaataa and the Soul Sonic Force, a record that I first encountered at a party soon afterwards. A girl we sort of knew had told friends to invite anyone else they thought would make the party good. On a bad night that might have been a recipe for disaster. But this wasn't a bad night and 'Planet Rock' was one of the reasons.

A couple of times at the start of the party I heard people ask about 'Planet Rock', but it meant nothing to me and I ignored it. Later however the room was suddenly stopped in its tracks by a metallic call for party people to get funky. Then a beat burst out, trebly and blurty, joined by an electronic refrain which drifted in and out of the voices and effects that were popping out everywhere. The guy who had put it on quickly arranged everybody in two lines facing each other, then lead us all in a formation dance. We stepped side-to-side in time to the beat, as he introduced a carousel of upper-body movements and passed regular, highly entertaining judgement on our performance. The delightful oddness of the record helped our laughter along. But odd it was: a few minutes in, I was still waiting for it to start properly - then I realised that it wasn't going to. This was it - the heralded 'Planet Rock'. The track is a milestone and is built on Kraftwerk samples.

Nine months later, four of us were sitting in my bedroom having left the pub for a board game and a lump of black. We smoked, we played and we listened to an album called *Electro 1*. It was pure, brilliant escape

- a bundle of electronic mischief, contrasting with the changing mood of the world outside; a treasury of grinding electronic beats, gently harmonising electro-melodies and massive breaks, peppered with all kinds of robot vocals, samples and effects.

The opening track, 'I'm the Packman (Eat Everything I Can)' by the Packman, was based on the arcade game Pac-Man - it doesn't matter where you hide or how fast you run, he's gonna getcha. It segued into 'Jam On Revenge (The Wikki-Wikki Song)' by Newcleus, a series of scenes involving the high-pitched chattering of electro-men and an intergalactic savant called Cosmo, with a rousing, chanted chorus and occasional, gratifying cry of *wikki-wikki-wikki-wikki!* This then transformed into 'Break Dancin' – Electric Boogie' by West Street Mob: big, heavy beats and horns on a loop, sampled - although I didn't then know it - from the Incredible Bongo Band's version of 'Apache'; punctuated by deep robotic chanting and regular visits from a sexy female voice.

These sounds were incredible – a continuation of what 'E.T. Boogie' had promised. I couldn't do robotics, I couldn't do the Moonwalk, I couldn't show off at parties; but I wanted to be part of a scene full of records like these. I taped my friend's copy.

I saw this soundscape as distinct from rap, even though other bits of *Electro 1* had straightforward rapping on it. Yet this music, plus body-popping and tagging, was all part of what we would eventually call hip hop and, for many, responding to any manifestation of it was already a mark of identity. I would discover this quite by accident.

Having worked for a year, I was now back at college making a second attempt at 'A' levels. My earnings had enabled me to buy a drum kit. Thanks to the tutoring I'd had years before, I got up to speed quickly, practising in my room to stay sharp. I found break rhythms, like the one on 'Break Dancin' – Electric Boogie', great fun to use. Soon I was getting involved in various jam and demo sessions. The following spring I was asked to be a temporary member of the pit orchestra at a local secondary school for rehearsals of *Bugsy Malone*.

On my first visit, the assembly hall was crowded with excited, overwhelmingly unruly pupils, ignoring teacher pleas to settle down, many of them racing across the floor at breakneck speed as I set up quietly in the corner, surrounded by a small crowd of intrigued onlookers. Other adults and senior pupils arrived to set up music stands and open instrument cases as the mêlée continued. We struggled to hear each other speak.

But when, quite innocently, I began warming up with my take on 'Break Dancin' – Electric Boogie', everything changed. Within seconds, all loud voices had been extinguished and the hall was full of robotics - earnest concentration gripping the faces of kids moving up and down the floor in their own little bubble, feeling their way along invisible walls and doing the Moonwalk, all trying to out-perform their neighbours. The sound of my drumming filled the air. It was obvious that I had no idea what I had done, because I then switched to a rock rhythm. The chaos returned, continuing until one kid leaned across and, flicking his hand at me, said "Go back, go back, go back." I did so, and, instantly, the noise disappeared and robotics reconquered the hall. It was like putting a coin into a machine.

I loved those tracks from *Electro 1* and with limitless funds I might have got them on vinyl. I was firmly of the opinion that having a record properly was having it on vinyl: not only that, but that having it properly was having it as a single, preferably a seven-inch (I have aired my views on twelve-inch singles elsewhere and will come back to them). But I hung on to my pirated *Electro 1* tape. My money could only go so far and its first port of call was always the current hit parade.

My reverence for the singles chart was enormous and deep-rooted. I had grown up following the Top 30 which, due to changes instigated by Radio 1 in 1978, was now the Top 40. It was the stage upon which great tales unfolded; heroes and villains, angels and demons, clowns and scholars, all parading before us, all doing battle in a never-ending carnival of action. It had been this way for decades.

Being number one in the charts carried massive status, and the incumbent seemed to set the tone for the world around it. This had affected me since the age of eight. I had been overjoyed when the pure pop of 'Mamma Mia' by Abba brought down the sententious tyranny of 'Bohemian Rhapsody' by Queen. I held my head in despair when Lena Martell's 'One Day at a Time' ended the reign of 'Video Killed the Radio Star' by the Buggles after just one week. I basked in the splendour of 'Don't You Want Me' by the Human League lording it up at Christmas following an autumn during which the top spot had been occupied by an endless parade of depressing dross. The chart had a history, one to be proud of, one full of outstanding, meaningful drama.

My collection was only a patchy representation of this. It was the story of my purchases since 1975, the point at which I had started caring for records properly, plus what was salvageable from the years before. It had been added to by three fortuitous hauls, two being from school summer fairs and the other being a pile of clear-outs from a family friend. I wanted more, but I didn't yet know about the record-collecting world, so I concentrated on current music, the stuff that was played on the radio every day. The singles chart and its attendant trappings were still my barometer of importance.

Singles sales had fallen about 17% since their peak in 1978-9, but, in terms of quality, at least for now, the chart retained a broad balance between the glorious, the horrible, the workaday and the just alright. However, since this is early 1984, everything needs to be put into the context of Michael Jackson and his *Thriller* album.

Jackson had launched himself as an adult concern in 1979 when the single 'Don't Stop 'Til You Get Enough' exploded across the firmament. Since then, I had watched his stature and influence expand. He was now the complete showbiz package: a gleaming, sizzling entertainment monolith with trademark moves that youngsters longed to perfect, trademark vocal embellishments that made his sound unique and trademark photoshoots that rendered the brooding portraits of others wooden by comparison. People from any walk of life, and of any age, could pass comment on Michael Jackson from a position of knowledge.

None of this happened to impress me, but, if I voiced any dissent I was shot down. The biggest star in the world was black and brilliant. In the circles I moved in, this was what mattered most. So, if you were put off by the glitzy, family-friendly displays of omnipotence, you kept it to yourself. If you found any of his recent hits dull and emotionally hollow, you kept that to yourself, too. You could sit in pubs or stand at bus stops taking the piss out of Duran Duran, the Police, or just about anyone else that had been at the top of the charts in the last few years, but you never took the piss out of Michael.

'Don't Stop 'Til You Get Enough' had been the lead single from the previous album, *Off the Wall*, which had been a street-level sensation. *Thriller* appeared at the end of 1982. Its first two singles, 'Billie Jean' and 'Beat It', number one and number three respectively, were wolfed down by fans. I loved the third, 'Wanna Be Startin' Somethin'' - a sizzling chunk of energy that helped my summer along nicely. Yet it got no higher than nine, making me wonder whether I would be out of step with this phenomenon no matter what happened.

Albums were producing more singles nowadays. Convention had once been that albums released two: three was pushing your luck a bit. Yet *Off the Wall* had released five singles - *five* - and four had made the Top 10. This was new territory and many saw it as ludicrous, but it didn't matter. This was Michael. *Thriller* would yield a staggering six, the lowest position reached by any of them being eleven. Incredible. And there was the Moonwalk, there was the sequined white glove and there were the videos - all cementing the status of the self-proclaimed King of Pop. Devoted congregations of Michael's People could now be found in every part of the world; leaning in, hoping for a sign.

Perhaps the next sign would be a new video. MTV (Music Television) had been launched in the States in 1981 and, though successful, had come in for early criticism over the shortage of black acts on its schedules. The big-budget videos rolled out to support the singles from *Thriller* began changing all that, none more so than the one for its title track.

The album had been out for over a year when 'Thriller' was released as a single. The idea of important records with supernatural overtones was one I found tantalising. Being creeped-out by old Hammer horror movies had been a regular, late-night TV treat – the menace, the doom-laden bleakness and the not-particularly-happy endings. More recently there had been *American Werewolf in London*, following this tradition but with shocking new special effects, most unforgettably in the scene where the hero turns into a werewolf, an agonising transformation that the viewer sees in sensational detail. In 1983, its director, John Landis, was hired to make the video for 'Thriller'.

The single was in the Top 10 in December and the anticipation surrounding the video was off the scale. MTV aired it for the first time at the start of the month and, during the Christmas holiday, Channel 4 became the first to show it in the UK: at midnight, in keeping with the theme. I went out with a group of friends, one of whom set the video to record it. We returned to his flat rubbing our hands at the prospect and squashed together on the sofa, making sure we had all been to the toilet and had something to munch or sip. But when he pressed play there was some other bollocks on. In disbelieving silence, he wound the tape backwards and forwards looking for Michael. To no avail. He had set the wrong channel.

Those able to see it, which eventually included us, were wowed by its mega-budget slickness and colour. The costume design, the make-up and the widescreen synchronised choreography were like nothing seen before in pop. Its storyline: Michael is walking in the night air with his date, teasing her with terrifying visions of bloodthirsty, yellow-eyed zombies, to which the audience is lavishly treated. After we have seen it all, he relents, reassuring her that he was just kidding, but in a final twist he turns to camera, grinning, and with yellowing eyes.

It was a champion package: a known song, a sparkling new video - a synthesis of the familiar and the completely new. The widescreen synchronised choreography was intoxicating if you were impressed by widescreen synchronised choreography. The whole thing was intoxicating if you were impressed by Michael.

I was suspicious of music videos anyway. Everything paled beside what was on the vinyl. I knew what records were capable of doing, all by themselves, in their own context, unaffected by videos, unaffected by the public image of the artist. Music videos were a discrete form of entertainment with no obligation to recognise the subtleties in the song they were supposedly promoting. Often, these subtleties weren't particularly subtle and they still failed to recognise them.

I didn't *avoid* videos, I just didn't seek them out. I was always more comfortable with the radio. While at secondary school, I had heard almost all my new records on the Radio 1 *Breakfast Show*. Many of my peers listened to London's commercial station, Capital Radio, which I occasionally dipped into for as long as I could stand the adverts. BBC Radio 1 was home turf. The current presenter of the flagship *Breakfast Show* was Mike Read, whose straightforward, cheery style I was perfectly comfortable with, but he had been doing it for three years now and straightforward-cheery was doing less for me these days. I was going off the *Breakfast Show*.

I had similar feelings towards what was still the main televisual diet for fans of chart music, *Top of the Pops*. This had once been a showcase for new songs performed by artists on sparsely decorated stages which you could enjoy without distractions. The fact that they mimed to the recordings was something you accepted as part of the deal; it was better to hear the actual record than an inferior version for the sake of it being live.

The jiggling studio audiences were a curious mix; some clearly fashion-aware, some wearing clothes apparently loaned from parents, sometimes dancing coolly to the beat, sometimes looking as if they had got into the lift looking for *Gardener's Question Time* and pressed the wrong button. At any rate, it was all comfortably familiar and, for most of the time, you could ignore the bits you didn't like.

But I was becoming less tolerant. The bits I didn't like now included the expensive and aspirational fashion exhibited by performers. This was typified by the gloves. There were gloves everywhere - tight little leather gloves for guys, silky little gloves for girls, with the occasional pair stretching silkily up towards the elbows. It was an integral part of the up-levelling of public display. They now all had to look like they were going out on the town, to win the approval of sniffy doormen and be waved inside. In their fucking gloves.

The studio audience dressed smart rather than expensive, but there was something else - floor managers were handing them flags, balloons and plastic bowler hats, and ordering them to whoop and grin. The result was a studio full of gratuitous whooping and grinning. Artists performed their hit songs in clearings amidst this nonsense, or on stages surrounded by it, or up in gantries with balloons and grins bouncing against their shoulders. It didn't make the records any better. It did make viewing painful. The presenters - all Radio 1 disc-jockeys - joined in with the fun because it was in their contracts. This fun was very hard to understand. It was just whooping and waving balloons.

The presenters nevertheless got into the spirit. All except one. One who, although introducing each item as per the script, injected enough individuality to let you know that he thought it was all a bit silly. He actually thought more than that, but the contract forbade. He would scarcely have played a note from it in his show, a late-evening shopfront for the different, the non-conforming and the objectionable, which, for many, was a haven of sanity and reassurance. His name was John Peel.

His programme was an institution. I kept tuning in, only usually to find that I couldn't stand it for long. It had occasionally introduced me to things that I genuinely loved; and genuinely loving something on John Peel was a good feeling. But as far as most people were concerned, his show was "weird stuff". It was harsh electronica, winding deserts of bare beats, roots reggae, thrashy late-punk and a whole mass of other curiosities.

Its audience was a genuine community and Peel read out letters from listeners, almost regardless of their tone and purpose. Sometimes he would break with his characterful northern English deadpan to exclaim "Now this is the type of letter I like to get..." and then read a note from someone saying that they never used to like reggae until a certain track on his show made them curious and they were now avidly exploring the genre. Moments such as this seemed to confirm his purpose.

One hit record huge in this community was 'Blue Monday' by New Order, a track I knew well: a heavy electro-mechanism with sharp edges made for the dance floor - equal parts menace and positive charge. It had been a big favourite at certain clubs I'd visited and was the reigning number one in Peel's established end of year listeners' poll, the Festive Fifty. It was unusual for a John Peel favourite to be a hit on the pop charts, but the twelve-inch-only 'Blue Monday' had reached number twelve in the spring. On the alternative scene, New Order were a big deal.

Other names were familiar to me from the show's introduction, but I rarely found out what they sounded like. I formed mental images anyway. There was a group called the Cocteau Twins. The fact that there was also a successful chart act called the Thompson Twins made me suspect that "Twins" was some kind of band name fad. But I knew that someone called Cocteau was, or had been, an artist or writer or something, and was almost certainly French; it brought to mind drifting images of fey youths in silk shirts gesticulating from loungers in an attic. In the realm of John Peel music, their sound could be anything - I wasn't motivated to find out.

Likewise the Smiths, whose name brought to mind men with neat side-partings in plain jumpers. But I knew what they sounded like: there had been a single before Christmas, a skippity beat and twiddly-widdly guitar with a nonchalant voice saying he hadn't "got a stitch to wear". It annoyed me, particularly the twiddly-widdly guitar. It would be ages before I found out it was called 'This Charming Man' and had got into the Top 30. It was on an episode of *Top of the Pops* that I hadn't seen and had made quite an impression. They were already heroes, both in their home city of Manchester and among the John Peel community.

Peel was choosy and challenging. Steve Wright was not. I listened to *Steve Wright in the Afternoon* from start to finish almost every day. I had study time after lunch and would race home to collate notes and write essays in an empty house with the radio right next to me. His playlist was pure Top 40, like just about everything on Radio 1 in the daytime. But between records, and in addition to traffic reports and other announcements, you'd hear a knock, the creak of a door, and in would come some comedy character, to comment on the show, utter a catchphrase, or simply make a noise.

There was a whole load of them. There was a Sloane Ranger, a personification of city-dwelling wealth and privilege that was now admired when once it had been ridiculed: his job was to say "Okay, yah" in as many convoluted ways as could be devised. There was the Professor, who dropped by to be obtuse in a German accent; there was Gervaise the hairdresser, who dropped by to be camp; there was Mr Angry from Purley, who phoned up to rant.

These characters were established types. But then there were the geese. The geese were surreal and chaotic and were simply geese, a whole gaggle of them. They bust into the studio at random, aggressively, until ushered away, with Wright yelling "Get the geese off!" The geese were wicked.

Radio history is dotted with stuff like this. Wright was no doubt heavily influenced, particularly by Americans. There had always been characters on music radio - I could remember Tony Blackburn's barking dog Arnold and Noel Edmonds' gravel-voiced milkman Flynn.

More recently, Lenny Henry, one of the first black performers to enter the UK television mainstream, had a weekend show on Radio 1 in which a character called Delbert Wilkins broadcast from a pirate radio station called the BBC (Brixton Broadcasting Corporation). Hearing black accents doing good situation comedy on the radio caused a real stir of excitement. Years before, Radio 1 DJ Dave Lee Travis had put forth a black character called Edwin Claat, whose mocking dumbo-darkie voice he did himself. Delbert Wilkins was a token of progress.

But *Steve Wright in the Afternoon* trumped all these with its sheer pace. The whole show was sustained quickfire. In the same way that, six years before, I had buzzed listening to Adrian Juste pepper his Saturday morning programme with comedy extracts, Wright used his parade of characters to keep adrenaline levels high between records. Indeed, they often made the records seem better. This is straightforwardly done with adrenaline. That dull record we hear as we're trooping out of the football ground sounds great today because our team got a late winner. At a party, we suddenly see merit in some soppy load of rubbish because that girl kissed us as it came on. Steve Wright yells "Get the geese off!" and suddenly we want our own copy of 'Get Out of Your Lazy Bed' by Matt Bianco.

Matt Bianco were, in many ways, the quintessential early 80s chart act. Their keyboard-based sound was a bit jazz and a bit Latin; they were well turned-out; they moved with cool control and clicked their fingers (their girl singer wore gloves). They had a saxophone and a double bass. We were seeing the double bass more often these days. It had been unthinkable in the previous decade, when hairy-arsed rock had given way to electrified glam and then to electrified new wave. Even in the orchestras backing soul and disco records, the double bass had been the chubby dork in the corner. Now it wore a tilted hat, drew the eye and smoked without coughing.

This was because it no longer meant rockabilly-revival. It meant jazz. Or at least jazz *flavour*. Jazz was cool, it was sophisticated and it was expensive. It evoked classy, go-gettin' mid-century USA - in particular, its cities, in particular, New York and the affluence of those that had made it there. Fashion shoots, music videos and advertising campaigns gave us visions of white-cloth suppers on Manhattan rooftops, or strolling through shin-high breakers on a Caribbean beach - or being *en route* from one to the other. These visions were of mixed origin but, in the same way that our Christmas is a Dickensian snowscape, this new affluence coalesced around the zing of Eisenhower's America.

Images of an elevated existence, where cocktails were being served and the double bass was being lazily thrummed, moved centre stage. Girls became several parts Audrey Hepburn, with a concentrated, businesslike femininity; guys became several parts Frank Sinatra, with stares that suggested they were going to get their way. Latin intertwined with this, providing flavours of exotic, palm-fringed destinations that only those with wealth had access to and only those with style would be interested in. Tropical vegetation had once been the reserve of naff theatre reviews and cruise ships, but now it framed stages, adorned video shoots and decorated night clubs from Dover to Dundee. Jazz and Latin were dangled before us. Aspiration was in.

Artists didn't have to be explicitly jazz or Latin to be affected by this. It was in the air. You could catch a full-on fever or merely suffer the odd sneeze. It translated into the Top 40 in various ways. The insistent, driving beats of new wave, ska and late disco, so dominant in 1980, had been swept away. Rhythms now belonged on bongos rather than floor toms. The Bossa Nova formed the basis of many, the most glaring of which went *dit, d'diddit, dit-dit d'dit*. A record called 'Oblivious' by Aztec Camera, modelled this rhythm and its success depressed the hell out of me. I needed music to mirror and soothe my churning early-adult emotions - I didn't need to be doing the bloody cha-cha.

Some records used the feel explicitly, others merely had a whiff of it; but it drifted around us as we slept. A few years earlier, bands had been scowling beside pock-marked brick walls on council estates: now they were relaxing at a glass table beside a cappuccino and a packet of French cigarettes. It was just fashion, a change driven by the aspirational zeitgeist. Still, during the following few years, I would see more than one music fan mocking the sound of a record by going *dit, d'diddit, dit-dit d'dit* while shaking a pair of invisible maracas. It wasn't only me.

Paul Weller had been front man for the Jam, a thrashy new wave band who emerged from the punk explosion to become figureheads of the 1979 mod revival, racking up an impressive list of hits including

16

four number ones. The anger and disdain displayed by the young Weller had chimed perfectly with his vast audience. In a shocking move at the end of 1982, he suddenly broke up the band and was now in a group called the Style Council, cooling his demeanour and signing his sleeve notes "The Cappuccino Kid".

Following the loud intensity of their first two singles - which may, we imagined, have fallen off the back of the Jam lorry - their sound lightened, too. They embraced continental chic and made reference to classic, non-stompy soul artists. It could be argued with good reason that this was all firmly in the footsteps of the early mods, which was okay, because it was the later mods they now wanted to distance themselves from. In doing so, they were fully embraced by a contemporary crowd, and they certainly had a *dit, d'diddit, dit-dit d'dit* side to them.

Matt Bianco, on the other hand, were *dit, d'diddit, dit-dit d'dit* from head to toe. Their music was crammed with tropical leaves and expensive sunglasses. The album *Whose Side Are You On* could have been accompanied from start to finish by a bartender deftly shaking a margarita to the beat. Its best single, 'Half a Minute', peaked just outside the Top 20 at the end of the year and it featured the most *dit, d'diddit, dit-dit d'dit* sound of all. It came from a South American percussion instrument called the cuica. The cuica made some think of a wood pigeon in a grass skirt; it made others think of an asthmatic donkey.

Whatever it made you think of, early-80s pop was its day in the sun and it was one of the most annoying sounds ever conceived. Two years before, the number two hit 'Annie, I'm Not Your Daddy' by Kid Creole and the Coconuts (from the album *Tropical Gangsters*, note) had it going throughout the chorus. Now it was on 'Half a Minute' and in far too many other places. It remains an emblem of the days when people were ready and willing to release singles with cocktail umbrellas stuck in them.

'Get Out of Your Lazy Bed' was Matt Bianco's first hit, a fast-swinging slice of cheerful electronic jazz that was climbing the chart in mid-February 1984, when my enthusiasm for *Steve Wright in the Afternoon* was at its peak. That week's top 40 was representative of an important transitional time. Let's look at its detail.

It included the new Style Council single 'My Ever Changing Moods', a candified take on early-70s soul hero Curtis Mayfield with a few horns thrown in. It was a high new entry at number eight, one of only two records to enter the charts inside the Top 10 in the first quarter of the year. The other was right above it, spending its second week at number two – 'Radio Ga Ga' by Queen.

Queen had been visiting the upper reaches of the chart for over a decade, but 'Radio Ga Ga' was their first chart single for a while and anticipation was high. Its lyric praised the power of radio, recognising its purifying effect, both as a matter in itself and as a counterbalance to the imagination-narrowing onslaught of music videos. This reflected my feelings about music video and provided comforting echoes of 'Video Killed the Radio Star' by the Buggles.

But it sounded dull and, ironically, its meaning was somewhat overshadowed by its video, the main scene of which featured the band coldly leading an audience in regimented handclaps for the chorus, its setting reflecting early-century science fiction but the tone reflecting one of 1984's main preoccupations, the novel *1984* by George Orwell. This had been written in 1949 as a fascistic nightmare but, now the year had arrived, we were alert for signs that its premonitions were materialising and Queen seemed happy to provide one with their video. Given that its chorus sequence is what people remember, you might conclude that the point of 'Radio Ga Ga' had been so well-made as to render it unnoticeable.

There was also something austere and automatous about the Eurythmics, mainly due to the androgyny of front woman Annie Lennox, whose moulded, orange hair and hard cyber-expression had made huge impact a year before. Their first success was the synthetic chant 'Sweet Dreams (Are Made of This)', a single which had impressed just about everybody and reached number two here, but had gone to number one in the States. Together with the singer's look, it seemed to announce that the new decade was now properly underway.

'Here Comes the Rain Again' was the latest in their subsequent string of hits, closer in feel to 'Sweet Dreams (Are Made of This)' than those in between, and far less objectionable than the previous one, the shockingly jolly, steel-pan-wielding 'Right by Your Side', which, if not quite *dit, d'diddit, dit-dit d'dit,* had certainly cast admiring glances in its direction. I accepted 'Here Comes the Rain Again' as an apology. It got to eight.

Above it as it dropped away was a new single by the Smiths, 'What Difference Does It Make?' This was much more like it – a rousing, twanging guitar riff with both feet planted on the floor; swaggering momentum, big drums, a powerful, droning vocal full of pained meaning - I was mad about it. I played it over and over, high as a kite. Its peak of number twelve seemed like nonsense.

'(Feels Like) Heaven' by Fiction Factory had gone all the way to six. This was a heavyweight keyboard super-lovely, full of melodic and vocal contrast; a glorious tune that I've never heard anyone say a bad word about. It was slipping down the chart now, but I was still playing it loads and so was Steve Wright.

The best of the (few) explicitly danceable singles was 'Let the Music Play' by Shannon, a piece of thumping, sparkling electronic soul which sat neatly alongside *Electro 1*. Just as rhythmic and noisy, but far poppier, was 'Girls Just Wanna Have Fun' by Cyndi Lauper. Instantly appealing, although it made me pause to wonder: does "fun" mean sex or just laughter? I went on from here to imagine the circumstances under which sex and laughter would combine from a girl's perspective and ended up retreating from the whole question.

Just below it in the Top 10 was something more clearly meant for the dancefloor: an upbeat sound, an upbeat mood and an upbeat message on a record called 'Holiday'; a simple declaration of happiness and anticipation. It would be nice to have a day's holiday, to get together and celebrate. Just one day. Perfectly reasonable. Its sound was a blend of bright citrus and back alleys. Its beat raised the spirits. My happy soul-weekender friends liked it.

It was by a singer called Madonna, a name which, at that point, I had only ever associated with the Mother of God. I allowed it to amuse me. On *Top of the Pops* she did a funny, slightly clumsy dance with high-swinging arms which I did my best to forget. It was on the distinctively yellow Sire label, which had, in its time, been home to early punk notables the Ramones, noisy new wave scamps the Undertones and brainy new wave band Talking Heads. Such company rendered 'Holiday' even cuter.

Among these newcomers were more established acts. Duran Duran, early starters in this new era, were number nine with the rollicking 'New Moon on Monday'. I got the feeling of songwriting-by-numbers listening to it, but it didn't make me like it any less. Madness, who really belonged to the previous era, were maintaining a presence with the subdued, reflective, eponymous 'Michael Caine', featuring the actor himself saying "My name is Michael Caine" before each chorus. Puzzling and captivating.

For this round-up, I've saved two number ones until last. Rocketing up to eleven and due to take the top slot in two weeks was '99 Red Balloons' by Nena. Who was German. We were still being funny about Germans. Popular opinion had it that she was nice-looking but probably had hairy armpits. It was an anti-war song set against Cold War tensions in Berlin, with hard-chugging guitar rhythm and keyboard flavours reminiscent of early Kim Wilde records. This made it odd, but it created its own atmosphere to match the subject matter. The writer had been at a West Berlin concert as balloons were released into the sky, and had wondered what someone in uniform on the other side of the wall might suspect if they drifted their way - going on from there to imagine military response and nuclear apocalypse.

We remained in the shadow of the nuclear threat inherent in the Cold War. Friends of mine had a huge wall poster, depicting a parody of the movie-hoarding for *Gone with the Wind*, with the embracing co-stars replaced by US president Ronald Reagan and UK prime minister Margaret Thatcher and a giant mushroom cloud filling the sky behind them. This kind of thing remained part of our consciousness. I had been terrified of nuclear attack four years earlier, while the Americans and Soviets had been squaring up to each other in the Middle East. But my feeling now was that, if we hadn't been blown to bits in 1980, we probably weren't ever going to be, and that a kind of mutually-assured-destruction chic had set in. It didn't make me sceptical about anti-nuclear views, but it did make me relax.

Speaking of which, the record at number one in this chart was 'Relax' by Frankie Goes to Hollywood: the first number one to be overtly and uncompromisingly gay in a way visible to everybody. Prior to this, homosexuality in pop had been merely muttered about - tolerated because it was a mere component in something that happened to appeal to a broad audience. At the end of 1978, the gay inference in 'Y.M.C.A.' by the Village People had been made clear, but it was a jolly, clap-along disco tune that granny quite liked. 1981's 'Tainted Love' by Soft Cell was for everyone but it was quickly recognised that singer Mark Almond was gay. Rumours circulated maliciously about his personal life, and yet 'Tainted Love' was - rightly - adored by so many people for so many reasons that it all seemed insignificant.

"Poof" and "queer" were everyday terms, usually referring to anything judged less than masculine; they were often synonymous simply with "idiot" or "wally". But because of Britain's pantomime tradition, flamboyant camp found a safe haven in various corners of the entertainment industry. If someone made you laugh, or sing, or do a silly dance, you smiled and applauded.

Using the word "poof" was a long-standing habit of mine, but times were changing and such things were being challenged. Gay bashing was no longer laughed about. Two people I knew completely surprised me when they told me they were gay, so any prejudice I might once have harboured was gone. Yet violence was still common, verbal abuse was all too easy and sniggering behind the hand was even easier. Advancement required caution. It was all very tenuous. Gently does it. Then 'Relax' by Frankie Goes to Hollywood came crashing through the wall like an out-of-control Sherman.

There was nothing understated, hesitant or apologetic about any of it. It was a mid-paced throb of measured, four-to-the-floor stomps and huge, swooshing effects from the latest technology, all piloted by production man of the hour Trevor Horn. The word "relax" exploded from the start of each chorus; the lyric then advising on what to do "when you want to come". Probably innuendo: the kind of thing we were used to. The word "come" could easily be explained away and the band publicly denied any sexual meaning. However, there was a subsequent line that could be heard as "When you want to sock it to it" or, alternatively, "When you want to suck it, chew it". You believed what you wanted to believe.

In truth, only two of the five were gay – the tall moustachioed one and the lead singer. The others were just group members enjoying the limelight. One of these had a moustache too, but it wasn't a *gay* moustache. None of this mattered, though: they were Frankie Goes to Hollywood and they had made 'Relax'. It had already rocketed into the Top 10 when Mike Read, in a splutter of disgust, removed it mid-play on the Radio 1 *Breakfast Show* and it was thereafter banned by the BBC. This kind of thing does a record no harm at all, especially when linked to the burgeoning alternative and overseen by a producer whose work is defining the sound of the moment. It went to number one and stayed there for five weeks.

I was beginning to see anything alternative as a kind of ally, so I wanted to like 'Relax'. I bought it, because I was in the habit of buying records that I thought were important. Certainly, 'Relax' felt important. But it also felt dull and plodding and I hardly played it, particularly when '(Feels Like) Heaven', 'What Difference Does It Make?' and 'Holiday' were elsewhere in the record box. The scale of its popularity was hard for me to understand. I would feel very differently about the next Frankie Goes to Hollywood single.

That, then, was the breadth of the soundtrack in that mid-February week. I partook of it. But I didn't really belong anywhere in it. It didn't really apply to me. There was nowhere that I could feel I was *participating*, beyond liking some records and disliking others. I had been here before and, as then, I turned to the past.

Annie Nightingale is a legend. She was the only regular female presenter on Radio 1 and had been for ages. But she was above the common herd of daytime chart jocks. I got this feeling not from experience of her shows (since I rarely listened to them) but because I knew she had once presented *The Old Grey Whistle Test* on TV, a serious music programme for serious music fans, featuring artists bearing the stamp of credibility. It was on late at night and consisted of live studio performances with a few videos thrown in; or, alternatively, collages of early-century cartoons and other odd clips, to accompany tracks for which there was neither live band nor video. All this gave it a sense of gravitas. Annie had form and status.

I happened to catch her on the radio one day, doing an analysis piece about how youngsters were now habitually referencing the 60s. Having enjoyed the 1979 mod revival, kids had gone on to idealise the decade.

But what she actually said was: "... many teenagers today wish they had been born in the 60s". As this was 1984, most teenagers actually had.

I myself was no longer a teenager but I had good 60s credentials. I had been born in 1963. I could, so my mum told me, operate the record player before I was three, and I had formed big opinions on a long list of current records prior to starting infant school. When, in 1969, I started getting pocket money, my mum assumed I would budget to spend an amount each day on sweets. But I saved it up and bought more records. In the summer that I finished primary school, I fell in love with mid-60s Motown and spent the next three years imbibing it.

At the end of 1978, I acquired a copy of the *Guinness Book of British Hit Singles*, the first book which enabled me to look up any chart hit by any artist, from any year, and find its catalogue number, highest chart position and number of weeks on the chart. I began using it to build a solid base of knowledge about the decade which, at that point, dominated its pages. I digested statistics concerning the Beatles, the Hollies, the Seekers, and anyone else that had ever meant anything to the early me. Then, suddenly, at around the same time as Annie Nightingale was discovering the need for a calculator, I had a new line of enquiry.

Like most other 80s families, we were members of a video rental club. This enabled us to hire, for anything from 50p to £2, a plastic brick containing a tape that ran between two internal spools, with a movie, or a TV series, or a documentary on it. You fed this into your video player, either via a contraption that rose from its centre like a theatre trap door, or by now more commonly, by feeding it into a slot at the front. Once in, it paused, thought about it, then gave a series of metallic mutterings to let you know it was ready for the play button to be pressed. Decades down the line, it's easy to snigger at such clunky technology, but in 1984 it was still exciting to watch a movie that you could pause if you needed the loo. Once, all we had was TV and cinema. Now we had this. Videos were brilliant.

A few hundred yards east of the Sun and Doves, beside a building that had once been a cinema, was a hut that housed the video club. I was in there one day when something unusual caught my eye. It was a documentary called *Girl Groups: The Story of a Sound*. On the cover were pictures of the Supremes, a group I knew very well, the Ronettes, who I knew because of *Phil Spector's Christmas Album*, plus the Angels and the Dixie Cups. I took it home.

The interviews and clips provided a narrative on songwriters in early-60s America, clustering together in the employment of music publishers and producers who creamed off the best of their work to ensure a continuation of hits. It was a production line. The most famous address on this scene was in New York: 1619 Broadway - the Brill Building – where the likes of Neil Sedaka and Neil Diamond made their names, as did young couples Barry Mann and Cynthia Weil, Ellie Greenwich and Jeff Barry, and Gerry Goffin and Carole King. Between them, this crowd wrote a list of songs that you will know just because you are walking around and breathing: 'You've Lost That Lovin' Feeling', 'I'm a Believer', 'Do Wah Diddy Diddy', 'River Deep – Mountain High', 'The Loco-Motion'. With a little investigation, you might discover that you know several times this many.

The publishers farmed them out to whoever needed them, with the result that the same song could be a regional hit for one artist, a nationwide hit for someone else, then go to number one in the UK with a band from a British city. The songs directly addressed the concerns of teenagers, who were still a relatively new phenomenon. They had emerged in affluent, post-war America as a distinct demographic - independent, energetic and passionate, not yet married, and with money to spend. Entire industries sprang up to cater for them. The primal energies of rock 'n' roll had provided an electrifying soundtrack with its crazy noise and intoxicating rhythms. It had delivered the additional benefit of alarming the older generation with its wildness and rebellion, its associations with drink and debauchery, as well as the fact that it was rooted in black music, when any link between whites and "negroes" was taboo.

However, by the end of the 50s, things had changed. The leading lights of rock 'n' roll were off the scene: Buddy Holly was dead, Little Richard was working for Jesus, Jerry Lee Lewis and Chuck Berry had fallen foul of personal scandals, and Elvis Presley was in the army. The industry, now fully aware of how much money could be made selling records to teenagers, filled the gaps they had left; replacing primal energy with dewy-eyed longing and stuffing the charts with male pop idols and girl groups.

Every era has had its hit factories. A percentage of record people will always take a hard-nosed, direct route to the approval of young listeners, working with as close to a formula as they can manage and, if they find a good one, milking it to the last drop. And when I say "record people", the last thing I mean is performers - when the Beatles first landed in America in 1964, the fact that they had their own personalities and wrote their own songs was revolutionary. In the half-decade preceding Beatlemania, record people organised and manipulated everything to maximise the flow of dollars. This cynical marketing of pop happened on TV, radio and the pages of magazines, but it usually happened first in the recording studio.

However, there is a case for saying that it happened first in the cubby-holes of the Brill Building. These songwriters had to market their songs to producers who were under no obligation to take them. If it didn't sound like a hit, it was rejected. One way of telling if a new song had potential was to listen to the janitors pushing brooms and mops around the place - perhaps a little slowly as they were older and going grey - as fresh compositions were being tried out on pianos and guitars. If a new tune caught their ear and they started whistling it, the writers were thrilled. It was going to be a hit - it had passed the old grey whistle test.

Cynically conceived, approved by the middle-aged, forced on performers reared on gospel or rock 'n' roll who really did not want to sing such saccharine ditties. Doesn't sound great does it? And yet out of it came some of the most thrilling records in history. It fed mainly on themes of clean-cut romance and happy-ever-after, but the writers and producers knew enough about their audience to give them something truly riveting, vividly reflecting their longings for falling in love ('Be My Baby' by the Ronettes), wedding days ('Chapel of Love' by the Dixie Cups), intense melodrama ('Leader of the Pack' by the Shangri-La's), gritty soap-opera action ('My Boyfriend's Back' by the Angels) and pre-liberation teenage sex ('Will You Love Me Tomorrow' by the Shirelles). Okay, so 'Chapel of Love' is a bit wet, but these others bloody aren't. They plugged into their audiences in the most direct way possible and slammed the voltage up. They are works of genius.

There was more where this lot came from. We haven't even mentioned Motown yet. It was all illustrated by *Girl Groups: The Story of a Sound*, and it swept me up like a janitor's broom. This new interest coincided with learning about a record shop in Croydon called Beano's, which, since I lived in South London, was only a bus ride away. It was a *secondhand* record shop, which was a new one on me. I had collected original oldies from here and there, but never from a dedicated outlet. Of course, there was a whole population out there who knew about record fairs and collector's shops. But I didn't. My first visit to Beano's was my first inkling.

I found it in the late winter gloom behind canopied market stalls. The frontage had an old, tumbledown look, but behind the door was the feel of a library, except there was a record playing - the Beatles' "White" album, I think. It was dark and the atmosphere was close. I had spent my life buying records from big, flash record stores in the West End, or brightly-lit branches of Woolworths or WH Smith, or small local record stores that let in plenty of natural light. My most frequently-visited outlet was A1 Stores in the Walworth Road, an electronics shop with a record department deep at the back, but even that had light and space. This was all drifting cigarette smoke and disapproval.

Serious, brooding men leant across long stacks of album covers arranged at midriff height in wooden racks. The walls were plastered with old gig posters and caked-on pages from the music press. It was the first time I had seen this but in time I would come to recognise it as default décor for certain types of establishment. Apart from the Beatles, there was no sound save periodic muttering between sullen customers and the two sullen members of staff behind the counter, beside which was a sullen door leading to some other sullen area.

I peered through the gloom, wondering where the singles were. Finally, I went to the counter, waited until someone looked at me, and asked about singles.

"Upstairs" he mumbled.

I gave a jovial chuckle. "Oh, there's an upstairs, is there?"

He made a big, unsmiling gesture towards a large sign on the wall, which said: "More upstairs." I couldn't get through the door quickly enough.

On the first floor, the ceiling was lower and there were singles everywhere. Wooden racks full of them went right along one wall. I can't remember how they were organised, but it was perhaps by decade, because I quickly became distracted by hits from my primary school days; mid-70s glam-pop, big hit records that I hadn't been that keen on at the time but which I now revered, either for their status or for their time-machine qualities - three beats in and I'm ten again, seeing what I saw, feeling what I felt. Brilliant.

I got 'Devil Gate Drive' by Suzi Quatro and 'Jealous Mind' by Alvin Stardust (consecutive number ones from early 1974, which, in some moods, is my favourite ever pop year). I think they were £1.20 or something each. I had taken £10 out of my Post Office savings and had an additional pocketful of silver. I flicked on, slipping deeper into a mid-70s mire, oblivious to my surroundings and, before long, I had a pile that needed thinning out.

On the other side of the room stood an open cubicle, inside which sat a man with a beard and long straight hair, who could have been anything from forty to eighty. He reminded me of the hermit in *Monty Python's Life of Brian*. The turntable beside him was providing the background sounds for the room. Between having to change records, he was quietly sorting through a pile of singles, occasionally taking one from its sleeve to look it over, perhaps give it a careful wipe with his cloth. The singles in this pile were instantly recognisable as 60s – I remembered the designs from the box of seven-inch treasure that my aunt and uncle occasionally got out; they were a far cry from the plain sleeves that contained mid-70s ones. Suzi and Alvin had been exciting enough, but this really raised the stakes. I lingered, peering awkwardly to see more. Then I saw the crates.

Wooden crates originally made to carry certain brands of soft drink were the perfect size and as tough as hell. The singles in my bedroom were still stored in converted crisps boxes, one inside another, cut down at the sides so that the records peeped out, with a hardback book at each end for reinforcement - just about okay for a private collection in a bedroom. But it was different if you were selling them or lugging them in and out of venues. Wooden drinks crates were just the thing.

Up behind the hermit, there were maybe twenty of them, each with a label denoting their genre. I can confidently imagine that one said "Beatles", one "Bowie", a further one "Tamla-Motown" and another "reggae", but the one I remember for sure was the one that said "girl groups". My heart leapt. I had only considered non-Motown girl groups as a specific genre because of that video, but here they were: long-considered, long cared-for.

The hermit didn't look up. I was perhaps occasionally guilty of overbearing enthusiasm on a given day but muttering and mumbling seemed to be the requirement here and I was learning to be cautious. I lingered, hoping he would look up. He didn't. Perhaps you needed a special pass to get access to the crates. I didn't feel worthy of any special pass. I was clutching a pile of singles on RAK, Bell and Magnet and was aware of how people generally felt about the 70s, with its industrial action, its flared trousers and its hairy chests. The prevailing winds were glad to be away from it.

I had to ask. I can't remember what I said, but it would almost certainly have combined hesitation, resignation and self-deprecation in one short sentence. The hermit turned, made a non-lexical noise that I assumed was one of annoyance, then turned back to his pile. Just as I was about to creep away, he stood up and extracted the girl groups crate, setting it on the counter before me and turning away again.

I flicked through various curious and exciting things on a range of labels and at a range of prices. But then I found an original UK version of 'My Boyfriend's Back' by the Angels, on Mercury. This tough, street-corner love story had serious status. I checked the condition was good. It was £8, which was a lot. I managed to get a look at the Tamla-Motown crate too, but despite some exciting items from a canon that I knew very well indeed, there was nothing in it to match 'My Boyfriend's Back'. A few minutes later I was carrying it from the shop along with Suzi and Alvin.

Shopping at Beano's opened up a whole new world. Not only did I begin to develop new knowledge about artists, labels and great records that had not been UK hits, but I also began a practical module on removing sticky price labels from record centres. Beano's used those little price labels familiar from corner shops – rectangles with the corners missing – and stuck them directly on to the paper centres of the singles in the long racks. I quickly learned that peeling up the edges and pulling them off ripped the label, which was demoralising. If the label was black, it could be sort-of fixed with marker pen, but that wasn't the point. In response, I developed a painstaking method of scratching and easing them away over a period of minutes, but that didn't always prevent ripping either; and even when it did, the process often left behind an unsightly, puffed-up patch on the (otherwise) original label.

Those stickers were a pain in the arse. I suppose they ensured that customers bought the records at the asking price – if they had been on the sleeves you could easily switch the sleeves. I had seen record stalls in street markets where prices had been written on the label in marker pen, which was straightforward vandalism, so at least it wasn't that. And it was permissible to swap the sleeves anyway, in order to get better-condition sleeves.

I went back the very next week, with money I had set aside for clothes, browsing with the zeal of the newly-converted, picking out, among other things, anything curious on the Red Bird label, especially if it was by the Shangri-Las. In terms of where, and how, I was acquiring records, I had turned a massive new corner.

Once again, I was investigating a specific aspect of the past while continuing to enjoy new releases. It was a balance I had been used to for years. That spring, I worried the balance was beginning to tip too far towards the old stuff. But at the start of May, two new and very different singles eased all such concerns.

It had been nice to have the Mother of God in the Top 10, but I had suspected 'Holiday' to have been a one-off, a refreshing but transient distraction. When Madonna released 'Lucky Star' in mid-March I thought only: *Oh, so here's the follow-up.* I bought it, because it was catchy and fresh, contrasting with the dull fug of adult worthiness that filled so much of the rest of the chart. But suddenly I found that when I went into my room and switched on the record player, it was the first thing that went on. Sometimes I went to my room just to hear it.

It was song of simple adoration. The shrill youthfulness of the voice, the crispness of the rhythms, the tightness of the arrangement and the strength of its chorus, all contributed to an acceleration of the pulse and brightening of the surroundings. It reached number fourteen, which wasn't particularly high, but, actually, it was in the weeks following its peak that I played it most. I listened out for more Madonna, but when it came, 'Borderline' was a disappointment; it seemed to lack the vital elements that had made the first two so good and it didn't even get in the Top 40. But that was not going to be the end of it.

I mentioned *The Old Grey Whistle Test* earlier. I occasionally tuned in on the off-chance that there might be something I liked. Frightfully earnest singer-songwriters never did much for me, but the show had its weirder and more striking moments, sometimes involving one of the show's home-made videos. They produced one of these as the visual accompaniment to the first thing I ever heard by the Cocteau Twins.

As well as being aware that they were one of John Peel's preferred acts, I had somewhere, somehow, been told that they didn't use lyrics, only vocal sounds, like they had made up their own language. This was something I instinctively disapproved of: I took lyrics seriously and was open to their effect. So, blithering or yodelling or whatever the Cocteau Twins did was just going to be bloody silly. I could imagine a certain portion of John Peel's audience contemplating it all with studious frowns and slow nods of the head. I scoffed at it.

But then I heard this track. The accompanying visuals were merged scans of stained glass and stone. It was late, I was half asleep, and these sounds drifted into me like mist: tinny, eerie guitar and a voice like none I had heard before, a mournful holler of wonderful power, carrying melodies which, against the backdrop of these drifting images, seemed like piety. The title, which I only vaguely remembered afterwards, was 'Millimillenary': an obscure word, a real one, although I first assumed it was made up. It also apparently had real lyrics, but I thought it was this fabled Cocteau Twins language. I didn't care. It was too late to care. I had been claimed.

The track wasn't available – it had been put on a compilation cassette and distributed via one of the music papers. But I didn't know that yet. I went into a record shop somewhere in Lewisham and asked for "the new one by the Cocteau Twins". I was duly rewarded with a seven-inch single in a pleasingly robust card cover covered in maroon imagery, like some fake Victorian ghost photograph. I liked the jaggedy, similarly spooky style of the lettering forming the band's name.

The single wasn't 'Millimillenary', it was something called 'Pearly-Dewdrops' Drops', which kind of dejected me, but off home I went, and played it. By the third listen, I was utterly in its grip. It was low-rattling bass and drifting, chiming guitar; it was a doleful vocal dipping and swooping, dignified and assertive; a procession of gorgeous, noble strangeness from a parallel universe. It was exquisite.

I was getting tingles I recognised from Siouxsie and the Banshees, from Kate Bush, from other things I couldn't name. It flooded me just like that first spliff in the Sun and Doves. It got into the Top 40, reaching number twenty-nine. But not much from John Peel's playlist ever made the charts. Many years later, on a druggy lads' weekend, a friend would beg me, almost tearfully, to put 'Pearly-Dewdrops' Drops' back to the start, but I couldn't work out what to do on the laptop because I was as mashed up as he was. It was special.

In the midst of all the ups and downs that the 1980s had in store, there would always be Madonna and there would always be the Cocteau Twins and, of course, at that point, I had no idea what either would become. There were entire galaxies between them, but that didn't matter. All I wanted was more euphoria and wonderment. All I wanted was for great pop to win.

Pop, however, was beginning to see its role as something greater than merely providing empathy for stoned young men.

Two

The end of the Cold War was still several years away. The Soviet Bloc of European countries glowered at us from the east and for even the most adventurous of travellers, it appeared an unattractive zone - sinister, grey and stifling. Yugoslavia, however, was a socialist state that existed outside of the Soviet Bloc. It was on relatively genial terms with the west; so much so, that you could go there on an Interrail ticket.

You can still get Interrail tickets as I write. In 1984, they gave you almost unlimited train travel across Europe for a month. Three of us did it that summer: myself, the LSM and a university friend of his. I wasn't a university student, but I was hoping to become one in a few weeks when I got my exam results. In the meanwhile, I had sold my Vespa motor scooter to do Interrail. After a few days in France and Italy, we decided to board a train at Trieste that would take us all the way down to Greece.

Unfortunately, an entire, over-stuffed trainload of youngsters had the same idea. There were no seats. Every gap and passageway was rammed with people pressed against their rucksacks; twisting into contortions whenever a train official had to get past.

Between Italy and Greece stood Yugoslavia. Our arrival at the border was like a scene from an espionage drama. As the train halted, guards with red stars on their hats pushed aboard, bashing the panelling with rods, loudly demanding to see passports and hauling people off onto the platform. These unfortunates were lined up and we briefly worried that they might be shot. As the guards edged close to us, we were more than a little nervous; but a British passport seemed to make a difference. As we held ours up, they just grunted and pushed past.

In time, it all calmed down to being merely tense. The train pulled away, but few of the Americans, Australians and other bewildered souls on the platform had been allowed back on. Did this mean we could now get a seat? Did it heck. The prospect of enduring this for the best part of another twenty-four hours was too much to bear and so we got off at the next stop, spent the night waiting for connections, and ended up at a campsite on the Adriatic coast.

We had struck gold. We camped on a peninsula covered in huge conifers, with mountain streams collecting in the bay on one side and ocean waves washing in on the other. It was unbelievably cheap. The days were hot and the nights warm. We stayed there for two weeks.

Most of our fellow campers were either Yugoslavs enjoying a final fling before entering national service, or Austrian tourists. We met one family of Brits. We also met two German-speaking Swiss girls, with whom we held the only conversation I can remember there about music. It wasn't much of a conversation, just a swapping of lists. They each had their own lists, but they both agreed on Kate Bush, or, as one of them pronounced it, "Kah-tay Boosh".

The impact of Kate Bush on people of our age is hard to exaggerate. Her sound was unique, her records startling and absorbing - she was phenomenal. When I was fourteen, her album *The Kick Inside* was a game-changer; when I saw her in concert the following year, my mind was blown and my heart lost.

But her singles were no longer charting highly and her most recent album, *The Dreaming*, now two years old, had seemed to relegate her to cult status. She nevertheless remained an important figure and role model. She was clearly important to these Swiss girls, but for me she was on the backburner. Few people were now thinking about Kate Bush. But almost everybody was thinking about Frankie Goes to Hollywood. Their new single, 'Two Tribes', was dominating the summer.

This record had serious context. It was the follow-up to 'Relax', which by the end of the year was the biggest seller of the two, although for the life of me I can't think why. The "tribes" in question were the two snarling world superpowers. In the video, actors playing US president Ronald Reagan and Soviet supremo Konstantin Chernenko fought in a baiting-ring, two old men grappling laughably, summing up the feelings of many about the Cold War and its nuclear threat.

Frankie Goes to Hollywood were being overtly political, in what was an increasingly political time. Internal divisions over the power of trade unions had been splitting the Labour Party since the 60s. Its moderate wing had fractured and broken away, leaving a bare doctrinaire socialism, now licking its wounds from a thumping in the 1983 general election by Margaret Thatcher's Conservatives, who were attracting former Labour voters with visions of personal advancement and wealth creation. This was all that the working class had ever wanted and they had once got it through the unions with broad public sympathy. That sympathy was now harder to come by. It was a period of significant transition and a bloody mess. Slogans flew through the air in every direction, like the missiles we all hoped never to see.

Certain kitsch segments of fashion incorporated Soviet paraphernalia: winter hats sporting red stars or the hammer and sickle, long coats evoking guard duty on the Eastern side of the Berlin Wall. It was a provocative badge of youthful protest. Or it was irony. Or it was just another fashion. But there was a kick to it. Few would have been happy living under the Soviet regime, but neither did people have any time for the insistence that we should all either fall into line with the Conservatives or bugger off to Russia. By donning a mock-sable hat, they were following that most British of traditions – the raising of two fingers.

Frankie Goes to Hollywood will, for the rest of this chapter, be referred to simply as Frankie, an adjustment which was happening then anyway. Billowy white t-shirts bearing Frankie slogans in shockingly large, black lettering became a fad. Other pop stars wore them. They said things like "Frankie say relax". Frankie were a cultural phenomenon, riding on a new, shiny, fashion-savvy kind of protest, fuelled by clothes, videos and, importantly, an extremely modern, ground-breaking sound.

If I had found 'Relax' something of a dull plod, I felt very differently about 'Two Tribes'. The record was simply incredible. It rocketed along on a wildly percussive and dirty-sounding bassline, creating a core rhythm powerful enough to blow you out of your chair. The vocal was all slogans and sneers; spoken here, sung there. Synth sounds exploded all around. The arrangement was busy – super busy, *deliciously* busy – with lots of studio trickery enhancing lots of bits, including the one where the parade-ground march built into a hysterical crescendo of xylophones before crashing back down to the bassline and vocal. That was just one bit. If we mentioned the full list, we'd be here all day. As with 'Relax', the producer was Trevor Horn and it was on Zang Tumb Tuum, a label which was in itself something of a sloganeering fashion statement. It was mad and brilliant and left you blissfully exhausted. It went straight in at number one and stayed there for nine weeks.

I'm tempted to call it the best thing about 1984. But, really, the best thing was that my exam results were good enough to make me the first member of my family to go to university. I packed my bags and headed north, with little preparation apart from making a tape of my all-time favourite tracks, a C90 to represent me, like a *Desert Island Discs* selection.

Lists of all-time favourites change regularly. If you did one per week, they might be different every time. Mine have always had the shimmering tear-stains of 'Baby Love' by the Supremes, the beautifully-formed '(I'm Always Touched by Your) Presence Dear' by Blondie and the record whose release I still like to think was the ultimate purpose of punk, 'Babylon's Burning' by the Ruts. But the rest have been subject to shifting taste and perception. I no longer have this tape, but I know for certain that it contained 'Leader of the Pack' by the Shangri-Las, 'My Boyfriend's Back' by the Angels and 'Will You Love Me Tomorrow' by the Shirelles, representing the girl groups. It definitely had 'Bridge over Troubled Water' by Simon & Garfunkel, 'Tammy' by Debbie Reynolds, 'Maggie May' by Rod Stewart and 'Mama Weer All Crazee Now' by Slade, for the hall-of-fame element. 'Life Is a Long Song' by Jethro Tull also slipped on. I'd be guessing at the rest, but I think it probably had 'Pearly-Dewdrops' Drops' by the Cocteau Twins. It was going to be my way of introducing myself and I fully expected people to be intrigued.

I suppose I thought that, in terms of musical leanings, any university environment would be steeped in late 60s and early 70s rock with a bit of Atlantic soul thrown in – the mightiest volumes on pop's polished oak shelves, the musical equivalents of Aristotle and Newton. It would simply be in the air. I expected to be well-versed in Led Zeppelin and Pink Floyd by Christmas.

But there was far more than that. I was amused by the fascination of some with Peter Gabriel-era Genesis. I was surprised by the widespread reverence for punk. There were plenty of lank-haired, denim-wrapped metallers. There were plenty of Bowie people that you wouldn't lose in the snow. The number of fist-happy, shiny-shirted soul boys proved that my alma mater lay closer to cold pavements than to dreaming spires.

But I got soul boys. What I didn't get was Bruce Springsteen. This name had long been familiar because he had written, or co-written, songs for other people, and the fact that he had written them was always mentioned. So, in 1976 it had been 'Blinded by the Light' by Manfred Mann's Earth Band, *written by Bruce Springsteen*; in 1978 it had been 'Because the Night' by Patti Smith, *co-written by Bruce Springsteen*. It was almost as if *Bruce Springsteen* was part of the title. These were good records, very grown-up pop.

I had imbibed images of him from copies of *Melody Maker* that my mum had once had delivered because of its folk section. These images had coalesced into the picture of a guy with faraway eyes, stroking his beard as he pondered his next lyric. In America, he was hailed as one of the modern greats, with a back catalogue of albums covering more than a decade. They told tales of the struggles and desires of ordinary guys on long factory shifts in the Land of the Free; tough towns, broad highways and big skies as seen through the bottom of a beer bottle. I had heard his 'Hungry Heart' single on the radio at the end of 1980 and hated it, but the album it came from, *The River*, had got to number two. Now, as I hauled my bags to the top-but-one floor of my tower block hall of residence, he was beginning to make forays into the UK singles chart. He had a cult following and I seemed to meet representatives of it everywhere I turned.

This had not happened in South London. I had a taped Springsteen spoof by comedian Alexei Sayle with a chorus that began "Every cloud has a mailbox" and I had bought 'Blinded by the Light' by Manfred Mann's Earth Band, *written by Bruce Springsteen*. That was it. As I made undergraduate friendships, however, I was invited into rooms and made to listen to *The River*, surrounded by youngsters for whom this was serious shit. I learned not to go in those rooms.

One day I would come to recognise Springsteen as an individual who genuinely cares about his fans and looks at important things in the right way. It's a great shame that, with the exception of 'Candy's Room' from *Darkness on the Edge of Town*, I find his records so horrible, the sound of his revered E Street Band such pudgy fug. But they were loved, and high in the collective consciousness.

Part of the initial round of undergraduate socialising involved attending hall of residence discos. These were usually advertised on flyers, one of which I remember bearing the central image of an erect phallus being stroked by a female hand. Lovely. Attendance levels at these discos varied, but the main one was on Friday nights: the University Union Disco, or as we quickly began calling it, the Dick Show. My group of friends were frequent visitors. You can draw your own conclusions.

Current tunes played in these places included 'Freedom' by Wham!, their second number one, with its four-to-the-bar snare in the Motown tradition, and 'Pride (in the Name of Love)' by U2, featuring a classic rock-star bellow of a chorus, which caused unattractive grimaces round the venue as it was almost impossible not to sing along and there seemed only one way of doing so. Also prominent was the anti-drug 'White Lines (Don't Don't Do It)' by Grandmaster Flash and Melle Mel, and the home-grown funk explosion of 'Hot Water' by Level 42, which I bloody loved. 'Blue Monday' by New Order was always included. They also played 'The Passenger' by Iggy Pop, an oldie I had never heard before and which occasioned outlandish styles of dancing tolerated at no other point.

To accompany the slow dancing and the consequent setting-off of most of us for the cloakroom, they usually played 'Careless Whisper', the solo showstopper by Wham! lead singer George Michael, which had been number one in the summer. The song was organised around a jazzy saxophone motif which, thanks to the enormous success of the single, took the sound of the exclusive and upmarket to unprecedented levels. There had been others, but this one was particularly smarmy and I hated the record as much for that as for the repeated reminder that I had no one to slow dance with.

The UK number one as term began had been 'I Just Called to Say I Love You' by Stevie Wonder. The saccharine horrors of this record have been amply recognised elsewhere, as has the shocking contrast with the bulk of his legacy. You need to know the number ones on important dates like starting university. But, due to all the distractions of my new environment, I had little idea of what else was in the singles chart that autumn if it didn't get played at the Dick Show.

But everybody knew the sharp, juddery synth-soul number one 'I Feel for You' by Chaka Khan. It had Melle Mel on it, rapping through an intro that made everyone say "chicken curry" instead of the actual "Chaka Khan", in the same way that we were "made" to say "Dick Show" instead of "Disco". It also had a harmonica part that had given Stevie Wonder something more positive to do with his time. To complete the star cast, it had been written by Prince, a performer about whom I knew nothing apart from a strikingly atmospheric single from the summer called 'When Doves Cry'. He was a guitar-wielding showbiz guy with a mop of black hair, a thin moustache and garish costumes. Adulation was mushrooming all around, in the same way as for Bruce Springsteen. Once again I looked on, puzzled.

His was a world of high-octane drum machine patterns and keyboard sounds with the texture of jacuzzi water, coalescing into rhythms to which performers clicked their fingers, either swinging from side to side or contorting themselves into dance shapes that made you worry for their spines. Other hit acts occupying this space included the Pointer Sisters, who had, in their time, made good records, but whose recent 'I'm So Excited' made you fear that the sound of pop was in the process of fizzing away into nothing, like an orange lolly left in the sun.

But Prince had other sounds. His new one that autumn was the broody, reverb-heavy ballad 'Purple Rain', which, it transpired, was the title song from a new movie in which he was starring. A movie. He had been around for five minutes and he had a movie.

On the subject of movies, the current hit with the greatest impact was 'Ghostbusters' by Ray Parker Jr., the title tune from a spooky action comedy just released in the cinema. The film was good fun and made you like the song even more. Awareness of 'Purple Rain' was patchy, opinions on 'Pride (in the Name of Love)' were somewhat divided, some people couldn't tell you who 'Hot Water' was by - but everybody knew 'Ghostbusters'. Its mood-lightening beats were well-received at the Dick Show, and its hook line – *Who you gonna call? Ghostbusters!* – was adapted for whatever use people saw fit. You could be passing someone you knew in a corridor and, instead of them saying 'Alright?', they would point a finger and demand to know who you were gonna call. The most dignified response was to roll your eyes. Meekly responding with "Ghostbusters!" would only diminish your status.

Status was something you had to watch in this environment. I was coming into contact with incredibly confident, witty people who greeted lower-league attempts at humour with loud derision. You get over moments like these, but I was unfortunately prone to putting myself in the firing line.

I had already met most of the group that would be the spine of my social life for the next few years, but we were still getting to know each other. As we were discussing records, one girl mentioned that she owned a copy of 'The Land of Make Believe' by Bucks Fizz with a special fold-out picture cover. She was slightly giggly and inhibited as she revealed this, almost certainly understanding that Bucks Fizz were not the most credible of acts in an environment where Pink Floyd and Joy Division were held in such high esteem. The fact that the record was almost three years old by that point was scarcely a defence - she had been sixteen, not six.

I, however, was not only noisily happy to reveal that I liked 'The Land of Make Believe', but that, in full recognition of the importance of picture covers, I was jealous because mine had been only the standard issue - no fold-out, no special. This made her giggle and redden even more, but I was aware of everyone else pausing, taking a micro-step backwards, watching as I voluntarily lowered my status before their eyes, waiting to see what would happen next: perhaps I would reveal more childish preoccupations; perhaps it was just a ruse for getting her into bed. It was all a bit uncomfortable for a moment. Happily, all it turned out to be was a brief conversation about a Bucks Fizz picture cover.

So now everybody knew I was a poppy-pop fan. But I was not the only such creature. Some in long raincoats and fur-trimmed boots that weren't done up properly could talk at earnest length about Duran Duran. Others in high-street cottons were going to continue loving Wham! no matter what anyone said. There were plenty of Madness fans and, in the various album stacks behind hall of residence doors, *I Just Can't Stop It* by the Beat was close to standard issue. And then of course there was 'Ghostbusters' which, by the start of the following spring, would have spent a total of twenty-four weeks in the Top 40.

It hadn't quite made it to number one – 'I Just Called to Say I Love You' had held it at number two for three weeks – but the final two number ones of the term were significant landmarks. That is particularly true of the first, if you are a lover of chart statistics. For, if Frankie's next single got to number one, it would be the first time since 1963 that an act's first three singles had all made it to the top, the last to achieve the feat having been Gerry and the Pacemakers.

Frankie fever was such that it was almost certain to do so. 'The Power of Love' was an intense, lingering ballad. Coming as it did at Advent, it had vaguely Christmassy elements, mainly in the presentation: crucifixes on the outer packaging for the single, a Nativity oil painting on the picture cover, silhouettes of the Magi on the video. The "Love" of the title was indeed romantic love, but there was a mixture of imagery in its lyric. Some bits evoked parental love, others godly love. Its over-arching slogan was "Make love your goal".

This had contemporary resonance. Healing was needed. The Cold War had split the world in two. The hard-nosed economic reforms of the Conservative government and the abrasive style of Margaret Thatcher's leadership had split the country along lines marked with suspicion and resentment. We were in the midst of the most bitter industrial dispute of modern times, the 1984-5 miners' strike, an entrenched stand-off in which no quarter was being given. Everybody understood that the outcome would determine which side of the split would get its way from then on.

Meanwhile, growing attention was being paid to another kind of split, that between the world of plenty and the world of disease and starvation. Ethiopia was being battered by famine. Harrowing footage appeared on the news. Striking miners' families may have been living at the extremes, but they were living; they might not know where their next meal was coming from but they knew they would get one. The families huddled together in the Ethiopian dust didn't. Here, it would soon be Christmas, when, in line with our traditions, we indulge in more than our usual enough. This time, instead of shaking our heads at the footage and then turning back to the feast, something different was going to happen.

Bob Geldof, front man for new wave band the Boomtown Rats, and Midge Ure, front man for synth notables Ultravox, wrote a song called 'Do They Know It's Christmas?', which listed all the comforting details of our festivities and contrasted them with the realities of the starving. Just like the Frankie song, it had a rallying slogan: "Feed the world – let them know it's Christmastime". A long list of music celebrities were invited to join its choir for the recording. These were not dribs and drabs, they were the biggest stars of the modern UK chart - Brits, Irish, and a scattering of Americans. A few sang lead parts. The act was called Band Aid. The music business appeared to have formed a united front.

Geldof, with unwavering assertiveness and energy, soon became the spokesperson for a whole fund-raising movement. As it grew in momentum, accusations flew back and forth about his misguidedness and self-importance, as well as about the government's unwillingness to make any significant effort of their own to alleviate the suffering. It was depicted as Caring Versus Not Caring and emotions ran high. Record stores and other industry bodies were urged to waive costs and donate proceeds from the sale of the single.

In the first week of December, Frankie's 'The Power of Love' crashed into the Top 10 at number three and was number one the following week. The week after that, Band Aid went straight in at number one, the only single that year apart from 'Two Tribes' to do so. Straight in at number two behind it, was 'Last Christmas/Everything She Wants', the new one by Wham!, who were also part of Band Aid, but whose festive offering was a contrast; representing, thanks to its video, the kind of exclusive and upmarket lifestyle that Band Aid was wagging its finger at.

'Do They Know It's Christmas?' stayed at number one until mid-January, selling over three million copies. It was the biggest-selling UK single of all time. Opinion was divided over whether it was a good record or not, but united on the point that it had an essential reason to exist. This did not stop some taking the piss out of it. People did unflattering impressions of the solo parts. Some Scouse wag entertained our town-bound bus one night, singing the part about "There won't be snow in Africa this Christmas time" and adding "Except on the top of Mount Kilimanjaro...", to tangible approval. In London, I heard the additional line "And there won't be any fucking snow here, either", sung angelically to the tune. The one really good bit of the record is the emotive final chorus. There's nothing wrong with an emotive final chorus. There's nothing wrong with enjoying the luxuries of Christmas either, as long as you make a contribution. The last two number ones of the year had made a unique impression and had given the dominant forces in pop a new and specific role. Make love your goal. Feed the world.

Having bought both, the luxury I was planning to enjoy that Christmas was the first release by the Cocteau Twins since 'Pearly-Dewdrops' Drops': a new album, *Treasure*. The cover artwork was all old lace and artefacts from haunted houses, and the sound, although it began in a similar vein, rose gradually towards the stratosphere and then on to outer space. Its titles were all single-word and - you eventually realised - all girls' names. 'Lorelei' was stomping pop, 'Amelia' was a gothic mini-melodrama and 'Donimo' was a series of goodwill messages between planets. I sat, I soaked it up, I let myself acclimatise. I loved it for being so different. I loved it for being so lovable. I had half hoped 'Millimillenary' would be on it, but no matter. Their hit single wasn't on it, either, and not just because its title had too many words. The Cocteau Twins were clearly a new kind of proposition. *Treasure* got to number twenty-nine in the album chart and I got to tour the cosmos.

I didn't view myself as 'alternative', although I was enjoying my place in the outer reaches of the John Peel community. I certainly wasn't on any pre-set diet. The Smiths were the big new stars of alternative, but, since they had not become the band that 'What Difference Does It Make?' had hinted they might, I had stopped paying attention. It would be years before I would properly "get" the Smiths, and even then, it didn't make me want to buy any of their albums. Being a voice for the marginalised and disregarded, a rallying-point for those alienated by the mainstream, is a fine thing - being misunderstood and disallowed is horrible. It's something of an irony then, that the massed ranks of Smiths fans contain some of the most intolerant chest-prodders I have ever encountered.

Patchy though my involvement in the alternative was, I was alert to any media attention paid to the Cocteau Twins. I bought issues of the music papers they featured in, learning that the singer and guitarist were, respectively, Elizabeth Fraser and Robin Guthrie from Grangemouth in Scotland, which was an industrial behemoth, so no wonder they wanted to make this strange, ethereal music whose meaning was entirely open to interpretation.

Among the things I had missed was that Elizabeth Fraser had been the guest vocalist for an act called This Mortal Coil, who had released a haunting cover version of 'Song to the Siren' (which I had never heard of) by Tim Buckley (who I had never heard of) and it had been a favourite on John Peel in 1983. If I was truly alternative, I would have known that. I discovered it in the end, and the track is incredible. But liking it didn't make me alternative. At Christmas 1984 I was listening to *Treasure*, plus what was good in the charts. And the best thing there was the new one by Madonna.

Having seen 'Borderline' sink without trace, we might have been forgiven for thinking that would be it. But suddenly she was back in the Top 10 with 'Like a Virgin'. The first striking thing about it was the title. Obviously, there was the Mother of God-virgin connection. Equally obviously, for most people, it was going straight in the drawer marked "Sex". The video had her writhing in choreographed abandon at the bow of a Venetian gondola, in a way which, by 1984-5 standards, was explicitly sexual. The tabloids lashed out. Steve Wright nibbled energetically at the bait, routinely referring to her as "the sleaze-bag".

The song was about how the touch of her new lover was so magical that it was as if she had never been touched before, and so, in effect, her love life was only now beginning. A great, romantic idea. But people heard the word "virgin" and went a bit funny. The 1992 movie *Reservoir Dogs* contains a scene in which Harvey Keitel's deranged character discusses the song, banging on earthily about how many guys she must therefore have shagged beforehand. Many people at the time complained that the girl was, in effect, saying: *I don't want to be a virgin any more – you may now fuck me senseless.*

Some around me, the supposed intellectual cream of society, didn't even get that far. I got into conversations like this:

"She's not a virgin though, is she?"

"No, it's *like* she is."

"Yes, but how can she be a virgin if she's had boyfriends before?"

"Because he makes it seem as if she is, because he's so special to her. She's not really - of course she's not."

"So why does she say so?"

"She doesn't".

"What do you mean, she doesn't? It's the whole song. Jesus."

"She only feels like it."

"But how *can* she feel like it? She *knows* she isn't because she's slept with people."

"You know when you're hungover and you say you feel like shit?"

"What's that got to do with it?"

"Well you know you're not actually made of shit, don't you?"

"What are you fucking talking about?"

The record was more than a wind-up. Its big, crisp synthetic sound was pop concentrate; aspiring to be polished but not quite getting there, which added to its allure. Mid-paced, with whiplash snare and a relentlessly bouncing *bob-bob-bom* bass line, it wasn't really a dancer, but it got played successfully at the Dick Show anyway. The vocal was instantly recognisable as the one from 'Lucky Star'. It dominated the sound. It was the most hummed and sung-along-to song for two months. We were subjected to sporadic outbursts of "Now you may-ee-ay-aid me fee-yull, shiny and neeeeewwwww..." from all but the most commandingly cool. It had a certain something that you couldn't put your finger on. It sparkled all over and it got to number three.

45

Another captivating Top 10 record from the same weeks was even rougher at the edges. This was 'Since Yesterday' by Strawberry Switchblade, with its mid-70s horn sample, its machine-gun drum fills and its refreshingly plain female vocal. If it caught you at the right moment, you could be utterly transported. All sorts of people fell under its charm, including many among the most commandingly cool. One of them told me "I really liked it – until I saw them on *Top of the Pops*".

I now only rarely watched *Top of the Pops*. But I had a small pile of recent singles in my room and this was one of them, its picture cover showing two women dressed in enormously layered, lacy and frilly polka-dot dresses and head-gear, like a pair of dolls in a Balkan souvenir shop. This was clearly a gimmick, but even so, this guy's response stopped me in my tracks. Why let a set of costumes ruin your enjoyment of the record?

It bothered me. One of the reasons for so rarely watching *Top of the Pops* now was my deepening belief that any visual representation of a song threatened to spoil it. Having said that, I did enjoy the fact that the gratuitous sexiness of the 'Like a Virgin' video had ruffled so many of the right feathers. The reaction had given Madonna all the publicity she could possibly want and it made me smile. Her next single, however, seemed to demonstrate how context and presentation are capable of powering a record to a greater extent that its intrinsic quality.

'Material Girl', which appeared in early spring, had no groove – it was all cold mechanics and functionality. It told us that the world we now lived in was all about material and financial wealth, and that she was happily in tune with it. She still fancied cute guys, but it was those with cash that really did it for her. In the zesty backstreets of 'Holiday' and 'Lucky Star', this could have meant buying an extra milkshake at the drug store, but we were moving into an age where it meant something very different. It was reflected in the video, where, in expensive evening wear and a jazz-era hairdo, she was hoisted and carried by beautiful boys in suits. It was the victory of money over everything else and it was roared on by aggressively reforming conservative governments on both sides of the Atlantic.

I had arrived at university with many assumptions that proved to be wrong, one of which was that it was a hot-bed of leftie protest that could have no possible truck with conservatism. Well, it didn't take long for that to be blown out of the water. The leftie groups and societies were still the most visible: you did not – I mean *did not* – do anything to upset the Gay and Lesbian Society. But the general mood was pro-Thatcher. This, to my mind, was shocking in an environment full of youngsters, but it had already been normalised. It may have been the case that nobody stood in student elections as a Conservative - the Conservatives stood as "Independents" - but the campaign to elect a president for our hall of residence, won by an arch but charming Tory, was conducted on the basis of personality and was well attended as a result. Nobody seemed to be getting too wound up.

However, the end of the miners' strike occasioned large doses of partisan triumphalism. The dispute continued into the new year. The government had been well-prepared, stockpiling resources and mobilising the police. The stand-off went their way and the miners, after months of hardship and with hopes of victory fading, began returning to work. The strike ended on March 3rd 1985 and, on the day of the announcement, Conservative students held a raucous champagne party in our junior common room, making every effort to be noticed by those who had been putting change into miners' collection buckets throughout the winter. The battle was over. Amidst the bewilderment and despair of the defeated, a period of unfettered change had begun. Less than two weeks later, 'Material Girl' was in the Top 10.

Madonna was dubbed "the material girl", which was a change from "the sleaze-bag". But she was simply a pop performer at a particular time, and these new times were unselfconsciously businesslike and serious about making it in the prescribed way. People would don smart suits and get to the office at eight on the dot in the same way that they had once chosen an Afghan coat and shared cosmic thoughts in a circle. It was fashion. As is often the case, it was linked to significant social change, but it was just fashion.

I didn't like 'Material Girl' anyway; I only bought it because I felt I should have it. I wanted our age to produce big stars making great, classic records that would soar to the top of the charts. Madonna was now certainly a major figure, featuring in tabloid newspapers and on the lips of the general public. She had made it to a level where people in their tens of thousands were buying 'Material Girl' in homage to her very existence. It, too, got to number three.

She would make more un-likeable, annoying records that year. 'Crazy for You' was next, a dour ballad-by-numbers which made it all the way to number two, and which I hated because I knew she was capable of better; any old Joan could have made that drivel. In the autumn there would be 'The Gambler', a song so featureless I can't hum a single part of it to this day, which had come from some movie, the title of which escapes me. That reached number four. I had no intention of buying either of these. But she would begin to redeem herself before the year was out.

The general hum of that year's soundtrack was clean, smooth-edged and inoffensive. Records that stood out, did so by not being bland, although very few achieved that by anything more than a short neck. They were neither explosions of adolescent rage, nor jabs of mischievous irreverence: it was their sound that made a difference. 'Like a Virgin' and 'Since Yesterday' were each good, but most importantly they had distinctive sounds that cut through the dull fug surrounding them.

So, too, did 'You Spin Me Round (Like a Record)' by Dead or Alive, which hit the chart like a hurricane early in the spring. Its energy swept you to the dancefloor in a euphoric wave and its powerful hooks made you stay there; wherever you were on the Happy Scale, it lifted you further. Few things that year raced the pulse to such an extent - it was a wonderful moment when it reached number one.

Most of the time we just chugged along, rather like 'Material Girl' did. The biggest number one pre-Easter was 'Easy Lover' by Phillip Bailey and Phil Collins, a duet between the American bloke with the high voice from Earth, Wind and Fire, and the British bloke with the thunderclap drum sound, whose albums were as essential to front rooms as pot pourri. 'Easy Lover' was bursting with arrangement set-pieces but was almost unbelievably dull. It fit the general soundtrack perfectly - with 'Material Girl' sitting snug alongside it.

Speaking of Americans, the success of 'Do They Know It's Christmas?' was not going to go without a response. Heavy-hitters Stevie Wonder and Lionel Richie wrote 'We Are the World' and assembled a who's-who choir under the name USA For Africa to record it. It removed 'Easy Lover' from number one in late spring, with barely a flicker from the bland-ometer. Equally dull, relatively speaking, was the title track from the eagerly-awaited Frankie Goes to Hollywood double album – yes, *double* album – *Welcome to the Pleasuredome*, released as a single in the same weeks. The rest of the album didn't get great notices, either. The single got to number two but they would never get so high again.

For me, the scene-setter for disillusionment in this period had been a new Cocteau Twins EP, *Aikea-Guinea*. The very thought of a new Cocteau Twins EP had been intoxicating, but the title track lacked something vital. You could see what they were trying to do: it had grand ambition, but something about it didn't quite work. Still, it *was* a new Cocteau Twins EP. This would not be the last time that they would disappoint, but the next occasion was many years in the future. They were about to enter a period which, if not exactly prolific, was certainly golden.

So, as was usual when frustrated by current pop, I turned to the past; but this time it was with help. A group of guys in our hall of residence began planning a covers gig and needed a drummer. I was invited to become interested. The result was the formation of Springboard Brucesteen and The E Floor Band.

Its leader was a physically imposing, enormously confident Manchester lad with an expensive Fender bass and boundless enthusiasm. Over cups of tea in a room crowded with technology including a full stereo system and an impressive bass amplifier, I listened to him exalting rock bands that I had always struggled to take seriously. This included Queen, with whom he was something close to obsessed. I thought their best was way behind them; that their output since 1979's 'Don't Stop Me Now' had rarely been more than curious.

This guy, though, was Queen mad. I got catalogues of detail about each member, especially guitarist Brian May, with his self-built, customised guitar. I was shown rare records, including a Polish greeting card with a spindle hole and the 1980 hit 'Play the Game' stamped on it in clear vinyl - as he then demonstrated, you could play it on a regular stereo. I was given an appreciative guide to their recent releases, through which I nodded and smiled politely. He went on to tell me that the room we were sitting in had recently hosted a game of Rude Scrabble, in which the best word had been "Madonnasmeg". Through it all, he leaned back luxuriantly in his chair, smiling gleefully. It had the desired effect. I felt privileged.

We got down to business. I was given a cassette tape containing songs we were going to do, including one by contemporary star Nik Kershaw called 'Shame on You', chosen because it had a particularly groovy bassline. Another was 'Distant Early Warning' by rock band Rush; chosen to showcase the musicianship of the line-up, the glory of which wasn't expected to extend to me. "Just keep the beat," I was told, "and make sure you come in at the right time."

Also on the list, however, was one of my favourite olden-days Queen songs, 'Now I'm Here', which I had often used as a warm-up when practising at home. I couldn't wait to get stuck into this. We began rehearsals and it soon came around. "Bloody hell," he exclaimed after a second run-through. "You can play!"

Having exceeded expectations, I then lowered them again by turning up shit-faced after sampling a little too much of the home brew organised for our floor. A Rugby Club type had burst into my room and helped himself to the bag of sugar by which the enterprise found itself short. My reimbursement was a share of the spoils. I certainly spoiled the rehearsal.

I didn't repeat this mistake and the gig went ahead. As preparations gathered, people came forward to offer their services, enabling us to add a trombonist and three backing singers in co-ordinated dress, one of whom had the job of holding the mic stand across the drum kit so we could do 'I Wanna Be Like You' from *The Jungle Book* as an encore, with me growling out the lead vocals as I swished the brushes. The idea for the Springboard Brucesteen name, like just about everything else, had come from the bass player, giving rise to more gleeful laughter, undeterred by the fact that nobody else was doing any more than rolling their eyes.

Working through such an eclectic set list was enormous fun. Variety was proving to be just the ticket and this was further enhanced by what was starting to appear on television. Everything about *Top of the Pops* was annoying me too much now. By the summer there were two new shows to enjoy.

The first was a UK version of *Soul Train*, presented by Jeffrey Daniel, a member of hit American soul act Shalamar, renowned for his nifty dance moves. The show was a step up from *Top of the Pops* because, although it was a platform for show-offy dancing, it was also a platform for the most interesting genre of the moment. Performing artists were often invited to join the dancing after their spot, which gave us the chance to see if they were any good at it, and they sometimes weren't. But at least it was proper dancing.

The second provided a far greater contrast. *The Max Headroom Show* was a series of videos presented by the eponymous host, a computer-generated, handsome blond with a top-of-the-range showbiz grin, modelled, so it was revealed, on chiselled Canadian actor Matt Frewer. Music television had been hijacked by the interminable prancing around of whooping idiots, but now here was a heartening alternative - the juddery, staccato prancing of a two-dimensional piss-taker.

Max messed around like a kid, in between (and often during) videos chosen for their marginality and oddness; as well as those for hit records whose spirit fit the bill. He laughed loudly at his own jokes, praised his own performance lavishly and tossed curt asides to unseen studio hands. He also malfunctioned regularly: stammering, distorting and oscillating. Our hall of residence television room had a more interesting crowd when *The Max Headroom Show* was on.

Liking other aspects of 1985 was more of a challenge. There were a few memorable moments. A Duran Duran single called 'A View to a Kill', the theme to a new James Bond movie and possibly the best thing they ever did, peaked at number two. On a whim, I bought a single by Propaganda called Duel' whose idiosyncrasies would grow enormously on me over the coming months. The Dick Show spun both of these, along with soul highlight 'Feel So Real' by Steve Arrington, and 'Obsession' by Animotion, possibly the most 80s-sounding record ever made. But it was thin pickings.

I remained alert for new leads on 60s girl groups. The number of girl group compilations being released at that point - usually on the Kent or

Impact labels - made me think I might be in some kind of vanguard. But there was little else to support this idea. Friends before whom I waved these collections usually smiled and said "great" without ever referring to them again. Sadly, having listened to them, my responses were often similar. Genre compilations sometimes scrape the bottoms of very deep barrels.

The disaffection I felt was best summed up by a record that got to number one just as we were packing for the start of the summer holidays - 'Frankie' by Sister Sledge (nothing to do with the 'Two Tribes' lot). Back in 1979, as disco was reaching saturation point, Sister Sledge produced a string of slightly cheesy hits whose appeal would prove surprisingly resilient. Records like 'He's the Greatest Dancer' and 'Lost in Music' were perfectly in tune with their 1979 surroundings. 'Frankie', in the summer of 1985, was definitely not.

In a world of big, frizzy hair, glossy jackets, reinforced shoulders and chandelier earrings, here, suddenly, was the sound of bobby-socks, finger-poppin' and preppie cardigans, like *Grease* had been out for seven weeks rather than seven years. Sure, my peer group was now the right age to be nostalgic for 1978-79, the days when disco was challenged only by a concurrent nostalgia for the pre-Beatles world that *Grease* presented. But 'Frankie' was number one for four weeks, making it the biggest-ever Sister Sledge hit. And they didn't actually wear bobby socks, pop their fingers or don preppy cardigans when they performed it, either - they wore 1985 mall fashion. It was all very odd.

Disaffection remained simmering throughout the summer, and it affected my response to its biggest event. The Band Aid and USA For Africa singles were to be followed up by two huge, open-air fundraising concerts, one in London, one in Philadelphia, on the same day. Live Aid took place on July 13th, with top stars playing crowd-pleaser sets. The landed gentry of British and US pop were all invited. Some - Michael Jackson, Frankie and Bruce Springsteen included - didn't make it. Prince sent a video. Madonna appeared. Phil Collins played in London, then boarded a plane and flew to Philadelphia so that he could appear on both stages. The Cocteau Twins were somehow overlooked.

For most, it seemed that simply turning up and playing in the name of the cause was more than sufficient. But then there was the set by Queen, who pulled off what is widely held to have been the performance of the day, electrifying Wembley and fitting themselves as pre-eminent stadium rockers, as well as establishing their generation of maturing fug-merchants as the pre-eminent musical force.

Bob Geldof and Midge Ure organised Live Aid, just as they had organised Band Aid. It was intended as a brand; an ongoing donation-gathering vehicle with the July concerts as its first major events.

Geldof was by far the most conspicuous of the two, bluntly grabbing the limelight, making impassioned appeals for attention and money right across the media. He thumped tables, adopted aggressive - often profane - turns of phrase and generally jarred with the composure of interviewers and presenters, as well as with the smugness of politicians. For the sake of the starving and the struggle against complacency, this was a good thing. But he rubbed others up the wrong way: people thought he was a bit too gobby, that he was a bit too impressed with himself.

I liked Geldof for the very reason that he wound people up. It's what makes me still think of him as an authentic punk rather than just a self-promoting chancer, which he undoubtedly also was. The Geldof we got with Live Aid was, as far as I was concerned, a more mature and focused version of the one growling 'Lookin' After Number One' at us in 1977 with a sneer on his lips. Then, he seemed not prepared to put up with wankers. Now he was not prepared to put up with wankers unready to help the starving with hard action and hard cash.

But the whole July thing irritated me, which, given its purpose, also racked me with guilt. The performance of Queen may have been a genuine high point, but, to me, Queen were just hanging around without bringing anything new to the party. You could say the same for most of the rest of the line-up. There was nobody there to upset granny. It was just showbiz. As the cameras zoomed in on well-groomed, expensively casual young women sitting on the shoulders of their well-groomed, expensively casual boyfriends, pinching their eyebrows together in sincerity as images of the starving were screened in slide shows between acts, my confusion deepened. I could neither participate, nor bat it away. I gave some money. I kept buying records. I felt angry.

This feeling continued to varying degrees throughout the summer.

The soundtrack had little if any of the sparkling pop that I thought of as my right; it was smoothed-off and self-consciously restrained. I looked back on the weeks of 'Like a Virgin', 'Since Yesterday' and 'You Spin Me Round (Like a Record)' as a lost age of wonder.

I couldn't even safely slag off records I hated. During a session in the union building pool hall a few weeks earlier, I had been told rather aggressively that 'Johnny Come Home' by Fine Young Cannibals was "fucking brilliant" in response to my (not altogether reasoned and measured) verdict of "this load of shit" when it came on the jukebox. Those of you glowing with fondness for this thoroughly irritating track, with its muted jazz trumpet and painfully affected vocal, will now be smirking with satisfaction. It seemed that all I was doing was moaning.

Madonna released a new single, 'Into the Groove'; a song linked with the movie *Desperately Seeking Susan*, in which she had a role. Clearly, it was time she had a number one and 'Into the Groove' achieved the feat. But it wasn't the stomach-melting, head-spinning classic I had been hoping for: it seemed to me an unremarkable get-on-the-dance-floor-and-show-me-you-love-me affair, a record without much of a hook, either in the melody or the arrangement. It has grown on me in the years since, but in a summer of being left feeling flat, this was one of the prime culprits. It held the top spot for a month and her debut hit 'Holiday' roared back into the Top 10 to join it, at one point giving her the top two in the same week.

Not even the return of Kate Bush could reverse the trend. The release of the first new single for three years, 'Running Up That Hill', put her straight back at the top table and the event got a lot of coverage. Its sound was richly atmospheric; there was a gently rumbling beat, a vocal of sharp reverberation and a lyric that seemed spiritual, even aside from mentioning God in the chorus. But it had a feeling of restraint, of incarcerated energy - it was intriguing rather than exciting. There was a glossy, fold out sleeve. There was a terrific B-side called 'Under the Ivy': just her, a piano and a ton of drama.

The rumbling beat of 'Running Up That Hill' meant that it got played at a club I went to with my sister and her friends. I imagine that the DJ put it on it in a moment of over-exuberance brought on by the fact that it was Kate Bush and it had a regular beat. I loyally took to the dance floor with two or three other souls, but it just didn't work. It was not a dance record. I was soon alone, not enjoying myself and not impressing anyone.

Of course, the vast majority of her audience no longer bought singles and were waiting for the album, which duly went to number one in late September. This was *Hounds of Love*, now revered as a classic. But really, 'Running Up That Hill' was no chart-topping single. It crashed in at number nine; but then only got as high as three. In a Top 40 of head-nodding arena fillers, slick club beats and knobble-kneed novelties, it was the uncomfortable guest at the party.

And I knew how it felt to be one of those. I was a thoroughly sociable and popular chap, but parties and night clubs didn't seem to suit me. I went because everybody went. Some nights were better than others, but, generally, I was uncomfortable, which was a shame because the music played there could feature the very best of what was around. I loved those records at home on headphones, but I often heard them first during nights out. Nights out were what youngsters did, so I kept going. I was one of the party people whether I liked it or not.

Three

My coping strategy at night clubs was to get sozzled on lager and drift off into thought, either staring into middle-distance from a vantage point, or dancing as neutrally and inoffensively as possible, staying alert both to the threat of trouble and the threat of being caught having a second look at an eye-catching girl.

This would all work better if I was enjoying the music, although this could, actually, be an additional threat, since overt pleasure would alter the manner of your dancing and defeat the whole object. But experience was beginning to deliver. I no longer mouthed the words or prodded the sky when favourites came on. That kind of thing never went down well, especially not amid the mirrored panels and clumps of potted rainforest that were standard issue in mid-80s clubs.

When you first entered the main chamber of these places, you were hit by a tsunami of treble: until your ears acclimatised, that was all you got – spiky and wall-shakingly loud. Above you, piercing beams of colour flew in all directions, often straight into your eyes, thrown out from lighting units spinning and pitching like fairground rides for the fearless. Dry ice made its first chemical assault on your sinuses. You tried to make out what this record was.

You stepped forward and kept going; to get past the blinding glare, to get to safety. Up staircases with lines of pin-head lights in the steps, along walls of mirror-strips, past fabricated Amazonian flora. The closer you got to the bar, the less the somersaulting lights got in the way. The closer you got to the bar, the more bass you could hear. The closer you got to the bar, the nearer you were to neutralising the dry ice with a gulp of something. Getting closer to the bar made sense.

Even after your senses had settled, the sound maintained its sharpness and attack. It did so at, or close to, 120 beats per minute. Sequencing technology had made records slicker; they were now also bigger, sharper and brighter; all kinds of new sounds were possible. Club PA systems belted them at you as if trying to reorganise your skeleton.

The 120 bpm phenomenon was well established. It was epitomised first and foremost by Prince and the Revolution's ubiquitous '1999', but now also by 'Sussudio', one of Phil Collins' livelier moments which delighted those in the habit of buying Phil Collins records but made others wonder what the fuck sussudio was, while wrestling with the fact that finding out would involve scrutinising a Phil Collins lyric.

The media highlighted the 120 bpm consensus in a disapproving tone, pointing out by inference that whole genres and types of rhythm had been abolished to facilitate it, like medieval buildings being bulldozed to make way for a shopping centre. There was no doubt that the jungle drums, growly guitars and emotional vocals that had characterised many of the most exciting records of my mid-teens had been swept away, their memory frowned upon. But they wouldn't have worked here; controlled cool fit the bill for these clubs. At 120 bpm, you could do that left in, left out, right in, right out thing with your feet without having to animate your upper body; or you could do it with a slight bending of the knees, adding arm and elbow twiddles as confidence allowed. Either way, at this tempo, it was done comfortably.

The only other dance you saw was the one that looked like one of those puppets with jointed knees dancing on the end of a plank: an intense blur of skips and jiggles with the body rigid, the hands cupped in front of the torso and the gaze fixed on the floor two metres away. It didn't lack rhythm, but it lacked cool. It was a badge of non-conformity and safer at the Dick Show than deep in the plastic tropics.

Music played at mainstream clubs had a qualifying sound. Synthesised soul was its bedrock, dispensing a range stretching from rich slices of

American class to street-level, garagey grooves with rough edges. But plenty of pop met the requirements; Madonna, Phil Collins and Duran Duran all got played. 'You Spin Me Round (Like a Record)' usually found its way in. Clubs also tended to have one novelty muckabout record saved for a carefully-chosen part of the night, when patrons were permitted to drop their cool. Friends from the West Midlands told me about 'The Hayrick Song' by Eddie Tenpole Tudor, others from Humberside reported 'Destination Zululand' by King Kurt; in London you might get a bit of Irish jigging via 'Sally MacLennane' by the Pogues. Meanwhile, 'New York New York' by Frank Sinatra continued its reign as the undisputed call to prayer in this new, exclusive and upmarket world, the sound of its intro quickly organising the faithful into wide circles, their arms across each other's shoulders, their feet kicking up Tiller-Girls-style, their frowning faces straining out the words as accurately as memory and sobriety would allow.

But the standard offering was soul, plus records that sounded like soul but weren't quite; ones with soul's production values but lacking its refinement, falling short on some critical point of credibility, perhaps in its lyrical content, perhaps in its commercial intent. Soul aficionados might tolerate such a record, acknowledging its popularity by way of a short rendition; but it would be a rendition involving playful voices and parody dance moves, proving that this stuff just wasn't serious enough to be soul. In club music, there was soul and there was not-soul.

Soul was safe ground and, also, it happened to be the genre producing the goods. Records like 'Thinking About Your Love' by Skipworth and Turner, 'Let's Go Together' by Change and 'I'll Be Good' by Renee and Angela were capable of setting the tone for wonderful nights. But if one track ruled this world above all others, it was 'Ain't Nobody' by Rufus and Chaka Khan, a rollicking tub of US love-bubbles from the spring of the previous year which was still going strong. It was one of the few records to inspire communal singing among club crowds, tolerated to the extent that DJs would lower the speaker volume so that punters could hear themselves belting out its joyful chorus.

These were exotic, overseas sounds, almost all American; but British-grown talent was moving among them. Younger soul kids had been swept off their feet by the space travel love fantasy 'Clouds Across the Moon' by the Rah Band, masterminded by Richard Hewson from Teesside. There was the grinning, finger-popping 'Spend the Night' by the Cool Notes, and the smooth class of 'Hangin' on a String (Contemplating)' by Loose Ends, both from London. Birmingham's Jaki Graham slipped into the summer Top 10 with the luscious 'Round and Around'. A few weeks later, Total Contrast from somewhere near the M25 made it into the Top 20 with the urgently percussive, American-sounding 'Takes a Little Time'. Then there was the measured stomp of 'Say I'm Your Number One' by Princess, crafted by English songwriting and production team Stock, Aitken, Waterman - also responsible for 'You Spin Me Round (Like a Record)'.

With the exception of Jaki Graham, none of these would go on to maintain a presence in the Top 40, but another home-grown act, Five Star, would be a different matter. These tightly-choreographed, costumed siblings from Romford - three girls and two boys - looked like the real deal. Their mid-year hits 'All Fall Down' and 'Let Me Be the One' blended American poise with British exuberance and both reached the Top 20. Their next one, 'Love Take Over', peaked at twenty-five, but it had more zip and polish and seemed to move them up a notch. It no doubt helped to make up the minds of many dithering over whether to buy the album *Luxury of Life*. I was one of them. There must have been plenty of others - it stayed in the album chart for seventy weeks.

This, then, was the soul and not-soul that soundtracked the contemporary mainstream club scene, with all its pressures and expectations. It didn't apply to all of clubland; various niches were served in various places. When at university, the students' favourite town centre venue staged a range of themed nights and put on gigs featuring all kinds of acts; it was both proudly alternative and extremely well-attended. When back in London, one of the biggest draws was Wendy May's Locomotion, held in the cavernous Town & Country Club in Kentish Town on Fridays; a celebration of oldies stretching back across the decades and sequenced skilfully in a playlist culminating in 'I'm a Believer' by the Monkees. There was an easy-going dress code; nobody really cared how you were dancing - nobody went there to be an alpha anything. But if you were young, that was kind of the problem; it was merely a bit of time out, a short break from the core business of hacking it in the mirror-lined jungles of mainstream night life where opportunity and threat lurked in equal measure.

This chapter chronicles the period in which I began getting to grips with it, at house parties, clubs and various other events in my second and third years as a university student, a period that happened to coincide with what was - eventually - a terrific soundtrack, and one that would end with a big decision. Of course, I have long lists of anecdotes linked to long lists of records; but even the friends they involve now consider them insignificant. This chapter won't cover those. But it *will* tell stories. It will cover emerging trends. It will address the nerdier aspects of buying and owning vinyl. It will cover typical-student stuff. It will cover some of the most important and memorable 45s of the time, some reflecting the political backdrop, some simply filling our waking hours with colour. As always, I'm forced to leave loads out. But it *will* cover Madonna and it *will* cover the Cocteau Twins.

When we got back for the autumn term, there were new lodgings to settle into. We had signed up for a three-storey terrace house split into bedsits, with shared kitchen and (also shared but rarely visited) bathrooms. Six of us moved in together as an unregulated lifestyle experiment. The whole place was cold, with varying degrees of damp. Mildew grew unchallenged on the bathroom walls. Invertebrates left silvery trails on the ground-floor carpets. The back yard was full of tall weeds, with around thirty milk bottles stretching along the wall beneath the kitchen window, filled with yellowing matter, never to be removed. During one holiday a human corpse would be found beside them. On dropping off their son for the start of the new term, one parent ordered that he be out of there in two weeks.

He stayed, along with the rest of us, for two years. We drew lots to allocate and re-allocate rooms. We took turns to prepare meals and to have the television in our bedrooms, each of which had a sink that saved us inconvenient trips to the toilet. Pissing in someone's sink was okay as long as you asked permission first and rinsed the basin thoroughly afterwards. We did have female visitors, but they always made sure they had gone to the loo before they arrived (as, for the record, did we).

All of us smoked, so the place stank of that, too; but, as has been noted, so in those days did just about everywhere else. It was conveniently close to the town centre and the union building, and therefore to showers and laundry facilities. A local youth sold hash door-to-door like a milkman. His family were not to be messed with, and there were more like them elsewhere along the street. We got ripped off, but we got supplied. For everything else, there was a small shop directly opposite. It was paradise.

It was also within walking distance of that aforementioned students' favourite town centre venue, an un-fussy, relaxing haven. It sold café food and seemed to be hollowed out of stone. On some nights you couldn't move in there. Wednesday night was oldies night, Thursday night was serious new stuff night. Every playlist was marbled with the alternative and - essentially - with soul.

Thank heavens for soul because, with very few exceptions, the singles chart that autumn was otherwise full of junk. The number ones following 'Into the Groove' by Madonna had been half-arsed celebrity cover versions of 60s favourites, namely 'I Got You Babe' by UB40 featuring Chrissie Hynde (a pointless and painful corporate snuggle) and 'Dancing in the Street' by David Bowie and Mick Jagger (like a pair of drunks doing a dare).

Midge Ure would replace this at the top with 'If I Was'; a square-jawed love song with a droning melody that obviously appealed to some, although you couldn't help wondering how much of its success was down to Live Aid. It was number one for a week. Then came 'The Power of Love' by Jennifer Rush, which stayed there for five; one of the most horrible records of a largely horrible year; an ear-splitting ballad with toe-curling lyrics, including the word "forsake".

Obviously, there were people buying all these 45s. It's easy to leap to conclusions about the type of person that wants to own a record you hate and the chances are they won't be accurate. But music in 1985 was characterised by a blandness that hung in the air like fog, and this seemed to be epitomised by a series of conversations I had at Christmas. I got a holiday job in a South London off-licence run by a young Asian couple with soft voices and gentle smiles. Music played all day, Capital Radio rather than Radio 1, but I wasn't complaining too much about adverts as I lugged crates up and down wooden steps and stacked shelves.

In quiet moments I was invited to sit down to chat. They wanted to know about my degree course and my family and my plans for the future, but I gradually managed to steer the conversation towards what had been on the radio. These exchanges seemed to pretty much sum up 1985, with anything quirky or innovative glossed over, and anything established and polished patted on the back. They were extremely good-natured but neither husband nor wife stopped grinning for a second. She was itching to start talking about Michael Jackson.

We agreed to like the recent number one by Wham!, the stompy, gonna-love-ya-baby sound of 'I'm Your Man'; and also the record which had replaced it at the top, 'Saving All My Love for You' by new name Whitney Houston, a jazzy sway capped by a forthright voice. But then there was 'Say You, Say Me' by Lionel Richie, a stroll along a lamplit boulevard in a big coat, at the mention of which the couple let out a unified gasp of approval; and 'Separate Lives' by Phil Collins and Marylin Martin, an anguished adult relationship saga, barely a song. "Yeh, but, you know, it tells a story. Lots of people really like that" insisted the husband, with a beaming smile.

The last two records we spoke about were different. They hinted at 1986 possibly being better than 1985. The first was 'The Show' by Doug E. Fresh and the Get Fresh Crew, a bunch of rappers clowning around in the throes of - supposedly - putting on a show. Crew members took turns to do their bit; there were funny voices, mad sound effects and bursts of instrumentation that enhanced the looseness. It had galvanising echoes of *Electro 1*. "I don't get it" said the husband. "What's it supposed to be about? It's a bit crazy." Indeed so.

The second was going to be my favourite record for the next two months: 'Girlie Girlie' by Sophia George. This was a bright, un-laminated reggae tune about a guy with girlfriends dotted all over the globe. It had me after one listen and I was wide-eyed as I mentioned it. "Yeh," nodded the woman, in a way which strongly indicated she would much rather be listening to Lionel Richie. "It's a bit of fun. It's good". She went straight from this to Michael Jackson and that was the concluding part of the discussion. Nothing could compare to Michael.

Earlier, she had said she supposed that I liked "student things" and I kind of knew what she meant. I thought immediately of the Cocteau Twins, and there was good reason to be talking about the Cocteau Twins at this point, but we'll come back to that. I asked if they had heard of them. The slow, synchronised shake of the head with which they responded indicated that this thread of the conversation was going no further and I took the hint.

Most people had at least a vague idea of what "student things" were. Aside from the specific tendency to fiddle with political topics, broad perceptions probably had it that the student mindset was given to the over-analytical, the frivolous and the ironic, although, as we have seen, the take-up on this was not universal among undergraduates. We were preoccupied with the same issues as most others in our position: making ends meet, managing a reasonable diet, making the gear last, not falling too far behind with course work, not having your clothes stolen from the launderette, not having your food stolen from the fridge; maintaining peers status through cool, maintaining peer status through being a bit 'ard, maintaining peer status through being funny; copping off, dealing with the fall-out from copping off, counselling friends through the fall-out from copping off, longing to cop off, failing to cop off, avoiding copping off - and all the emotion that went with it. And, of course, much of this stuff is what pop music had always been there to address.

Broad perceptions were, it has to be said, generally on the money. There was a studenty attitude, there was a studenty sense of humour, there were studenty clothes – and there was certainly studenty musical taste. A preference for the musically alternative was not the exclusive province of those with A-levels, but more students that non-students I knew had records by, for example, the Cure and Talking Heads. The Cure were in a rich vein of Top 30 form that autumn, following up their rumbustious 'In Between Days' with the edgy mischief of 'Close to Me', accompanied by a video featuring a wardrobe. Far out. Many of our student contemporaries arrived at uni already owning one or two Talking Heads albums and this New York group, led by family-friendly weirdo David Byrne, now brought out 'Road to Nowhere', a good old weirdo singalong with a military-style drum pattern that you could just about dance to, as proved repeatedly at the Dick Show. It got to number six.

It wasn't just the alternative cuts that went down well at the Dick Show. Neither Phil Collins nor Duran Duran, for instance, were ever very far from the turntable. Frankie Goes to Hollywood always hit the spot, as did the Eurythmics, particularly their energetic stomp 'Would I Lie to You?' Jacki Graham and Five Star sneaked onto the playlist, and space remained for Grandmaster Flash, Iggy Pop and the Buzzcocks. They also occasionally made room for Lynrd Skynrd's 'Freebird', giving long-haired rockers, of which there were many, something to throw their head-whips around to.

The mix was always eclectic, but usually it was the broad-appeal chart material that won out. By the end of the winter, one of the most reliable floor-fillers was 'When the Going Gets Tough, the Tough Get Going' from Billy Ocean, who had re-kindled his career with a string of Top 20 hits that matched your parents' wallpaper. This, his biggest success, came from the movie *Jewel in the Nile*, which did nothing to mitigate it. It was number one for the whole of February.

One of the things it now reminds me of is snow. That winter was piled high with the stuff. Going more than a couple of streets away was hard work, so we spent a lot of time in the Union Building, specifically in the Lower Refectory pool hall, where there stood a jukebox stuffed with recent Top 20 hits. For 50p you got three songs, one of which, if it was my 50p, would be 'Girlie Girlie'. It was often joined by 'System Addict', a good new one from Five Star; perhaps also 'How Will I Know' by Whitney Houston, the likeably springy follow up to her number one, or something more subdued and wistful like 'Leaving Me Now' by Level 42 or 'It's Alright (Baby's Coming Back)' by the Eurythmics. Some would have gone for the atmospheric 'West End Girls' from newcomers the Pet Shop Boys or 'The Sun Always Shines on TV' by newly-established Scandinavian heartthrobs A-Ha, both recent number ones. But if it was me: 'Girlie Girlie', 'System Addict' and 'One Vision' by Queen.

Having dismissed Queen as a band hanging around for the sake of showbiz, I had been quite happy to eat humble pie in November when 'One Vision' was released; a big fat rocker, at perfect headbanging tempo, centred on a dirty great guitar riff and with all kinds of up-to-date synth effects thrown in. The lyric, about bringing people together for one this, one that and one something else, was not yet the cliché it was destined to become. I bloody loved it.

The Queen-fan bass player began organising a second covers gig, with the act now billed as the Should Be Band. It was to be bigger than the last: in the same hall, but with the stage at the end rather than along the side, enabling the walk-in storage cupboard behind it to be used as a dressing room from which we could emerge like stars. A full PA and lighting rig were hired from the union building, accompanied by a four-strong technical crew. This was going to be the dog's bollocks.

There was little doubt that 'One Vision' would feature. It was chosen to open the show. The plan was that the long, unravelling intro from the twelve-inch would be played over the PA as we made our way on, donning our instruments in the gloom with just a few lights pulsing for effect. We would take over live on the first stroke of the guitar riff, with all the lights coming on in the same moment.

The idea actually worked – we carried it off and you couldn't hear the join. Such high professionalism set the tone, and some of the more amateurish moments that followed were forgiven, if indeed they were noticed. Around four hundred people saw a decent gig for a bit of pocket money, showing varying degrees of appreciation. Some merely chuckled and applauded, but during the encore, a cluster of mates performed ironic, alcohol-enhanced but deeply satisfying acts of fawning worship before my drum kit. If ever I hear 'One Vision' now, that's what I think of.

Despite some of us having the odd brush with pseudo-stardom, our lives often defaulted to frantic, lamplit rushes to get essays in on time, pathetic attempts to make one spliff's-worth go into three, or the budgeting of coins in the Lower Refectory, some of which were destined for the pool table, some for the jukebox, but some perhaps for the purchase of a thin, dry burger from the next-door bar, perhaps the only thing we would eat before sundown. There was also our desperately unhygienic house and the desperately unhygienic habits we practised there. In the lead-up to Christmas, we invited people round for a party. Heaven only knows why they came. We promised a cooked dinner, with turkey, sprouts and a nut roast for the vegetarians. The frozen turkey was taken out of the fridge in good time but the temperature in the kitchen was such that it wouldn't defrost without being immersed in warm water, the first time we had used either of the bathrooms in months. We cooked and served turkey. To my knowledge, nobody became seriously ill, but it was obvious that the vegetarians were the more relaxed ones.

This is not painting us into the most favourable of tableaus. Yet, at other times, we held forth in a manner fit for red carpets. Each hall of residence had its annual Hall Ball, where the dress was formal, the decorations lavish and the entertainment substantial. You could choose to wear your own dapper suits if you had them - most of us had at least a shirt and tie somewhere: but I, along with many others, opted for hiring the full black-tie outfit and getting my hair done in town. In our second year we got tickets for our old hall of residence Hall Ball and thus went twice. Additionally, there was the Union Ball, that everybody went to, staged in the sprawl of buildings on the central site. It took place in early summer and was massive, going from dusk till dawn with diversions including discos, stand-up comedians, magicians and movies. There was also plenty of live music. We saw current charting acts like Julian Cope and the Damned, plus a few who hadn't charted yet but one day would, including the extraordinary We've Got a Fuzzbox and We're Gonna Use It. But there were two other types of band: veteran legends from our childhoods, and the fledgling category of the tribute band.

Veterans first. In the space of two years, we saw Mud, the Sweet and Showaddywaddy, acts whose records I had spent a significant percentage of my pocket money on while at primary school. Les Gray was still Mud's front man, albeit a frail-looking version of the guy we remembered clowning around on *Top of the Pops*. He spent most of the performance leaning on the microphone stand surrounded by younger jobbing musicians. But it *was* Les Gray and he *did* sing and they *did* do the greatest hits and we *did* go nuts. The Sweet, with only two original members left, put on a solidly good rock show, doing the hits that had that heavier sound. Seeing them was undoubtedly exciting, but both were mere remnants of the bands we remembered.

Showaddywaddy on the other hand, with figurehead lead singer Dave Bartram still at the helm, looked just as they always had, rolling out the hits in full regalia. They were outstanding: slaying the songs, throwing the shapes and hoisting girls on to the stage for jiving lessons – a group of gentlemen guiding giggling damsels through their paces without putting a hair, a piece of gum or a brothel-creeper out of place.

There was a similar range across the tribute bands we saw. The Bootleg Beatles, who played at our first year Hall Ball, were probably the best known. They were clearly older than the Beatles had been when they had split up, but that didn't matter one bit. For the first half of their show, they dressed in faithful reproductions of the lapel-free grey suits from 1963 and did the early stuff; for the second half they donned faithful reproductions of the *Sgt. Pepper* costumes and did the later material. The attention to detail, in both look and performance, was impressive. They *sounded* like the Beatles. They *moved* like the Beatles. Each one even looked sufficiently like the Beatle they had the job of portraying and they stayed in role throughout.

But at another Ball we saw the Strolling Bones, who, by contrast, could have been a bunch of guys just sauntering in off the street because they heard there was free booze and grabbing bits of costume as they approached the stage. They could do the songs. They sounded alright. There was a designated Mick Jagger and a designated Keith Richards. They went down pretty well. But they were not like the Bootleg Beatles. One day, the world would be full of tribute bands of both these kinds and more.

Aside from these rare appearances in penguin suits, I was usually found in the standard casual combination of jeans, sweat-top and trainers. Plus, the typical-student topping of a knee-length, patterned raincoat. This was the most typically-studenty bit of clothing I ever owned. There was the odd spot of bother with locals starting on students when they fancied a bit of aggro, and if you went into town wearing a knee-length, patterned raincoat you were easy to pick out. It was wise to have a bomber jacket or something on standby, just to lessen the risk.

I would bet that when people saw us sauntering along in our studenty clobber they often made confident guesses about what bands we were into. Maybe they would have thought the Cure or Talking Heads. Perhaps they would have thought New Order, who by the end of 1986 would have had three Top 10 albums and a total of fifty-seven weeks on the album chart. Most people knew 'Blue Monday' (which was still getting regular spins at the Dick Show) and would recognise the group as a touchstone for the alternative – or indie – sensibility.

But the other band they would have thought of was the Smiths, whose national chart performance for an indie act then was simply astonishing. By the close of 1986, their four albums would have reached two, seven, one and two respectively, clocking up a total of 114 weeks on the chart. Add to that nine hit singles, five of these making the Top 20 and one making the Top 10 and you have a level of success that no one in the world of the UK alternative could get close to.

They were massive. They inspired devotion. People spoke passionately about Johnny Marr's guitar playing and made various - often floundering and inadequate - attempts to summarise the appeal radiated by front-man Morrissey. His songs formed a body of protest pieces unrivalled in 80s pop; ones which, importantly, depicted the real feelings of real people rather than what life's winners were apparently experiencing on a daily basis. Personally, I would always struggle to sit through a whole Smiths album, but I did understand all the fuss at the time.

There was something else that the Smiths represented. They were a band in that traditional format of drums, bass, lead guitar and focal-point lead singer, at a point where the industry had found these things no longer essential. Replacing them with new studio technology was, it seemed, overwhelmingly the way of the world; there was very little in the Top 40 to suggest otherwise. Some major acts did still feature prominent guitarists; but the point was the studio technology, not the guitars. People often say that the Smiths "kept guitars going" through the mid-80s, and that really tells its own story. Johnny Marr could twang and twiddle all he liked, but this would stubbornly remain the era of not-guitars until after his band had folded.

So: back to people watching students go by in knee-length patterned raincoats. I wonder how many would have thought: *bet he likes the Cocteau Twins*. I was perfectly happy being distracted by Sophia

George, Five Star and the occasional touring old-timer. But I kept looking out for the Cocteau Twins and, towards the end of 1985, it was announced that they would be putting out two EPs within a fortnight of each other; in effect, a mini album. These releases - *Tiny Dynamite* and *Echoes in a Shallow Bay* – would turn me from a mere fan into a pious devotee.

From their debut in 1982, each new release had seen some kind of shift in their sound. But this felt like a particularly big one. Each of their key elements - the synth-encased banshee cries, the haunted-house-on-Jupiter atmospheres, the lyric-free vocals, the effects-laden drum and guitar noise – were suddenly doused in the most advanced production. Usually when a band loses that initial rawness and smooths everything over with studio sophistication I mourn. But in bringing abstraction to pop in the way they were, I felt that the Cocteau Twins were doing something genuinely different, something that radiated vast promise. Suddenly it seemed to be the most worthwhile project in all of music.

It was the tracks on these EPs that put the idea into my head. 'Pink, Orange, Red', was a masterclass in control; everything arranged to achieve the richest possible effect from a simple idea. The stunning, shamanistic 'Great Spangled Fritillary' opened with long passages of wailing and lamentation over deep, dark beats, until joined by a looped melody that rose and trickled down in a rhythm like some otherworldly Flamenco. An instrumental, 'Ribbed and Veined', was a showcase for new guitar noise, its core refrain sounding as if made from sharpened platinum. Really the whole thing was a showcase, an exhibition of what they could now do, without lyrics or descriptive song titles to guide, and therefore limit, a listener's experience. This was a band in the process of honing a special craft. I now had an emotional stake in seeing what they could achieve.

Needless to say, neither EP made the Top 40. But they both went to number one in the Independent Singles Chart, as published in the weekly music press. I was yet to become an avid consumer of the music papers. I occasionally bought *Record Mirror* because it seemed to be the least snooty and had more pages of charts in it, and I had felt too grown up for *Smash Hits* at fifteen, let alone at twenty-two. But the *NME* and

Melody Maker had high status and sometimes I picked up a copy of one or the other, just for the buzz of seeing a chart where the Cocteau Twins were number one.

Their next new release came the following April. This was *Victorialand*, a nine-track, 45rpm album, with no listings or credits on the cover, just its title; and an atmosphere of warmth, drowsiness and security. There was no percussion, save the odd bit of drifting tabla drum. Voices wafted, warbled and wove honeyed harmonies. Guitars were gently strummed, or simply shimmered. Track titles included 'Lazy Calm' and 'Whales' Tails'. It was the first Cocteau Twins LP to reach the Top 10 on the national chart, getting to number ten and haunting the chart for a respectable seven weeks. Interesting. An unexpected direction, but another definite jolt forwards. I had faith. And it would be rewarded.

Another quintessentially studenty record from those weeks was 'Marlene on the Wall' by Suzanne Vega, a singer-songwriter of classic qualities; acoustic, feminist and earnest. This had a presence in our world out of all proportion to its peak position of twenty-one. There was an intensity about it, with chord changes of metallic spray and a vocal delivery of supressed anger; its protagonist reflecting on a love life that had, perhaps, become a waste of time. The *Suzanne Vega* LP was soon circulating. The best other thing on it was 'The Queen and the Soldier', an allegorical battle-of-the-sexes drama which you could see in whatever light suited your purposes. The album was an oasis, occasioning the kind of navel-gazing and self-absorption to which youngsters, and in particular young student types, are often prone. Suzanne Vega briefly seemed to be a kind of prophet. But only briefly. 'Marlene on the Wall' meanwhile remains a sensational single.

Before graduating, the lads in our house would each write out a top twenty records of our time at university, awarding points for each position and merging our lists into a single super-chart. 'Marlene on the Wall' would feature, but 'Sledgehammer' by Peter Gabriel would be its number one. In the spring of 1986, it spent four weeks at its peak of number four. It was a big, funky sound with a sturdy beat and a lead performance that was remarkable, given that Gabriel had made his name as the theatrical front man for Genesis, in the underground prog days before their commercial epiphany. The record had a memorable video: a stop-motion animation featuring the singer surrounded by morphing dough forms, including self-propelling tea sets and steam trains that swirled around his head as he sang - it won awards and got chatted about at dinner parties.

The lads in our house remember the single for a spontaneous dance that we burst into on one morning as it played; bouncing on the bed, grandstanding on the armchair, parading before the window as if it was a giant movie camera; with others arriving to see what the heck was going on and immediately joining in. It was like a scene from the kind of movie we all hated. 'Sledgehammer' is not remembered with universal fondness, but this was what it was capable of.

I remember the store where I bought both of these. 'Marlene on the Wall' was issued in a stiff cover made of textured card, with a centre consisting of a moulded plastic ring whose lettering was just about well-finished; 'Sledgehammer' had a slickly-designed paper centre, but came in a relatively vulnerable paper cover. This was all fairly typical of what you could expect when you went shopping for 7" singles now. Apart from the price creeping up to the £1.60 mark, the experience of owning them hadn't much changed in the previous three years.

There had been a sudden explosion of picture covers in 1978-9; now they were absolutely standard. I bought forty-four singles in the first half of 1986, all of them issued in picture sleeves. Twelve were made of robust, laminated card, but most were standard paper. This was important detail. The problem with unprotected paper sleeves was often that, as they rubbed together in the delivery boxes, a dark circle got printed on the next cover thanks to the raised ring around the centre of the disc. When you had spent years taking care to avoid rips and bent corners, dark circles were galling. I was, by now, buying protective PVC sleeves for particularly vulnerable covers and was prepared to be assertive with shop assistants who had handed me a new record with a circle showing, however noisily they sighed and tutted.

The other variable was whether the centre of the record consisted of a printed paper label like the Peter Gabriel one or a ring of moulded plastic like the Suzanne Vega one. Of these forty-four centres, twenty-eight were paper. I considered paper centres to be proper centres and assumed, grumpily, that the move towards plastic ones constituted gratuitous cost-saving at the pressing plant and an inevitable consequence of unfettered capitalism. Such were the times in which we found ourselves.

And yet they were good times. These Suzanne Vega and Peter Gabriel singles appeared part-way through a year which, for a long time afterwards, I considered one of the great years for pop, for the simple reason that the stream of interesting and enjoyable stuff coming out seemed to be unrelenting. In some years, good sounds bustle around you non-stop. 1986 *bustled.* We have already considered the frozen winter days that began it. As the snow and ice thawed, there was a new number one, 'Chain Reaction' by Diana Ross – yes, *Diana Ross* – who had left Motown for Capitol and was now at a latter-day apex with this rousing Bee Gees song, catapulting admirers old and young into starry-eyed delirium and filling the floor at the Dick Show.

Below it at two were the Bangles, an American all-girl band who I already owned three bits of vinyl by. Their song, 'Manic Monday', was a kitchen-sink mini-drama about being constantly late for work and having an unemployed boyfriend who wants sex at inconvenient moments. It was smart, richly orchestrated and almost universally popular. Guitarist and singer Susanna Hoffs had a distinctive voice and the kind of prettiness that the mid-80s could understand. She may or may not be the reason why Prince, writer of 'Manic Monday', had gifted them the song. In interviews, her bandmates seemed to think she was.

Prince himself was in the same Top 10 with 'Kiss', the quality of which perhaps explains why he was in a position to give away hit songs. Not everybody warmed to Prince; he was easy to take the piss out of and this song was really just an examination of his hard-on; yet its minimal, pinched funk and soft falsetto vocal sounded incredible. I bought it because it was something different - it took me ages to recognise exactly how good it was. It's still difficult to comprehend why it did no better than number six.

People now of course cite Prince as being one of the two major pop figures of the mid-80s, the other being someone we should now catch up with. Madonna was fascinating. It wasn't because I fancied her particularly, I just always felt like I was on her side: she seemed more naturally-equipped than most to provide the charts with the kind of excellence that I felt the charts should have. That feeling remained despite the odd bit of rubbish like 'Crazy for You' and 'The Gambler', which were, respectively, the third and seventh of her eight Top 5 singles in 1985. *Eight* Top 5 singles in one year – an incredible achievement by any standard. Since 'Into the Groove', there had also been the mood-lightening chug 'Angel' and the spritely 'Dress You Up', both of which got to number five and were the kind of Madonna I liked best. She got 1986 underway by re-releasing the 1984 flop 'Borderline'. This, we now decided, had been a little belter all along. It got to number two while Billy Ocean was number one.

So now, having exhausted *Like A Virgin*, resuscitated under-performing oldies and (for now) run out of movie links, she had to come up with something new. She came up with 'Live to Tell', a big change of tempo and a new mood; stately, reflective, restless – it had no decisive effect, it just kept drifting in and out of your head. It was number two for a week in late spring. She was one release away from a second UK number one.

Meanwhile, there was some quality not-soul in the Top 10, including the almost obscenely-hooky 'Can't Wait Another Minute' by Five Star, the first of what would be six singles - *six singles* - from a second album, *Silk and Steel*. Just below it in the Top 10 was a new one by Jaki Graham, 'Set Me Free', a foundation-rattling shouter with a pumping chant of a chorus. Alongside these stood the explosive 'All and All' by Joyce Sims, another one of those slices of American class, a record that we considered a kind of uber-soul - wonderful, state-of-the-art synth sound, deliciously groovy and well below 120 bpm. Late one Friday night, a handful of my London mates announced their arrival for a weekend visit by standing beside their car with all four doors open, dancing to the blaring 'All and All', with the drug-dealers peering past shutters and slowly-opened doors. We had to assure them that they were friends and not a rival gang.

In the week that 'All and All' peaked at number sixteen, the record one place below it was 'I Heard It Through the Grapevine' by Marvin Gaye, which had just paid its second visit to the Top 10, the first having been when it reached number one back in 1969. The rush of interest in this all-time-great oldie was due to it being used in a big-budget commercial for a certain brand of denim trousers. The ad featured a brooding young man with firm muscles and no body hair stripping down to his boxer shorts in a golden-era launderette, in order to wash his jeans while he sat in his boxers and waited for them to be ready - he was going to wear that pair of denim trousers and no other. Sam Cooke's 'Wonderful World' from 1960 had gone to number two a few weeks earlier due to a different advert for the same brand. 'Wonderful World' was a cute enough piece of fluff, but 'I Heard It Through the Grapevine' was serious.

Until now, my main memory of it had been its effect on my first drum teacher, who had drifted off into a parallel world when it was mentioned, stutteringly failing to do it justice with words. I had since come to understand why. In 1969, it was an epic saga of crushing betrayal and heartbreak. Now, however, it was about a cute guy taking his clothes off in a fantasy launderette; a wolf-whistle rather than an agonising turning-point. To sell jeans they needed sex; and to sanitise the sex they blended it with a classic record whose familiarity made it safe. 'I Heard It Through the Grapevine' had been rendered mere two-dimensional dressing. Pop had been used in adverts before, but this felt different. The commoditisation-proper of our musical history had begun.

Perhaps the biggest new release as the summer term drew to a close was 'Happy Hour' by the Housemartins. This was another quintessentially studenty record, engendering something close to hysteria among the undergraduate crowd. The group were four clean-cut, cosily-dressed English boys doing a little ankles-and-elbows formation dance in a line, the key element being their complete lack of glamour - any one of them could have been in the hall of residence room next to yours. They played at our favourite town centre venue and tickets were like gold dust.

In a fast, bouncy guitar rhythm, 'Happy Hour' parodied the early-evening bar culture in which young men in office suits flashed the cash, guffawing and ogling the bar staff. An emerging definition of the era was the amount of fun that everyone was having now that the political left had been quashed. Fun was now expected, fun was now demanded:

display your glassy-eyed delirium, your wealth and your lechery, or else you'll be suspect. But, as with other parodies, those being depicted saw it as a tribute and adopted it as an anthem; when it came on, they raised drinks, made eye contact with each other and started their own version of the little dance. It got to number three.

There was a political edge to two other memorable records in those weeks. 'Camouflage' by Stan Ridgeway was about a young soldier in the Vietnam War, rescued by a mysterious superhero, who turns out to be the ghost of a marine sworn to save a young life in action before he can rest in peace. It was a square-jawed, patriotic country record, but was oddly not a hit in the US, despite doing well all over Europe.

America was in tough-talking conservative hands and not giving an inch to the damn commies. In the cinema we were half-way through a succession of big movies including *First Blood*, *Platoon* and *Full Metal Jacket*, depicting positive qualities of endurance and togetherness amidst the horrors of war, almost always specifically Vietnam, a conflict which had ended with the damn commies getting what they wanted. 'Camouflage', with its narrative language of "swattin' charlies", fit this ambiguity.

A major concern about the conservative project on both sides of the Atlantic was the levels of unemployment accompanying the reorganisation of the economy. It had a dramatic effect on established communities and the results had been starkly depicted in television dramas - most memorably the BBC series *Boys from the Blackstuff* - as well as in coverage of the miners' strike. People had strong feelings about it, so 'Ain't Nothin' Goin' On But the Rent' by Gwen Guthrie was bound to cause a stir.

In the song, the woman was saying: *There's no point wanting to be my man if you have no money because my priority is paying the bills.* The chorus refrain of "You've got to have a J-O-B if you wanna be with me" was particularly provocative. You could now stigmatise the jobless by dancing and singing along, in a venue you can afford to dress up for and pay to enter because you're working. It was a not-soul club record and a good one, its energetic bassline and deep reverb underpinning a standout sound. It reached number five in August, a couple of weeks after 'Camouflage' had peaked at four.

The record at number one as the summer break got underway was controversial for more well-trodden reasons. It was a second chart-topper by Madonna and she was raising the bar. 'Papa Don't Preach' was about a pregnant girl imploring Papa to support her decision to have the baby. She doesn't want to get rid of it and the young man responsible has promised to stand by her. This is full-on girl group country, but the Shangri-La's and the Shirelles would never have released anything as explicit as this. It was perfect for 1986 and Madonna seemed to know exactly what she was doing in picking a controversy that would, at a stroke, both ruffle conservative feathers and win admirers for the feminine strength on display. The lyric implies that there's going to be a blazing row, yet it's impossible to decide whether an angry, vengeful father would be upholding family values any more than his determined daughter. Bloody clever. And a great record. Not a dancer, but a fully-orchestrated piece of class.

For that summer's holiday job, I once again managed to bag another environment where the radio was on all day, this time in an empty high school as an assistant caretaker. Good tune after good tune seemed to fly from the radio as I cleared strip-lights, scrubbed toilet walls, scraped chewing gum from floormats and drank stewed tea. An edited shortlist might include 'Let's Go All the Way' by Sly Fox, 'Smile' by Audrey Hall, 'Find the Time' by Five Star, 'What's the Colour of Money?' by Hollywood Beyond, 'The Way It Is' by Bruce Hornsby and the Range, 'I Didn't Mean to Turn You On' by Robert Palmer, 'Sun Street' by Katrina and The Waves and 'Breaking Away' by Jacki Graham. Just look at the variation in that line-up.

In the ultra-cheesy corner of this variation stood 'So Macho' by Sinitta, a song about hankering after masculine guys with big muscles. I hated it. There was nothing wrong with my muscles but stuff like this made me think there might be. Clearly though, it was aimed at gay men, especially since it was released as a double A-side with a song called 'Cruising'. Why gay men would want this crap any more than straight women seemed a mystery but, at any rate, it did very well in the charts. It was a big number two.

What then were the big number ones? Following 'Papa Don't Preach' came two that covered most of the rest of the holiday, and if you mention either you'll probably get groaned at. 'Lady in Red' by Chris de Burgh had a solidly sweet idea at its core, that of a guy seeing his wife from across the room at a party and falling in love with her all over again, but yucky detail wrung all the subtlety out of it. Clearly, it was aimed at the more mature listener. But 'I Want to Wake Up with You' by Boris Gardner sounded like it was for even older people - cod-reggae by a Jamaican star from the rocksteady era; one now boosting his pension by appealing to audiences who were beginning to draw theirs. It washed over me then and I have nothing more to say about it now. These two did for the top spot until the second week of September. It was a good job there were so many other things to distract and elevate. I will mention just two more. They came from different worlds.

First: 'Panic' by the Smiths. A short guitar herald, then bang-straight into two minutes and nineteen seconds of pure, swanky vitriol. Its lyric reported civil unrest in towns across the country, then urged us to join it and burn the discos, lynching those forcing us to listen to music which serves only to alienate us. The refrain "Hang the DJ" formed an angry, celebratory coda, swelled by the voices of children until it had become a baying, chanting mob pouring through the streets. As a fit of pique and a fleeting fantasy of revolution, it remains pretty hard to beat. It got to number eleven.

Second: 'When I Think of You' by Janet Jackson, sister of Michael. She had appeared in late spring with the number three hit 'What Have You Done for Me Lately', a breathless workout of abrupt rhythm and new-fangled synth, which she followed with the intense and playful 'Nasty', reaching nineteen. By the end of the summer she had enjoyed a third hit, which got to number ten and was arguably the best of the three.

'When I Think of You' was joyful: a rattling groove, a singalong bass line and a lyric about being happily in love. There wasn't another record that year which grew on me so enormously from such a modest starting-point. It played a starring role at just about every gathering I attended in the second half of the holiday, making everyone groove, making everyone smile. I was so impressed that I took the rare step of buying the twelve-inch.

As you may recall, I have banged on about twelve-inches elsewhere, largely condemning them as a rip-off; often because, despite there being nothing to add to the seven-inch mix, something gets bolted on anyway, contributing zilch to the tune you had been so impressed by on the radio. But they also have the habit of editing out features of the seven-inch that give it character. 'When I Think of You' is a prime example. Near the end, as it explodes out of the break, the singer produces a wonderful burst of laughter which seems to cap the whole mood of the record. Is this on the twelve-inch? Is it bollocks. I grumpily forked out another £1.59 for the seven-inch and redoubled my caution. I bought both formats of 'Smile' by Audrey Hall as well; the seven-inch of that is miles better, too.

Suddenly we were heading back to university, where the gathering cold and damp soon re-focused our minds on the inadequacy of our accommodation. To help us keep warm this time round, we had *Music Box* TV; a late-night broadcast on the independent channel showing music videos deep into the early hours. Staying up all night several times a week is really not what you need in your finals year, but this was an opportunity very hard to resist. Few people in the UK had access to non-terrestrial television and things like MTV. Indeed, it was only in this year that 24-hour broadcasting was first tried on our terrestrial channels - and there were still only four of those.

So the odds on us becoming regular *Music Box* viewers were short. And view it we did, huddled in our chairs for hours on end under blankets and coats, like beleaguered troops waiting for the promised airlift. This was how we quickly became familiar with 'Walk This Way' by Run-D.M.C. - the one rap act that seemed to have staying power. It was a very particular kind of cover version, effectively 'Walk This Way' by New England rockers Aerosmith with some of the singing replaced by rap. This made it mainstream-danceable - rap *and* rock – and whenever the term "cross-over" was used subsequently, this record was often cited as Exhibit A. The idea of cross-over bristled with possibility. The video that accompanied it was *Music Box*'s star turn. It showed Run-D.M.C. and Aerosmith doing their thing separately, in adjacent rooms, their rival styles causing friction, until Aerosmith front man Steve Tyler burst head-and-shoulders through the wall, yelling his chorus at the rappers in a haze of plaster-dust.

Run-D.M.C. were using rock to demonstrate rap's versatility and potential. But for most, rap still amounted to no more than a hotchpotch of novelties that were to be no more than tolerated. Hence 'Holiday Rap', not many places away in the same Top 10, a record about, well, being on holiday, which incorporated bits of Cliff Richard's 'Summer Holiday' into its piffle. It was by MC Miker G and DJ Sven. Grannies taking end-of-season breaks did cheeky things to it on the Med.

But the biggest record at the start of term - and for some way into it - was, without doubt, 'Don't Leave Me This Way' by the Communards. They were fronted by falsetto-voiced Jimmy Somerville, whose former group, Bronski Beat, had established themselves in 1984 with 'Smalltown Boy', a poignant record about a youngster whose homosexuality forces him to leave home. The gay scene has always been partial to energetic dancing (there was even an 80s genre called Hi-NRG, which featured early productions by Stock, Aitken, Waterman) and when Somerville's new group recorded a club-ready cover of 70s disco favourite 'Don't Leave Me This Way', entire sections of society lost their minds.

The word "anthem" has been badly over-used down the years with regard to pop tunes, but before it became thus corrupted, 'Don't Leave Me This Way' by the Communards was an anthem for our university's Gay and Lesbian Society and associated sympathisers. Dancing to it, and doing so with serious application, was a statement. There were some people that you never saw on the dance floor at the Dick Show except when that record was playing. They threaded their way urgently through the melee, past all those Level 42, Eurythmics and Five Star fans, to any space that they could make their own, and then gave it everything. We danced alongside them; but it wasn't our record, it was theirs. It was number one for four weeks to mid-October and remained hot thereafter.

At number three in the same chart sat another dance-worthy ditty, 'Word Up' by Cameo; solid, sparse funk with an outrageously affected vocal and spaghetti-western flourishes. It was hard to decide whether it heralded some kind of new dawn or was just a high-quality bit of mucking about. The video, with which we also became familiar during our long nights in front of *Music Box*, did nothing to settle the question. It was, to say the least, a bit tongue-in-cheek - but then again perhaps it wasn't. It was hard to tell. It had a bloke in a bright red codpiece, anyway.

'Word Up' was a very different dance proposition to 'Don't Leave Me This Way'. But then 'Walk Like an Egyptian' by the Bangles was something different again. It made people swarm onto the dance floor with no idea what to do when they got there. Well, almost none. In tribute to vintage dance-craze records going on about how "everybody" was "doin' the" whatever-it-was, the song claimed that, in public spaces everywhere, people were performing something akin to the Sand Dance, an old variety show routine inspired by friezes on the walls of Egyptian tombs. To walk like an Egyptian was to employ a similar gait, with your front hand up and jabbing forward and your rear hand down and jabbing back.

Amazingly, it caught on. Troupes of football lads did it on the way to the ground. Party-goers announced their arrival by doing it beside the cab. When you answered the door, you might find someone on the front step doing it. People did it if they were just stuck for something to do. But nobody of any sustained status did it on the dance floor. If you happened to be there when it came on, it was well-advised to adopt some manageable variation on the twist instead. Which is what most people did. So that they could enjoy an extraordinary record without looking like knobs. Over a period of seven weeks, 'Walk Like an Egyptian' fought its way steadily up the chart until reaching number three in mid-November. In America it went to number one.

I can't remember it being played among the serious new stuff on Thursday nights at our favourite town centre venue. There, we were beginning to get familiar with a new term: "house music"; due in no small part to a particular track, 'Love Can't Turn Around' by Farley "Jackmaster" Funk with Daryl Pandy.

These credits merit scrutiny. We would soon be acquainted with the term "jack" through other records - for now, it was enough to know that Farley Funk was its master. The inclusion of "Funk" placed it in a known tradition, but less traditional was the fact that the background guy was the main star. He'd got Daryl Pandy in just to do vocals.

The sound was equally fresh; with a simple, driving *thomp, thomp, thomp, thomp* rhythm, a synth bass made to sound like the lowest notes on a tuba, and the vocals a blend of Pandy's oceanic tones and the crisp coos of huddled backing singers. It had entered the chart at the end of August and had mileage in it yet.

Now playing alongside it, was 'Showing Out (Get Fresh at the Weekend)' by Mel and Kim, the latest Stock, Aitken, Waterman production. Many of us labelled it "house" straight away because of its predominant *thomp, thomp, thomp, thomp*. Two cool girls, who turned out to be sisters, doing crisp, simple moves in sync as they sang about getting fresh at the weekend and turning their noses up at boring stuff; with bright vocal hooks, machine-gun drum fills and sharp keyboard giving depth to the *thomp, thomp*. It swaggered to number three.

To summarise the rest of the autumn, Five Star had what would prove to be their best placing, a number two with accomplished sugar-sculpture 'Rain or Shine'. Madonna enjoyed a third number one with 'True Blue', the title track from the new LP, a gum-chewin', bobby-socks 45 in the grand tradition. We'll save a detailed compare-and-contrast with 'Frankie' by Sister Sledge for another time. As far as I was concerned, 'True Blue' was brilliant. As far as I was concerned, Madonna was *it*.

Before the end of the year there would be 'French Kissin' in the USA' by Debbie Harry for pop, 'Livin' on a Prayer' by Bon Jovi for dirty-denim rock, 'Experiment IV' by Kate Bush for out-of-the-blue oddity, and 'Love is the Slug' by We've Got a Fuzzbox and We're Gonna Use It, for pantomime punk revivalism. I bought and loved all of these.

It seemed that the only thing that could top it all would be an epic, rafter-rattling, authority-stamping single from the Cocteau Twins. Well, there was one. 'Love's Easy Tears' was their way of saying: *Okay - we've done all that experimenting; now here's something straightforwardly stunning*. They wheeled out the big stuff - massive, Spector-like beats dragged from the bowels of the earth, a leviathan of a riff and a chorus of cascading fireworks. The depth of its sound was maintained across the EP, most notably on the galactic, hurtling 'Those Eyes – That Mouth'. Its bass made the needle jump out of the groove on my parent's turntable, requiring a couple of 2p pieces to be balanced on top of the stylus to restrain it, which was important because I wanted to play it a lot. 'Love's Easy Tears' peaked at ... well it doesn't really matter where it peaked.

1986 *bustled* with action. The following year, by contrast, felt mostly flat and disappointing. Steve 'Silk' Hurley had a surprise number one in its early weeks with an oddly compelling chunk of tinny electronica called 'Jack Your Body'; essentially an instrumental with the title sung over the top, punctuated by the odd groin-thrusting grunt. It seemed to be missing something to make it a bona fide dance record. Later came the even less-obviously-dancey 'Jack the Groove' by Raze, which made it into the Top 20.

These "jack" things were different to the soul and not-soul of the mirrored panels and acrylic fronds. Some of us might have wondered what else might be done in a studio without the need for a song. We were given a clue with 'This Brutal House' by Nitro Deluxe, whose gravel-crunch electro beats and cute keyboard motif became very familiar to club-goers. Its concoction of sequences and samples hinted at the kinds of sound that would follow in the next couple of years – songs, it seemed, would indeed be essential no longer.

There *were* songs, though. There was 'Respectable', the new one by Mel and Kim, an exercise in how much fun you could squeeze on to one side of a seven-inch. You simply couldn't hear it without brightening up, and the sight of these terrific, smiley sisters had something for everybody; for one wonderful week in March, it was the UK's number one. Three weeks later, Madonna was there again. Having taken the rollicking 'Open Your Heart' to number four at Christmas, she now turned her attention to sun, sea and Spanish guitar for her next best-seller, 'La Isla Bonita', which made its way to the top with effortless charm.

This pair of number ones constituted a high point. The Smiths released another good single, 'Sheila Take a Bow', and then split up. That was the only other thing worth noting. There was a handful of other decent new singles. And a whole heap of old ones. In the chart of March 14th, five of the top six were either oldies or cover versions.

In the top spot was Boy George's perfunctory cover of Ken Boothe's 'Everything I Own'. At two, Ben E. King's 'Stand by Me' from 1961, revived by its use in another jeans advert, and having just ended a three-week stint at number one. At three, sat Jackie Wilson's 'I Get the Sweetest Feeling', which was already an oldie when it first became a hit in 1972, and with which he was now following up the re-release of his 'Reet Petite (The Sweetest Girl in Town)', from 1957, which had been number one at Christmas three months ago. Seriously. Number four was 'The Great Pretender' by Freddie Mercury, a cover of The Platters' 1956 hit, as pointless as the Boy George effort.

Finally, at six, having dropped from number two, was 'When a Man Loves a Woman' by Percy Sledge, from 1966, the result of yet another jeans commercial. Thousands of youngsters nevertheless got the chance to buy this amazing and powerful record in their local high street, which was a good thing. Whether it now makes them think of the thin line between overwhelming love and mental illness, or a skinny girl wriggling into skinny jeans, is something only they can tell you. At any rate, bombarded with all this, it's little wonder that 'Respectable' and 'La Isla Bonita' felt so precious.

I graduated in June. There were ceremonies and parties and then we all left. I went home and spent an uneventful summer. I occasionally got together with friends. But I felt surplus to requirements. My future was formless. My love life was a shambles. I was about to enter a big wide world that was nothing like the one I had grown up expecting.

The summer soundtrack had an air of weariness about it, with a few exceptions, such as the magisterial 'True Faith' by New Order, and yet another good one from Madonna, 'Who's That Girl', something from yet another movie that I had no intention of seeing, which took over at number one in July. I clung to both of these. Michael Jackson then claimed top spot with 'I Just Can't Stop Loving You', heralding an album with which finally to follow up *Thriller* - it was horrible. Everything else was dull or annoying. Or both. Even the new Mel and Kim one was a bit rubbish.

The one other thing I really liked was 'Heart and Soul' by T'Pau. Based on a rhythm reminiscent of Queen's 'We Will Rock You', it yelled at the heavens and let off steam for me. It would end up getting to number four, but the only other person I knew who loved it was the LSM's youngest sister. I was twenty-three and only able to share the best current record with a kid seven years my junior. The thought occurred to me that perhaps it was intended for sixteen-year-olds.

My mind drifted back to a Sunday morning when I was eleven and at a friend's house. We were talking about music while his dad, who had put some opera on the turntable, was coming and going in his dressing-gown. I was probably banging on about something by Sparks or the Rubettes. His dad paused and stared at me with a quizzical smile. "When", he asked, "are you going to start growing out of all this silly pop music?"

I can't remember my reply, but I loved Sparks and the Rubettes and was not about to abandon them at the behest of a dad in a dressing-gown. I understood that at some point this would change, but I wasn't sure when. Grown-ups liked boring stuff. I was only eleven.

Now, however, at twenty-three, deflated, disillusioned and developing a strong sense of needing a fresh start, I was perhaps ready to respond to that quizzical smile. I would stop listening to the charts. I would stop looking for thrills and deeper meanings in seven-inch singles and search for satisfaction elsewhere. I would finally grow up.

I noticed an ad in a national newspaper asking for graduates. That was one of the few things I knew for certain that I was. Warmed by feeling so wanted, I rang the number. I was invited to a group interview at a well-known organisation and spent two hours chatting with other young people around a huge polished oak table. I wasn't asked back, but they said nice things about me and I was sent to another group interview.

This was at an organisation about which I knew nothing. They impressed me. I impressed them. I was called in a second time, then offered a sales job which I accepted. The suit I wore to these interviews, with its rounded jacket hem and little grey flecks, would soon be replaced with something slicker, more angled and more going-places. I had made the decision to join a world I had once sneered at. I started work in the first week of September.

So, I had done it, and quickly. It was time to come to terms with the new way of things, both in my situation and in that of the wider world. Margaret Thatcher had just enjoyed her third consecutive general election victory and there seemed nothing to do but go with the flow.

Get a suit, get a money-making career, get a life sorted out. Get into different, more mature things. Forget about all that silly pop music.

That's what I decided to do. That's what I began to do. But then 'Pump Up the Volume' came out.

Four

The office was multi-storey, open plan and full of people in formal business wear making deals. You didn't skimp on the clothes. You didn't skimp on the hair. You didn't skimp on the briefcase. Your look and your attitude were your measure of professionalism - you were judged on your professionalism. Some looked on the culture knowingly, pointing out with a smile and a wink how slick and hard-nosed it all was. But others had found their true calling in the engine-rooms of the ethos; instead of smiling and winking, they scowled and glared, often while drawing aggressively on a cigarette.

Aggressively was just one way of drawing on a cigarette – there was a full range on display across the building. Non-smokers had to endure. Wherever your seat happened to be among the units of desks, you worked within reach of an ashtray the size of a cereal bowl that would be deep with fag-butts and ash by lunchtime. You learned the hard way about relaxing and being yourself - ignorance and innocence were buried, spontaneity and gratuitous cheer were supressed. It could be an unforgiving place. But the frothy coffee in the machines was free for half an hour from ten thirty.

The foot soldiery consisted almost entirely of graduates; hungry young bucks and buckesses, few of whom were in settled relationships. There was a recognisable split between niceys and dickheads; there was a lot of socialising in bars after hours. Football and music remained the dominant subjects as we got to know each other. Experienced troopers took hesitant new arrivals under their wing.

At the end of my third day, a gregarious, grinning nicey helped to embed my understanding-so-far over a couple of pints. He was a walking bank of knowledge and, once the subject of the training programme had been covered, he sniffed out common musical ground, alighting on Jethro Tull.

This quirky rock band had a well-publicised new album out, *Crest of a Knave*, but they were veterans; their era-proper had been late 60s to late 70s. I knew a few of their songs from when I was a kid but, shortly before graduating, I had been fully converted via a best-of and a couple of early 70s LPs. I thought this gave me some authority, but this nicey could discuss the merits or otherwise of their entire back catalogue, as well as the output of Blodwyn Pig, a late 60s band featuring a former Jethro Tull member, of whom I had heard not a crotchet. I might once have been put out by being so outgunned on music. But I was different now. This conversation was merely the means to a social end; its subject matter was almost irrelevant.

My family had left London while I was away studying - as I was preparing to leave the north, they bloody well moved there. So I had to find digs. I started in the spare room of a family friend and we regularly stayed up late, setting the world to rights in her lounge over cigarettes and Blanc de Blancs. She spoke with passion and stomping disgust whatever the subject: politics, the state of the neighbourhood, estranged friends, faulty goods and running out of Blanc de Blancs. It felt strange to be having these comfy-chair evenings without background noise; she wasn't a big fan of television. I asked about perhaps having music on and she said I could look if I wanted to; she couldn't remember what albums and cassettes she had and wasn't even sure if the stereo was plugged in. I thought there would be folk and classical. I can't remember any details beyond this and I didn't press the point.

A transistor radio had been left in the room I was using. Late at night, I explored the frequencies just like I had as a youngster, under the bedclothes, finding foreign-language stations with various inadequate levels of signal strength, moving straight past what for years had been my usual ports-of-call. I listened to bits of classical. Certain pieces of classical music were childhood favourites; 'Eine Kleine Machtmusik', 'The Sorcerer's Apprentice', *Scheherezade* and the mazurka from *Coppelia* were all things that I had known and loved for years. There could be truckloads more like these to find. I assumed there was. Classical music seemed a bottomless pit.

I started listening to Radio 3, the BBC's classical music station. Knowing so little made it difficult. I persevered for a while. I would one day experience bursts of enthusiasm for composers including Handel, Haydn and Vivaldi. For now, I found only sonic mush and it was no use to me. I had to do something to get the morning adrenaline going, even if it meant switching to Radio 1 for the sheer familiarity of it.

It was frustrating, but it proved useful. Fitting in alongside my new colleagues was essential and it seemed that pop records were able to worm their way into our daily routine regardless of any effort on my part to avoid them. The new number one, certainly, was sweeping all before it and saw no reason to pause at our office doors.

Stock, Aitken, Waterman (SAW) had come across a singer called Rick Astley with a soulfully throaty voice. They had given him a song called 'Never Gonna Give You Up', a measured sway of a tune over similar beats to those used on 'Respectable' and 'You Spin Me Round (Like a Record)'. The combination of measured sway and *thomp thomp* was highly effective and proving itself a hot ticket.

His voice had similarities to that of Daryl Pandy and so at first people assumed he was some burly black guy - there were stories about night club doormen turning him away from his own promotional appearances because he wasn't one. However true these stories were, the record was an extraordinary event. You would easily have forgiven yourself if caught humming the tune. It was number one for five weeks from the end of August.

One of the middle managers squealed with excitement whenever she was reminded of it. "I can't believe how brilliant that song is!" she would exclaim, in something close to delirium. She was not alone, not even in that building. I stood back, radiating civility but resolutely sober. It was a cultural phenomenon, no more. Having left pop behind, I could rise above any theatrics associated with it.

While in that narrow bathroom I had noticed a few other things to rise above: among them an unremarkable new single by Five Star ('Whenever You're Ready') and a return to the Top 20 for dear old Squeeze ('Hourglass'). There was also 'Bridge to Your Heart' by Wax, an act comprising two old timers from the 70s emulating the sound of 1985, which they did very well, except that it was now 1987. Its video, I would later discover, was like a public information film on midlife crisis.

But it was all just background noise, there only to kick-start the adrenaline. Top 40 music now was lightweight: various combinations of hazy, syrupy, dull and insubstantial - everything that I had once looked to it to supplant. This crop seemed to confirm that. 1986 had been my last hurrah and I would look back on that time with fondness. I had my career and my future to think about now. My focus was on building a client base. Other, younger people had their 1986 to come.

These feelings would prove untenable. They belong to a period of time that feels substantial and yet lasted less than two weeks. Chart music was about to enter one of its years of renewal; one capable not only of mobilising a new generation of young pop fans, but also of re-connecting maturing minds with wonder and pure delight. Normality would take a while to catch up with it and spoil it – it would be free to dance for months and months first. It would be powered by the freshest technology and most vibrant ideas, full of programming, sampling and rap; it would include sounds of Asian, African and Gaelic origin; it would raid pop history for some of its most scintillating treasure; it would flood the airwaves with bright melody. Dull fug, although not entirely eradicated, would be relegated to lowly status for long, lovely months. 1988 was about to arrive. And it got here three months early.

One morning in that second week, as I shaved in that same bathroom, 'Pump Up the Volume' by MARRS came on and everything changed. A beat and a bass riff, marching powerfully and unstoppably; with samples coalescing in dazzling sequences across the top, piping, chirping, issuing orders and thud-chanting the title by way of a chorus. The sound was compressed, anti-reverb, businesslike. And percussive. Everything was percussive. It put images in my head that belonged nowhere except together. There were no lyrics to narrow them, no baggage to hinder them. It was utterly new and yet all I had ever wanted. Everything else was instantly boring.

I was almost frantic. I had no turntable. Until I could buy a copy and get it recorded onto tape, I could only hear it if it came on the radio; and now I was working, radio time was severely limited. It was entering the charts and people were talking about it. I knew it would come on again soon, but when? What would I do until then? I was supposed to have left all this behind me.

In the week that I started work it had entered the lower reaches of the Top 40 and now it had shot up to number eleven. The following week, it was number two, behind Rick Astley. By then I had bought it and got it taped. The glossy cover had a slick, simple design: letters and shapes in red and white on black. Its label was 4AD, the same as the Cocteau Twins.

I found myself heart-thumpingly wishing and wishing for it to be number one. Now. At my age. And 'Never Gonna Give You Up' was capable of being number one for another month yet, such was its grip on the country's affections. Sure enough, the following week, 'Pump Up the Volume' was held at two. But then, another week later, it wasn't. I walked down the pavement fifteen feet high. 'Pump Up the Volume' was number one. In the office, people sang the bass riff and grooved in their seat as they got off the phone from a good call; they sang one of the samples as they extracted a mid-morning frothy coffee from the machine. The record ruled. *My* record ruled.

And things seemed to change around it. Gradually, here and there, I began noticing lights coming on elsewhere in the general soundtrack. The radio wasn't the only source of this. The friend who had once introduced us to *Electrc 1* played cassettes in his car as he drove us around, and that autumn he was repeatedly playing 'Paid in Full' by Eric B & Rakim, a rap track with an easy-going groove. It used a distinctive drum pattern with loosened hi-hat off-beats that would be widely copied. Its verses had lyrics about earning your money through honest endeavour. Among its samples were the key refrain from the as-yet-unknown 'Im Nin'Alu' by Israeli singer Ofra Haza, as well as the title sample from 'Pump Up the Volume', which, it would transpire, was a slowed-down version of an original line from Eric B & Rakim's own 'I

Know You Got Soul', sampled by MARRS for their number one. If you follow me. And you needed to start following things like this.

The other good source of new sounds was clubs. At this point, our main habit was Caesar's Palace in Streatham, a converted ballroom with modern fittings and an air of decay. On Mondays it was cheaper and billed as Students & Nurses Night; but it was virtually empty, leaving ample room in which to dance to soul lovelies such as 'I Found Lovin'' by the Fatback Band and 'Casanova' by Le Vert. Two incidents at the venue have stuck in my mind. My memory of the first is fractured, but the horror of it is easily re-kindled.

There are, in some dark corners of showbiz, populations of bands who, with slick professionalism and utter lack of character, perform covers for the patrons of supper clubs and elsewhere who aren't taking a blind bit of notice. Even if they tap their feet, they aren't taking any notice. Even if, when tables are cleared, they take to the sprung floor in pairs, they aren't actually taking any notice - the band's presence is mere facility.

This slick professionalism comprises fixed smiles, meticulously measured movements and sounds as clean as their attire. There's nothing that could possibly offend. Except for all of the above. That doesn't matter though, as long as they remain in their dark corners, where they make no impression whatever. If they venture anywhere else, the result can be carnage.

I am still scratching my head over how one such band, in the autumn of 1987, came to be booked for Students & Nurses Night at Caesar's Palace. Maybe the promoter lost a card game. Maybe the local drug baron's daughter was the lead singer. Maybe the promoter *was* the local drug baron and, having imbibed too much of the wares himself, decided it was a good idea. Regardless of how it came about, there they were, playing on an oval platform that had been wheeled into the middle of the dancefloor.

They began playing, their docility contrasting with the echoey slam of the sounds they had replaced. Their look provided a similar contrast. Okay, so you had to dress smart to get into a club, but we had high street garb that fit the times – these guys could have been from anywhere back to the early 70s, with their blazers, their heels, their full hair.

The girl singer had a chiffony dress with a wavy hem, that reminded me of a busy cuttlefish. With teeth on constant display and eyebrows aloft, she danced with arm movements of precision and economy as she sang; her knees moving but her feet rooted. The bass player, towering behind her in a pale blazer frizzy hair and a full beard, grinned a beaming grin as he swivelled smoothly to the beat, delivering backing vocals with studied sincerity.

Their audience had all backed away to the sides. There may have been a few students and nurses there, but none of them had come for this. Then there was us, we spliff-headed lager boys, standing close to a wall, suddenly concerned for our immediate future. They probably did some recent soul hits but I don't remember any of that. What I remember, and wish I couldn't, is that they also did 'Pump Up the Volume'.

They shared the vocals around. There are far more male voices than female ones in its samples but they altered this slightly to give the woman more to do. They used their voices to approximate the black urban delivery and ape the juddery effect of the gated parts. In the office, we sang these samples in giddy moments as individual pieces, but that only confirmed them as discrete, applied snippets. This lot did the whole thing in their supper-club style, with their supper-club grins and their supper-club moves, taking the same approach they might have taken to cover 'Easy Lover'. My heart sank and my soul shrivelled. I can't speak for the specific reactions of my friends, but there was a general sense of collapsing morale. I don't think any of us mentioned it afterwards. It was best simply forgotten.

The other Caesar's Palace memory is more positive. One night not long afterwards I was assailed by the most extraordinary combination of sounds I had ever heard at a mainstream club: a break beat of the kind I was familiar with, but twice as big and three times as heavy; a voice of handsome assertion rapping in strong phrases; a crisp, mob-chanted chorus; all of it exploding with energy; all of it with the most incredible sound over the top – a climbing screech on a four-beat loop, which I assumed must have been forced out of a synthesiser, but was actually a horn sound sampled from an oldie by James Brown's backing band. Such an overbearing, disharmonious noise should spoil a record, but this one absolutely crowned it.

I located and assailed the DJ booth; and within twenty-four hours I had bought my own copy of 'Rebel Without a Pause' by Public Enemy. I discovered that its spoken intro, itself sampled, contained the same "brothers and sisters" phrase as the title segment of 'Pump Up the Volume'. I would one day learn that its sound was hugely and directly influenced by Eric B & Rakim.

Michael Jackson, meanwhile, was continuing to influence all sorts of people. He had just released the title track from the new album *Bad* as a single. Its verses were great, with tension building stealthily over a great bassline. But then the chorus completely changed the mood, becoming something desperate to impress – he was telling us he was "bad", as if he was all too aware that we needed convincing; while at the same time shrill backing vocals repeatedly, loyally, insisted that he was "really, really bad".

Jackson, whatever face he pulled, was not a persuasive badass. Okay, so there is no uniform look for someone who might pull out a knife on the subway, but still. A hoodlum might even spring about in a succession of nifty dance moves before attacking you, but still. Yet the record was enjoyable; and the chorus pay-off - *who's bad?* - gave us something to deploy in a range of office situations, as represented, perhaps, by workplace sitcoms you may have enjoyed in the years since. 'Bad' got to number three while 'Pump Up the Volume' was at number one.

There was also a new release by George Michael, who had already enjoyed two solo number ones before Wham! split up. This was the retro-chic 'Faith', its Bo Diddley beat providing a showcase for George's habit of pronouncing the word "baby" as "bay-bear". He was not the first to have done this, but the affectation was now his trademark and a widespread excuse for piss-taking. The record was fun and it went to number two. The album of the same name was fiercely promoted and duly took itself to the top of the LP chart, amid heavy competition from Fleetwood Mac's *Tango in the Night.*

I can share a story about how ubiquitous it was. A friend in the fire service attended a massive blaze at a branch of Woolworth's. They were making their way through the interior with poor visibility, trying to work out why, when the heat was so great, they hadn't yet got to the source of the fire. They suddenly realised that it was on the floor directly above and that the ceiling could collapse at any minute. As the signal was given to get out, they discovered that they were in the record department and decided that, since the stock would be condemned as smoke-damaged anyway, they might as well grab some freebies. They opened a drawer full of cassettes and stuffed as many as they could into their pockets. Safely away, they pulled them out to see what they had. Every last one was *Faith* by George Michael.

Fleetwood Mac were not the only old-timers who hadn't quite finished yet. Because this autumn saw the final seriously good piece of work by the Bee Gees. 'You Win Again' was a fantastic upper-body workout of a singalong, built on a percussion sound like something from heavy industry. Its appeal was massive and caught everybody off-guard. It flew to number one for four weeks, and the final chart-topper of a legendary act played out to a standing ovation.

Its replacement was 'China in Your Hand' by T'Pau, an adult epic with plucked violins and cryptic lyrics. It was a colossus of a single; and its video, which included artful slow-motion footage of a vase smashing on the floor, became an exemplar of adult-oriented pop cliché. Like most people, I held back from making judgements because I suspected it might be brilliant. It was a few months before I decided it wasn't. I liked it mainly because I had liked 'Heart and Soul' so much.

I was more decisive about 'I Say Nothing' by Voice of the Beehive. Since the start of the decade, we had accepted the contemporary swirl of sequenced, synthesised sounds as being *the* modern sound of pop, while seeing any vestige of guitar marginalised, put under some niche heading and smiled at kindly. This had been a matter of recording convenience; synths and sequencers had simply come to comprise the technology with which pop was made. Often people had appeared on *Top of the Pops* wielding guitars but, from the sound of their records, you would never have known there were any. The only real exception had been the Smiths, but they had been an exception to everything – and anyway they were gone now.

That's why 'I Say Nothing' stood out. Here, suddenly, were hard, bright pop guitars, thrilling guitars, accompanied by friendly voices sharing hard-won wisdoms. It bounced, it yelled, it rang out with pride. The drummer played a real drum kit and used to be in Madness. It was unmistakably brilliant, but failure to quite make the Top 40 reflected its novelty. The two girl singers hugged each other on the cover, presenting a scene of spontaneous joy which these days seemed taboo. Having 'I Say Nothing' on the soundtrack for a few weeks felt like a holiday.

And indeed, we were now racing towards Christmas. Party season kicked in. There was little in the current chart to set dancefloors alight, but the classiest soul turn was 'Criticize' by Alexander O'Neal: huge, energetic beat, big voice, complaints about a deprecatory woman and a humdinger of a chorus. It got played everywhere.

Alexander O'Neal and Luther Vandross were the two-headed monster of everyman soul, appealing across boundaries and offending very few - Vandross for smoothness and poise, O'Neal for vim and vigour. Vandross had set the bar for the modern male soul voice early in the decade and his recent *Give Me the Reason* album was almost obligatory in any house with a record player. Both he and O'Neal poured from the windows of passing cars, some of which had me as a passenger, and many of which had furry dice. Certain sections of society found the temptation to dangle large furry dice from rear-view mirrors too much to resist and these singers became associated with the phenomenon, which neither deserved. Nothing from *Give Me the Reason* came close to doing as well in the singles chart as the number four achieved by 'Criticize'.

The record at the top of the chart on Christmas Day was another bloody cover version. The Pet Shop Boys, who had already notched up two number ones, were as dour and heavy as a winning keyboard act could possibly be. You won't have to go far to find someone keen to deliver eulogies about them; clearly, they were keyboard studio whizzes. This third chart-topper was a keyboard studio whizz cover of 'Always on My Mind', made famous by the Vegas-era Elvis Presley. I liked the song and thought its best version was yet to be recorded; a thought that remained having heard the Pet Shop Boys cover, with which there was really nothing wrong. Their next single I would absolutely love. But then that *was* from 1988.

Because 1988, particularly the first six or so months of it, brought a tangible change, an unleashing of fresh energy, vivacity and innocence

that for a while proved all-conquering; a set of sounds in the same spirit
- if not often with the same form - of 'Pump Up the Volume'. You
could taste it in the air. Perhaps, having wanted to ditch that silly pop
music only a few months before, I was now acting like a born-again,
seeing wonder and brilliance in everything, my reactions therefore
prone to exaggeration. But there *was* something about it. Suddenly,
there were more smiles, more clicking of fingers; more belting, pulse-
racing tunes. It was lighter, more inventive, less *uptight*. Its sexiness
and its showbiz were coated in irony and frivolity. Because sexiness and
showbiz were not the point. The point was pop.

If any particular record was the curtain-raiser for all this, it was
'House Arrest' by Krush, which rocketed up the chart in early January.
Its intro shoe-horned every fresh studio trick of the moment into a
twenty-second blast of electro-exhilaration that left you breathless.
It then settled down a bit - thank goodness, otherwise it might have
hospitalised people. Among its vocal samples were ones that went "I
know you're gonna dig this" and "bug on out", each of which would
spend the following months wandering onto record after record and
wearing themselves thin. It got to number three and spent five weeks in
the Top 10.

Suddenly, releases like these were everywhere. In the same Top 10 was
'Rok da House' by the Beatmasters featuring the Cookie Crew. Roaring
up behind it was 'The Jack That House Built' by Jack 'n' Chill. Later
there would be 'Doctorin' the House' by Coldcut featuring Yazz and the
Plastic Population. A whole generation of records now jostled to share
the fresh goodies that 'House Arrest' had so brightly showcased – the
rhythms, the sharp percussiveness, the congestion.

'This Brutal House' by Nitro Deluxe was given a fresh lick of
production paint, re-packaged as 'Let's Get Brutal' and sent to number
twenty-four. 'Beat Dis' by Bomb the Bass was one hell of a caper: almost
a carbon-copy of 'Pump Up the Volume'; less polished, but the same
set of ideas and almost exactly the same structure - one of its samples
was actually used in 'Pump Up the Volume' and another was the
identical screeching noise used in 'Rebel Without a Pause'; I sniffed at
it but it spent two weeks at number two. Another Public Enemy sample
provided the title and main hook for 'Bass (How Low Can You Go)' by

Simon Harris, a thumping backline-and-keyboard grind which reached number twelve in the spring.

This swath of new sounds was soon being parodied. 'Stutter Rap (No Sleep Til Bedtime)' by Morris Minor and the Majors took a shot at white rap act the Beastie Boys, as well as at people with speech impediments. Later in the year there would be 'Pump Up the Bitter' by Stars on 45 Pints, and 'Loadsamoney (Doin' Up the House)' by comedian Harry Enfield, in role as his braggart plasterer and Thatcherite standard-bearer Loadsamoney. Nobody of sound mind ever listened to these more than once.

Amongst all the new vocabulary involved, the term "hip hop" was being heard more often. But it was often badly misinterpreted. I fished a pair of cassettes out from a bargain bucket one day with similar cover artwork to *Electro 1* and with "Hip Hop" in their titles, specifically *Hip Hop Electro 13* and *Hip Hop Crucial 3*, both released two years previously. "Hip hop" seemed to suggest playful, skippity-dippity beats and the type of knockabout rush that had characterised the opening tracks of *Electro 1*. Naturally, I hoped these would be similar. They contained some good stuff, including the 1986 hits '(Nothing Serious) Just Buggin'' by Whistle and 'Amityville (the House on the Hill)' by Lovebug Starski, which were both terrific fun and featured prominent electro elements. But their lead vocals were straight, untreated rap. Most of the other tracks were straight, untreated rap too and my immediate reaction was disappointment. In the fulness of time, any urban music involving rap would be called hip hop. But back then, I wasn't the only one getting the wrong end of the stick.

A duo called Climie Fisher appeared on the cover of their new single looking broody and serious, the one at the front in a white under-vest and the one at the back in round shades with spiked-out hair. They were both as white as the under-vest. Their song, 'Rise to the Occasion' was delivered in a restrained, gravelly vocal and would have worked being played on an acoustic guitar in soft focus at a riverside picnic. But this single was billed as the 'Hip-Hop Mix', a subtitle justified because it had a soft-focus skippity-dippity beat under it and used samples – the "I know you're gonna dig this" one and an instrumental jiggle used at the start of 'Pump Up the Volume'. Few acts have ever been as un-hip-hop as Climie Fisher but the beat on the record seemed to qualify the claim. For a few weeks they convinced record buyers that they were at some kind of cutting edge.

If I had taken more to the sounds on those two cassettes, I might have seen straight through 'Rise to the Occasion'; joining the growing numbers of rap fans in the know, owning albums by Run-D.M.C., Public Enemy and the aforementioned Beastie Boys: former punk brats whose 1987 hit '(You Gotta) Fight for Your Right (To Party)' was the teenage moron's anthem supreme and whose 'No Sleep Till Brooklyn' had given Morris Minor and the Majors their half-arsed idea for a parody. They wore Volkswagen badges as medallions, a gimmick which led to a spate of vehicles being vandalised for trophies. They were turning other former punk brats onto rap and are therefore significant. They were on Def Jam, the same label as Public Enemy.

Some of the freshest pop sounds in these months used the new rhythms and intensity but by-passed the rapping and sampling in favour of conventional song structures. Dead loud number three 'Tell It to My Heart' by Taylor Dayne was one such record, another being the debut from fresh teenybop sensations, Bros. They featured a pair of excitable blond brothers with vocal affectations borrowed from Stevie Wonder and the bottle-top mechanisms from a certain brand of premium lager stuck to their shoe uppers. Their hectic 'When Will I Be Famous', likewise gave all that rapping and sampling a miss. It would reach number two.

Others came from likeable, clean-cut girls with likeable, clean-cut songs, bopping and bouncing around in defiance of the hard-baked seriousness of the decade. Debbie Gibson had made her mark as the female lead in the Broadway stage production of *Grease* and was now putting out records. Having briefly presented as a bargain-bucket Madonna, she had settled into a girl-next-door peddling pure, upbeat pop, as with 'Only in My Dreams', her second hit but her first good one. This niche had three main players and we will come to the other two shortly - they had records that were simply massive.

Because possibly the most remarkable thing of all in the first half of 1988 was its unbroken succession of good number ones, records that championed this sweeping freshness, rather than doing what number ones often do - defying it, thwarting it, reminding it that the old order is boss. I revelled in them. Right through childhood, almost every one of my favourite records had got stuck at number two. The number one position had seemed, for long periods, to be the reserve of the smug, the dull and the downright offensive. A succession of two consecutive good chart-toppers, such as 'Message in a Bottle' by the Police and 'Video Killed the Radio Star' by the Buggles from 1979, seemed like a little golden age.

Of course, when you look at chronological lists of number ones, you can almost certainly find a few sequences that you're able to approve of; and that is, clearly, all dependent on the judgements to which your taste leads you. But I bet if you're honest you hardly ever find more than three. Early 1988 trumped all that. Because, in early 1988, there was a run of at least five. I say at least, because I'm tempted to say there were seven. But the one at the end is a perennial audience-divider, and the one at the start, the one that ousted 'Always on My Mind' from the top spot, won my approval largely for personal reasons.

Belinda Carlisle had once fronted all-girl US guitar band the Go-Go's, whose surfy new wave sound had taken the post-Disco-Sucks America by storm, while being seen as out of date in a UK freshly enraptured by the Human League and Soft Cell. My peers had largely dismissed them for this reason; one had loudly proclaimed them "stone age". But I had loved them, tracking their repeated failure to breach the Top 40 with a bruised heart, while those around me slagged them off. Carlisle had already released solo stuff – her careering 'Mad About You' had added extra spice to my summer of 1986 – but this new one, 'Heaven Is a Place on Earth', would be her first significant hit. From one angle, it was contemporary big-sound stodge from the same drawer as 'China in Your Hand' and no friend of 'Pump Up the Volume'. But it was optimistic and uplifting and it went to number one for two weeks in mid-January. A Go-Go at number one. Vindication – all I ever wanted. That's an in-joke for Go-Go's fans.

The two number ones that followed came from Debbie Gibson's deodorised niche-mates. 'I Think We're Alone Now' by Tiffany was a salute to uninhibited teenage joy, sung by a teenage girl who could have been sitting next to us on the bus that morning. No sampling, no rap, just a zingy set of pop sparkles that I never imagined could be allowed to exist, let alone top the charts for three weeks. Everyone you met knew it. Plenty of my work colleagues with their smart suits and their business attitude liked it. Most of them would sing it at the drop of a hat - if one started, others would join in. Dull fug ran for its life. Few people had any idea that it was a 60s song.

It was replaced by 'I Should Be So Lucky' by Kylie Minogue, as cheesy as heck but like a cleansing shower after a clammy day. To have one catchy, upbeat pop tune replace another at number one was dizzying. Minogue was a toothy, disinfected article with a nasal singing voice, whose neutrality could not have been more perfect. She had made her name playing a slightly annoying, dungaree-wearing tomboy in a lunchtime Australian soap opera called *Neighbours*, whose stratospheric success in Britain hinted at a population with too little to do.

She had already had a number one hit at home, a thoroughly rotten cover of mod classic 'The Loco-Motion', re-titled 'The Locomotion', as if the hyphen had been a problem. It was drivel, but SAW recognised an opportunity. They snapped her up, gave her a song with a mockable, high-note chorus and a thumping house arrangement and, by their next day off, she was starting a five-week run on top of the UK singles chart.

This heralded a sustained period of big success for SAW. They would soon be considered a pop production line in the same way that Motown had once been, churning out sequences of hits by a whole roster of artists with a homogenous sound. My love for Motown made this promise exciting, but SAW would fall short. Over the next few years they would take a selection of tatty scraps - soap stars, ailing chart veterans and various combinations of grinning fizz-heads - and successfully launch them into the upper reaches of the Top 40. To begin with, the pop quality made it all okay. But with only three composers on your team, maintaining that quality was never going to be easy; and before long it became apparent that young pop fans just liked being young pop fans and would buy anything as long as it was by their favourites. Once SAW realised this, the imperative to make good pop records shrank by about fifty percent. And once SAW realised it, others would follow, many of whom would look on the remaining fifty percent as unnecessary bother.

The next number one was 'Don't Turn Around' by Aswad. They were known as a serious roots reggae act – "aswad" being Arabic for "black". I was used to them lurking deep in the background, but suddenly here they were in broad daylight with a pop hit, a plaintive lament served on a bed of bright reggae: *Go, then, if you want to leave, but don't turn around or you'll see me crying.* This idea had been used before, but not by any serious roots reggae act. It was an irresistible cocktail.

After two weeks it was ousted by 'Heart', a fourth Pet Shop Boys number one. For PSB devotees, and there were plenty of those everywhere you turned, it was business as usual. But I had until now been largely resistant to their charms and the effect of this single took me completely by surprise. It simply swept you along. There were no dull bits. Its alto-robot riff was brilliant. There was nothing to do but love it.

Then came 'Theme from S-Express' by S-Express. I can't remember exactly when I first heard the term "acid house", but I assume I had heard it by now. We were, in general, associating it with any house record using samples instead of sequenced orchestration and vocal arrangements. The yellow smiley face symbol was already being recognised as its crest and variations on it were popping up elsewhere. One had been on the cover of 'Beat Dis' by Bomb the Bass.

We thought 'Pump Up the Volume' was probably acid house, which was kind of correct, but *bona fide* acid house came from Chicago or Detroit and had a distinctive, disorientating flavour. These British chart equivalents differed audibly, using samples as a tasty variety pack rather than as embellishments to a trance-inducing underlay. It was the British ones I heard on the radio and at venues down the road.

Anyway, it was about time another one of these records got to number one and the infectious 'Theme from S-Express' duly obliged. It opened with the intro from an old Rose Royce favourite, laying the ground for its main riff while a voice invited us to "Enjoy this trip". I automatically linked the "trip" reference with drugs, therefore LSD, therefore a revival of the 1967 Summer of Love aesthetic and therefore the hippies, who represented everything the engineers of the 80s despised. I felt an instant affinity and I wasn't the only one; the warm months of 1988 would be dubbed the "Second Summer of Love". The groove and sexiness of 'Theme from S-Express' wowed the pop audience, its rise suggesting the onset of some kind of new dawn.

There is, arguably, a final record to add to this list of good number ones, although many whose views I respected hated it. 'Perfect' by Fairground Attraction was a piece of grinning jazz-ska complete with prominent double bass. I liked its message about not getting into a relationship for the sake of having one. It was heartfelt and a bit brainy. It was only number one for a week and five more months would pass before the arrival of another number one worth applauding. You can include it if you want to.

Whether or not you do so, this extraordinary run had been instrumental in setting the tone that characterised this period of unadulterated pop triumph. Most of the rest of the Top 40 reflected it in some way. It was like a luxurious lucky dip, one from which you might pluck 'Joe le Taxi' by Vanessa Paradis, 'That's the Way It Is' by Mel & Kim, 'These Dreams' by Heart; 'Could've Been' by Tiffany (her wistful follow-up single), 'I'm Not Scared' by Eighth Wonder, 'Love is Contagious' by Taja Sevelle, 'For a Friend' by the Communards, 'Who's Leaving Who' by Hazell Dean, 'Broken Land' by the Adventures, 'Every Angel' by All About Eve, 'Girlfriend' by Pebbles, or 'Everywhere' by Fleetwood Mac – records in various styles and coming from various traditions, but all connected by a tuneful, wide-eyed spirit.

And on top of all that, these weeks also saw the return to the charts of proper pop guitars, an event that would have implications for the next ten years, never mind the next few months. The Bangles had originally been a jangly guitar band, back before the determination to break into the Top 10 had seen them succumbing to general studio craft. In February 1988 they reached number eleven with a cover of Simon & Garfunkel's 'Hazy Shade of Winter', recorded for the movie *Less Than Zero*, turning its acoustic lead guitar riff into a distorted twang that made their version a blaring thrash. This made it stand out from the chart sounds surrounding it, yet it was probably just a retro gesture and a one-off.

But then we heard the Primitives, an English band with black leather and big hair, a real drum kit, a creamy, unpretentious female voice and distorted, growly, chugging, chiming guitars. They had a blistering tune called 'Crash' that picked you up and dunked you like a biscuit into two minutes thirty-five seconds of rock 'n' roll intoxication. Surely, though, this was just a transient airplay gimmick; surely it would ultimately be dismissed as "stone age" and sink without trace. Well it bloody didn't. Thousands upon thousands responded. We talk about some records as being a breath of fresh air. 'Crash' was more like a rocket-blast of the stuff.

When a girl fancies you, she makes sure she's in your line of vision every time you look up. 'Crash' seemed to do the same. When I turned on the radio it was the next thing on. When I chatted to people, they mentioned it. When I stepped into HMV Oxford Circus to buy my copy, its intro began on the PA system; and as I approached the singles section, the first blast of its full noise hit me full in the chest. While I queued to pay, I heard assistants laughing among themselves about how it was flying out of the store. I looked around and the guy behind me had one. Its *Top of the Pops* debut was a notable event: these surly guys and this blonde girl producing the kind of melodic blare that wasn't supposed to exist anymore. For many young pop pickers, 'Crash' ignited something new to their experience; for some older ones, it was like a homecoming. It went to number five. Something in the DNA of our culture had begun to thaw.

I would develop an enduring love for the Primitives. They released the album *Lovely* in April. Its songs had lyrics about love and friendship, barefoot walks on beaches and hazy strolls through flowers under blue skies. Sometimes it sounded like a house-wrecking party, sometimes like a nursery rhyme. It evoked 60s psychedelia, most explicitly on a track called 'Shadow', a woozy, shamanistic ramble backed by tabla drum and sitar. 'Nothing Left' had the sound and spirit of 'Crash'. 'Spacehead' was a rumbledrum fuzzbomb complete with *lalalas* and the unforgettable lyric "What is that boy on? /He's a strange pers-on".

A little way into side two sat 'Out of Reach', a gospelly clapalong with a *chang-chang-chang-a-lang* rhythm guitar part that gave the chorus a buzz. It was chosen as the next single. Not a bad choice, except that they re-did it and removed the catchy rhythm guitar part, replacing it with a bass run. Why this was allowed to happen is something that bothers me to this day. It just didn't leap out of the radio in the way that the album version could have. It got to twenty-five and no higher. But I remained full of hope. *Lovely* went to number six in the album chart.

So where was the dull fug? Well, those same weeks carried the ballad-by-numbers 'Where Do Broken Hearts Go' by Witney Houston, the perfunctory 'Get Outta My Dreams Get into My Car' by Billy Ocean, the meandering adult jog 'Love Changes Everything' by Climie Fisher (no hip hop labelling in sight) and 'Stay on These Roads' by A-Ha, who were now veteran heartthrobs – their first hit had been a mere two and a half years previously but next to Kylie, Tiffany, Debbie and all these samples, they looked like gnarled oaks. None of these hits were poisonous, just offensive in their mediocrity; but in the first half of 1988, they posed no threat.

This period also contained a moment which perhaps embodies the whole point of this chapter. It came on the day that I was standing in the HMV queue waiting to pay for 'I Should Be So Lucky' among other things. In the big stores you now gathered your singles before you queued up and this was a massive improvement. They were banked up in racks, ten or fifteen in each clump, so that you could select a cover without bent corners or black rings. Singles were now £1.79 each, so you didn't want blemishes.

Anyway, here I was with yet more records, and a thought occurred to me. Only six months before, I had been giving it all up as a sign of maturity. Now I was into it as much as ever – great new singles were popping up all around like corn in a hot pan and they weren't being spoilt by *Top of the Pops* performances because I hardly ever watched it. I looked down at the Kylie cover. I was used to the once-difficult recognition that some pop stars were younger than me, but this one was four-and-a-half years younger – if I met a girl that age and fancied her, it would be borderline indecent. Yet I had no compunction in buying the record and I could think of no reason why I should.

Did this therefore mean I would be buying singles indefinitely? If I hadn't stopped six months ago, when was I going to? I was familiar with the cliché of a man in mid-life crisis, going down to the local disco having memorised the Top 10, trying to impress the girls and prove he still had what it took. It was an image of desperation and tragedy and I could never imagine myself doing that.

But I could imagine myself in my sixties, standing in the queue at HMV Oxford Circus, grey and balding and in a sober suit, waiting to pay for a single by some future equivalent of Kylie Minogue, wearing a calm, self-assured smile and responding to curious glances by saying "Well, it's in the blood, isn't it?" My acceptance and my dignity. It would be okay.

All this was happening because these pop months were exceptionally good. But where does that feeling of heightened excitement over a soundtrack actually come from? It must be about the music more than anything else, yet it doesn't seem logical that the music in one succession of months can *per se* be so much better than that of another. Was it all down to coincidence? Was it all down to an illusion caused by my personal situation and state of mind?

Try and reason about it and you'll tie yourself in knots. Look again at how I had felt about 1986. I didn't chime well with the mid-80s. However, I was at university, with the relatively carefree life that came with the package - it may have relaxed my filtering systems. And yet I was also there in 1985 when the soundtrack was duller. Perhaps the soundtrack will always sound better when other things are going well, when anticipation amplifies your senses - a sudden improvement in your love life, for example. But I saw more action in 1985 and 1987 than in 1986 and 1988, so that doesn't make sense, either. It's complicated, this.

The truth nevertheless remains: when I'm pulling out boxes for a headphone session, it's easier to reach for some years than for others. The fact that any period of months carries a positive charge that changes the smell and feel of everything and wedges itself in your lifetime Hall of Fame must, in large part, be down to coincidence. The bright pop attack of the first five months of 1988 can be explained by the invasion of the charts by radio-friendly house music in its first flush of youth, along with the cavalry charge of SAW. But many things unrelated to either carried the same spirit. So if coincidence was all it was, give coincidence a cheer; because the soundtrack *was* brighter, it *was* more radio-friendly, it *was* more assertively poppy and dull fug *did* flee in terror.

106

If anything rammed this point home it was the success of 'Somewhere in My Heart' by Aztec Camera, which was a new entry in the week that 'Perfect' was number one. Five years previously, Aztec Camera's flimsy, Latin-lite guitar rhythms and affected vocals had put me right off: if I'd heard the name since, I made faces like I'd just bitten into an apple and seen half a worm. But 'Somewhere in My Heart' was simply fantastic: it had grandeur, it had stature: there were powerful horns and keyboards, there was melodic drama and a minor key oddness to the chorus, and it got to number three with my (somewhat humble) cheering ringing in its ears.

Unfortunately, these feelings were challenged and mocked by some of the number ones that came after 'Perfect'. We had to endure dreary cover versions in support of otherwise deserving charities and movie releases ('With a Little Help from My Friends' by Wet Wet Wet, 'Groovy Kind of Love' by Phil Collins) , life-coaching yell-ballads ('One Moment in Time' by Whitney Houston), slow-dancing slush-ballads ('Nothing's Gonna Change My Love for You' by Glenn Medeiros), and painfully sincere love songs with an enamel finish, adapted from ad campaigns for fizzy drinks in red tins ('The First Time' by Robin Beck). No fun, no encouragement, just a big fat finger in the face.

One chart topper seemed to sneer at the very business of being number one, belittling its value by seeking to prove how easy it was to get there by following a set of rules. 'Doctorin' the Tardis' by the Timelords had a very "new" title and a very "now" format; it used samples from stuff that people knew and it was as dumb as hell.

The duo responsible wrote a book about their adventures called *The Manual (How to Have a Number One the Easy Way)* which, I would later learn, was funny and contained a lot of truth. Its cynicism didn't go as far as denying the possibility of great records getting to number one simply through being great records, but it did land punches on the kind of romanticised views of pop that permeate the book you are now reading. 'Doctorin' the Tardis' was hollow and dripping in shit, yet both record and book had branding elements that we would see again. In future, the duo would find other ways of making their point.

So there were dampeners. But beneath these clouds, the 1988 party raged on. It felt like a revolution had taken place. My excitement had been re-kindled, my devotion cemented. This was it now; this was going to be me forever and always. So I would have to negotiate the hostility that came with the territory. I expected a lot of it just because of my age. But I would also attract it because of my taste, sometimes shockingly. The soundtrack was never going to please everybody. Not even in 1988.

Five

Talking about music can be a battleground; a hotbed of prejudice and one-upmanship where your status is often on the line. In the late 1980s, it was advisable to stay within touching distance of the approved list: early Elvis, late Beatles, Jimi Hendrix, Led Zeppelin, David Bowie, Kraftwerk, Atlantic soul, the leading lights of punk and a few irrefutably hot others. Anything else carried risk.

The subject delivers plenty of opportunity to those who consider it in their interests to slap you down and slap you down they will. Some won't give an inch to commercial pop under any circumstances: "It's shit" is often the beginning and end of their critical repertoire. They don't actually have to deliver a fully-formed opinion - in two words your preference has been stamped and relegated. Others prefer to smugly steer the conversation towards acts that were supposedly the key influence on whoever you've just been raving about. It helps, of course, if these are relatively obscure.

In my first post-graduate workplace was an overbearing, bombastic manager who had mastered these approaches and more, wielding each at need like a golfer selecting the right club for his next shot. Music was the only thing he took as seriously as sales work and, in his presence, you spoke about either at your peril - express a spontaneous opinion and you risked being buried under verbal masonry. I spent most lunchtimes wandering around HMV Oxford Circus, rarely gravitating towards anything he rated. On returning it was all but impossible to slip past him unnoticed. He just knew, as I entered the room twenty yards away, that I had a bag of seven-inch singles somewhere on me. He would drop whatever he was doing and canter over with a "whadya got, whadya got?" Then out would come Kylie or some such and it would be: "Oh fuck's sake, whadya buy *that* for?"

There were a number of ways in which I might reply. On a bad day, I might mumble something about not having asked for his opinion and shuffle away. But with the wind in my sails, I might insist that it was exactly the type of pop hit whose '60s equivalents I bet he raved about, before rattling off pertinent examples. And, in a few cases of transcendent delirium, I might wax lyrical about clouds clearing and evil being driven back to the shadows. He would just stand there, hands on hips, shaking his head: "You're a loser, a muppet, a waster..."

There was certainly a measure of harmless banter involved in all this, although I was never sure which parts. But others listening in would snarl and put their resentments on ice. I was unprofessional. I didn't have what it took. Because I had bought a pop record. On seven-inch.

To an extent, of course, we all have banners that we rally around. But some banners are bigger than others and the biggest at that time were the Smiths and U2. If you were a Smiths or a U2 devotee, you could walk into almost any situation, shoot your mouth off and hear confident cries of support from somewhere close by.

That definitely was not the case if you lauded the Tiffany and Kylie Minogue number ones for their pure pop quality. It might have been the case on some smaller scale if I had shouted about the Cocteau Twins; but perhaps the support would come from some fey, fragile specimen; or the grunt in the corner who, in replying, had just uttered his first syllables in months.

By contrast, devotees of the Smiths and U2 were well-dressed types with sun tans, biceps and good shades. They knew where to buy suits that were 75% better than yours for a 25% greater outlay. They had nice girlfriends and shagged other people on the side. Also, importantly, they bought albums, and therefore had an overview. I didn't buy albums by Tiffany or Kylie Minogue.

Being into the Primitives was a bit better. 'Crash' was tolerated, and some forked out for *Lovely* without regretting it. But there were no sun tans or biceps with the Primitives. Just a lovely dream of a different kind of pop purity. And who needed dreams, when you had the confidence of knowing what to say about *The Queen Is Dead* or *The Joshua Tree?* You were not alone if you rallied around these banners - they were planted high on the best hills.

'Voyage Voyage' by Desireless was not. It was Eurobeat: fluffy, in French and entirely plastic. Synth records had always sounded synth, but they tended to have some vestige of flesh and blood somewhere in the orchestration. 'Voyage Voyage' didn't seem to. The French was fine, but the backing vocal was a breathy echo of the female lead by a voice that sounded male. It had somehow been decided that this was okay. It was like a parody.

Perhaps due to a recent listen enhanced by intoxicants, I was open-minded on its behalf. I didn't exactly evangelise about it, but I did have a bee in my bonnet about snobbery and was willing to make a small point here and there, happy for my views to stand out from the crowd. Others were less happy.

One warm June evening, with the post-work crowd spilling out of pubs and onto the pavements, we gathered in drinking huddles at the roadside and intermingled. The huddle beside ours contained brash, scowling individuals with short fuses when it came to nonconformity. I was fully aware that many of those present was likely to dismiss 'Voyage Voyage' with a slamming, consonant-enhanced "shit"; but when the opportunity arose, I mentioned it with a few upbeat words, hoping to make one or two people reconsider.

No such luck. Down rained the slamming, down rained the consonants, and the other huddle both figuratively and literally turned their backs. I had disqualified myself from further discussion. Not only that, but I had spoilt the occasion for my huddle. I could sense the deflation. One of them raised his pint calmly to his lips and gazed into the liquid. "You shouldn't have done that", he said.

'Voyage Voyage' got to number five, thanks to a remix for which Pete Waterman of SAW had a half-share of the credit. Waterman and his label PWL were on a roll. In September he would be co-presenting *The*

Hit Man and Her, a late-night TV show featuring music and dancing live from a club somewhere in the UK. It didn't matter if PWL records happened not to be featured, their ascendency was already secure - the SAW production team were omnipresent. By the end of the year, they would have produced hits for Kylie Minogue, Rick Astley, Mel & Kim, Mick & Pat, Sinitta, Jason Donovan, Brother Beyond, Hazell Dean, Sabrina, Bananarama, Sigue Sigue Sputnik and the England Football Team. In a reflection of their performance at that year's European Championship, the latter stalled outside the Top 60.

But the rest did better. SAW records never seemed to be out of the charts. SAW records never seemed to be out of the Top 10. That crisp, clean production and springy house beat was everywhere, its brightness deflecting the hard stares from the sun tans and biceps. Jason Donovan was Kylie's germ-free love interest in *Neighbours*. Mick & Pat were leaping telly twits who added an extra dimension by sometimes being listed as Pat & Mick. Bananarama had made better records in the previous six years; Sinitta made slightly improving ones now. Hazell Dean stood alongside Mel & Kim and Rick Astley at the serious end of the SAW roster. Sabrina was less serious, there only for the two-dimensional summertime sex element. Sigue Sigue Sputnik were a fancy-dress party who had once convinced the tabloids that they were the future of rock 'n' roll: it was easy to imagine that SAW had signed them in a flurry of giggles after one pale ale too many – their mediocre chart performance was the hangover. Brother Beyond were a smiley band who got to number two with 'The Harder I Try', not a single note from which has stuck in my memory.

We rolled our eyes and sighed, remembering the terrific records Bananarama had once made and hoping that Mel & Kim might return to former heights. These were established stars who, alas, now stood in a line-up that seemed to exist merely to make mums and dads happy about how their children's pocket money was being spent. Any aspiring performer could fit the bill: you didn't even need a musical background – just a symmetrical face and white teeth. From this viewpoint, it looked grim; but almost anything could be forgiven if the records were good.

Which brings us back to Kylie. She followed up her big number one with the undeniably good 'Get to Be Certain', a song with similar lyrical purpose to 'Perfect', a cool melody and a wobbling bass hook that lent it plenty of charm. It entered the chart in mid-May and spent three weeks at number two. Kylie had become a megastar in the space of three months and there wasn't even an album yet.

Her clean-cut, girl-next-door peers were also busy in the middle of the year. Tiffany had her third Top 10 hit, an adaptation of a Beatles album cut called 'I Saw Him Standing There', but it was pointless and useless and she wouldn't see the year out. Debbie Gibson did better; 'Out of the Blue' sparkled delightfully, and her downtempo tale of heartbreak 'Foolish Beat' avoided enough cliché to merit a rosette. It reached the Top 10 in July. She went a bit rubbish after that.

The summer also saw the reappearance of relative veteran Kim Wilde. Her album *Close* yielded a succession of strong singles, of which 'You Came' was the very best; a big, rich song with a big, rich sound; an explosion of joy through love's redemption that oozed class and had that drone about it, like a hymn, that number ones often have. I was convinced it would become one. I told everyone who would listen.

But it peaked at number three and left me red-faced. Naturally, I resented the two records above it. The number one was 'The Only Way Is Up' by Yazz and the Plastic Population, a surprise package which I will come back to. I wasn't greatly keen on it, but it was far from the kind of record I hated most. That was, without doubt, pointless cover versions from acts so firmly on the rise that the success of the next single was in the bag, no matter how awful it was.

Which brings us back to Kylie. Because the number two was a SAW re-hash of her flimsy, gutless, wilfully destructive take on 'The Loco-Motion' - a mighty classic reduced to a piece of bunting. SAW had already given her two perfectly good original songs, so why they didn't just ignore this is a mystery. I actually felt sick when it came on. It was in the wake of this disgrace that the album *Kylie* was released and flew to number one.

'You Came' nevertheless greatly enhanced Kim Wilde's standing, just in time for her big assignment - as support on the UK leg of Michael Jackson's worldwide *Bad* tour. I saw her perform it there. A bunch of us went. Michael Jackson coming to town was a big deal.

It was at Wembley Stadium, and a huge crowd poured into its vast expanse; heavily congested at the front, gradually easing and thinning as you moved back, past huge screens providing close-up detail of the performance for those further away. Then you got to where we were, standing aloof in a huddle to one side, not participating to any significant extent, but swapping sober comments, sometimes being positive out of reverence, sometimes being positive out of caution. I don't remember anything specific about Michael's performance, but I do remember the roar from the crowd when 'You Came' fired up.

It had taken its place in a soundtrack that was more diverse and eclectic than any within memory. 'Im Nin'Alu', by Ofra Haza, a Hebrew poem framed in thumping modern production with English-language pop flourishes, was as exotic a chart sound as you could imagine. The key refrain had been sampled on 'Paid in Full' by Eric B. & Rakim. It was in the early summer chart for five weeks, reaching number fifteen. There was also 'Yé ké yé ké' by Guinean performer Mory Kanté, a thrilling record without a word in English, which was a massive hit across Europe. In the UK it was given a house beat but was still irrefutably African, its single edit being named the 'Afro Acid Mix', which played well to certain galleries. It got to number twenty-five.

Alongside these was more conventional exotica. Maxi Priest reached number five with 'Wild World', an old Cat Stevens' song excellently re-framed in a seductive pop-reggae that fit warm summer days perfectly. Fairground Attraction followed up their number one with the deft 'Find My Love', which a work colleague of mine dismissed as "too Spanish". In defiance of this indictment, it got to number seven, spending a month in Los 10 Mejores.

If you wanted alternative exotica, you had the long-resilient Siouxsie and the Banshees. They got to number sixteen with 'Peek-A-Boo', harnessing modern studio craft to create an unearthly, menacing atmosphere in which to excoriate men who peered through letter-box slots in backstreet rooms to watch writhing strippers. "Golly jeepers, where'd you get those peepers? / Peep show creature, where did you get those eyes?" sang Siouxsie. It was powerful and angry and had an accordion riff. In what would eventually be seventeen years of chart hits, this was one of their very best.

But there is rarely anything more exotic than the fresh output of fresh genres and, with dance music reinvigorated, the next new development was always just around the corner. We're saving acid house for later. From the rest, between June and September, three records stood out.

Among rap acts, Eric B & Rakim, the Beastie Boys and Public Enemy were making most of the headlines. But from the emerging UK scene came Wee Papa Girl Rappers, a duo whose number twenty-one 'Heat It Up' deserves its own place on the podium. It used conventional funk samples but also included dialogue from black-and-white British movies, the plummy tones of which were a stark contrast with all the "I know you're gonna dig this" stuff elsewhere in the charts.

The vocal delivery was just as recognisably British; but importantly, it was also pure percussion. Rap reserved the right to slur and stretch its rhymes across the beat, but you could play along to the rap on 'Heat it Up' with a pair of drumsticks and the effect was startling. Some people I knew insisted that rap simply wasn't music: you couldn't possibly level that accusation at 'Heat It Up'. In the autumn the duo would breach the Top 10 with the more conventional 'Wee Rule', which had its own orchestration, a rapped verse but a sung chorus. 'Wee Rule' is the one most people remember, but 'Heat It Up' is the more significant.

Above it in the charts was the second of this trio: 'Push It' by Salt-n-Pepa. This wasn't just a rap record; it was a sensational whole-body freak-out with massive, piping keyboard riffs and alternating vocals fuelling a nut-house party at which no crockery was safe. You were out of breath just listening to it and decades later it retains its impact; at the sound of that panting, scraping intro, you either roll your eyes, start laughing, or spring to your feet – perhaps all three. It was number two for three weeks, held off the top spot only by Glenn Medeiros' soppy-arsed 'Nothing's Gonna Change My Love for You'.

The third arrived in September. Kevin Sanderson was a leading light in the US club scene where acid was born and had a growing list of credits to his name (he had remixed 'Heat It Up' by Wee Papa Girl Rappers). He was now at the helm of Inner City, whose 'Big Fun' was yet another fresh chart sound and it kicked the autumn off beautifully; soft crunches of percussion, juddering keyboard rhythms and a smooth female vocal all contributing to a delicious groove – a balanced blend of acid and soul that was just the ticket. Shimmying coolly to this at parties seemed suddenly preferable to leaping around with Salt-n-Pepa. Its status was far greater than its peak of number eight.

Records like this could straddle the boundaries between scenes; but acid had its own crowd, with a distinct attitude and a distinct look: a uniform of comfortable casual wear, hippy wristbands, hippy shades and bandanas, and that yellow smiley face almost certainly incorporated somewhere. At clubs they danced in stiff bounces, sometimes with straightened arms steering an invisible ship, sometimes with folded fingers smoothing invisible lapels, sometimes with clenched fists kneading invisible dough. Many people I knew had friends like this. They brought them to meet us after work, like some postgraduate show-and-tell conducted on the pavement outside the pub: *Here's my mad friend*. The friends grinned and said "man" in slightly woozy voices. They showed us accoutrements of the uniform, perhaps the shades, perhaps a selection of wristbands. They had clubbing stories, but they never seemed to complete sentences, let alone tell an entire tale.

They were always friends-of-friends, presented as being off the rails, never considered capable of becoming one of us - we dullards who were holding down jobs. On return visits to my university town, I met old faces who were well into it and who were, indeed, properly off the rails; manically giggling girls in smiley-face bandanas, chewing gum at a million miles an hour and telling us about how their friend put an acid tab on her eyeball in a club and let it seep into her from there. I asked them once about the music. They ignored the question. Many, I guess, did take acid, but it wasn't too common. Because now there was the phenomenon of illegal "raves" outside of the club circuit where another drug was becoming popular: MDMA, or ecstasy, which you took as a tablet. We'll come back to raves.

As I write, you can search online for acid house and get lists of wonderfully mad records which, back then, I wasn't sufficiently involved to know about. They weren't on the radio shows I listened to so that was that. But the nonconformity, frivolity and plain silliness that seemed to run through the scene made it attractive. What we saw on record covers and in the media didn't always help to enlighten us as to where "house" ended and "acid house" began, but I thought it had to be acid if it had successions of riffs, sirens, klaxons and cartoonish samples in place of conventional song structures. These records delivered loopy fun of the kind that echoed my magic mushroom experiences, so if the idea was to evoke the effects of psychedelic drugs, this made sense. But if an acid house record was simply a house record with hippy-era embellishments, then I was equally happy. I saw hippy stuff as an important part of my heritage. Calling this the Second Summer of Love only served as encouragement.

Retrospective acid compilations seem happy to include any US house record from 1984 onwards, anything with odd, strange or woozy sounds; riffs that don't quite stay in key; barrages of electronic riffing. I have since been told that true acid house records were those made in a particular place (Chicago), on a particular synthesiser (the Roland TB-303) using particular techniques ("squelching"). But I'm still not sure that I could pick one out from a line-up.

Whatever they were, the difference made by these sounds was welcome. John Peel praised the anonymity of house music for rendering pop stars and image obsolete. It was an interesting observation. He might not have been speaking specifically about acid. Maybe he had as much trouble distinguishing acid house from other house as we did. Sometimes, however, identification was made easier. 'Superfly Guy' by S-Express for example was certainly acid: you only had to look at the trippy picture cover, hear the trippy lyric, move to the trippy groove and dig the trippy riff. It got to number five in what was a brilliant summer chart. Apart from the number ones.

Which is, perhaps, a little unfair to the already-mentioned 'The Only Way Is Up' by Yazz and the Plastic Population, a hectic dancer with the right bpm rate for its surroundings. It was a defiant, spirited yell from the down-at-heel, with a sky-punching chorus that caught imaginations far and wide. It was a cover but hardly anyone knew. I bought it. I tried to like it. At least it prevented 'The Loco-motion' by Kylie Minogue from getting to number one.

Back to the acid. Bomb the Bass apologised for 'Beat Dis' by releasing 'Megablast', with its explicitly acid packaging, its samples – including the already well-worn "Uh, uh... uh yeah!" one - and an almighty main riff that united club crowds for long, joyful moments, as well as threatening my cool outward display when it came on the Walkman during the bus commute. It was a double A-side with the more conventional 'Don't Make Me Wait', featuring Lorraine. It got to number six.

The influx continued throughout the autumn. 'Can You Party' by Royal House and 'Burn It Up' by the Beatmasters featuring PP Arnold both arrived in the Top 20, qualifying as acid by virtue of their packaging and a structure which enabled them to sit happily alongside 'Megablast'. 'Acid Man' by Jolly Roger, which got to twenty-three, had to be acid because of its title. However, 'Jack to the Sound of the Underground' by Hithouse, which reached the Top 20 in early December, simply took elements of every house hit of the year and stitched them together under a new title. But every scene has those.

By now the media had caught on to acid, and its drug-associated hippy heritage was never going to sit comfortably with the tabloid press. There was a backlash. In response, D-Mob released the ridiculous 'They Call It Acieed' which had an acid house beat, a rap explaining what acid was and wasn't (insisting it wasn't about drugs) and, most glaringly, had the singer manically yelling "acieed" throughout, in a tone that could have shattered windows. On the bus, I turned my Walkman right down the second it started. This threatened to remove the gloss from it all and, by Christmas, the chart presence of acid house was kind of over. Similar dance records would be called something different from now on.

But the acid year ended on a high, a grand finale in the shape of a UK acid house stunner and one of the best records of the year: 'Stakker Humanoid' by Humanoid. It started with a lot of low-key electronic twiddling, but then suddenly a robot yelled *Humanoid* at you and the whole thing burst into acid-soaked riffing of the kind that those Chicago guys could only dream about. It was like it had lifted you clean off the ground. There are stories of when it was first played in clubs, including at Manchester's iconic alternative venue the Hacienda, when people just fucking lost it.

Just as important as acid was the rehabilitation of guitar pop heralded by the Primitives. Now: indie aficionados like to bring up bands like the Jesus and Mary Chain and the Shop Assistants when you mention the return of guitars, insisting that the Primitives were a pale imitation of both. But, for me at least, there's no comparison: it was the Primitives who were on *Top of the Pops* and all over the radio and in the Top 10. Yet, if you remember, the first delicious chimes of resurgent guitar the previous autumn had come from Voice of the Beehive.

Since then, they had released 'I Walk the Earth', which peaked outside the Top 40 and which was okay, but in early summer they came up with 'Don't Call Me Baby', a post-breakup drama with a bittersweet tone and a superb main vocal hook. It sounded brilliant on the radio and went all the way to number fifteen, spending a total of seven weeks in the Top 40. Primitives fanciers naturally embraced it, but I also heard "Oh I like that one!" from soul fans with tightly-tied hair and big, tinted glasses.

There was an album, *Let It Bee*. Its lyrics described attitudes, dreams and experiences of love that I instantly recognised, and which had no hesitation in pointing out the role of girls in undermining their own cause as well as that of boys in being tossers. Its noise was wonderful. 'I Say Nothing' was re-released a few weeks later and got to number twenty-two. They played at the Town & Country Club that autumn and three of us spent an excellent gig diving in and out of the mosh pit in a state of delirium. When, over the next few years, I had occasion to visit girls' rooms, I often found *Lovely* and *Let it Bee* together beside the music player.

Some people inspired by 'Crash' went in a different direction. The guitar band/bouncy tune/blonde girl singer combination had sparked something. And so came Transvision Vamp, who put a definite twist on these elements. Their singer, Wendy James, was a pouting, bare-shouldered object of desire straight off a High Street peg, soon bringing meaning to the lives of fourteen-year-old boys everywhere. Their big 1988 hit was 'I Want Your Love', which had been stitched together from ten other records you'd heard before and ruthlessly refined in the studio, so that it became a bit less guitar, a bit more studio.

Much of it crossed over with the Primitives, but the overt sexiness was a major divergence. It was all done, we were at liberty to imagine, in the name of the kind of "fun" that the tabloids could make sense of. The result was profitable. Wendy pouted, the boys did their studied rock 'n' roll stuff behind her, and between them they exuded masses of dumb energy. They would call their first LP *Pop Art*. 'I Want Your Love' shot to number five.

People said: *If you liked the Primitives, you'll like this - and this is better.* Many saw it as the linear fulfilment of an idea, suggesting that pop is a package of which the music is but one, equally-weighted element. The idea seemed borne out by Transvision Vamp's success. In the next three years they would have another six Top 40 hits and a number one album. In September, the Primitives released the skyrocketing 'Way Behind Me'. It was brilliant Primitives, the very essence of them. It got good press reviews. I played it obsessively. It peaked at number thirty-six.

Was it because of this disparity that I resented Transvision Vamp so much? Possibly. But that was my problem. Transvision Vamp were what Transvision Vamp were: they had every right to be the soundtrack to saucy nights at the holiday camp if they wanted to. And after all, I wasn't fourteen. It should in any case be recognised that there was more than enough room for two guitar bands fronted by blonde girl singers. And while you're pondering that, here's the news: by October, there were three.

When 'Burst' by the Darling Buds first came on the radio, the first impression was how hectic it was, how *excitable*. The vocal in the verse was sometimes super-fast, cramming in the syllables to fit the tempo. The sound was clean and buzzy, closer to that of Transvision Vamp than to the warmer sound of the Primitives. But warmth came from elsewhere; from its wide-eyed bouncing, its explosive four-beats-to-the-bar chorus, and its sense of sincerity. It was guitar pop taken to an extreme and it made me as high as 'Superfly Guy' and 'Megablast' had. It didn't bother the Top 40, but the Darling Buds would have their moment.

More guitar-based sounds appeared. The Lilac Time had the cool, thoughtful 'Return to Yesterday'; the Wonder Stuff had 'It's Yer Money I'm After Baby', the first in a run of well-loved chart hits. Later in the autumn, I bought 'There She Goes' by the La's, which would be a Top 20 hit two years later and hailed as an all-time guitar great. But in the meanwhile, U2 re-entered the fray.

They had last been seen gazing around meditatively in the middle of a Californian desert, on the stylishly monochrome artwork for their monster album *The Joshua Tree*, which people had taken extremely seriously. U2 was, generally, an extremely serious business. They had started out as a guitar band; chief twanger the Edge was one of the guitar giants of the era, but it had all gone rather corporate and stylised during the synth years with the guitar-ness somewhat subsumed.

However, with pop guitars now growling, chugging and thrashing all around, it was as if they had something to prove. They did so with 'Desire', which went to number one for a week in October. It was a feast of cranked-up guitar noise and Bo Diddley beats, lasting three minutes and one second – a back-to-basics sound that was one of the main ideas behind the forthcoming album, *Rattle and Hum*. It's easy to yawn over U2, but 'Desire' was a reminder of just how good they were capable of being.

I have mentioned my Walkman a couple of times. I had finally got one. There still wasn't a turntable where I was living, so I was forever going to friends' houses and taping my vinyl. One particular friend had to put up with this more than most. I took a stash round there on a late spring Saturday and was made to wait my turn, because a guy from his work had brought round *Lovesexy*, the new album by Prince, of whom he was quite clearly in awe. Delirious superlatives burst forth as he rolled around enraptured on the carpet: *Listen to that! Oh my God-duh, just listen to that-tuh!* We uttered supportive comments in calmer tones. I had liked its lead single, the lite-funk ditty 'Alphabet Street' and without doubt 'Sign 'O' the Times' from the previous year had been brilliant. But I still didn't get the "genius" thing and the sight of him lounging across the cover of *Lovesexy* with his body out was making me want to delay my dinner.

Getting my stuff taped was nonetheless always worth the patience involved. I had a long, meandering bus commute into central London at that point and needed sustenance. Listening to music was still a minority activity among commuters, most of whom regarded the sight of spongey-tablet headphones as a threat and would wait anxiously for the chippering of noise overspill to start further ruining their already miserable morning. I tried to be considerate.

All of my tapes had new singles on. If I bought an album, I pumped it onto one side of a C90 and filled the rest with chart hits. I did precisely that with three new albums that year. One was *Lovely* by the Primitives. The second was *Let It Bee* by Voice of the Beehive. The other was *Blue Bell Knoll* by the Cocteau Twins. With all these other distractions, I'd almost forgotten about them. Pop had been busy purifying itself in line with core values, but now suddenly here again were the group taking what I had always seen as the purest path of all.

Because of those bus journeys, I was buying the music papers again and finding them an increasingly satisfying read. I wish I had kept the *NME* review of *Blue Bell Knoll*. It was nothing short of an exaltation, upholding all my feelings about the group; awarding the album a maximum score of ten and making me glow with pride; all before I had heard a note from the record.

When I finally heard it, it was as if all the music I had ever known could now be put into perspective. These were ten tracks whose sole purpose was taking the interaction between music's fundamental elements to new highs; relentlessly and from start to finish. The titles almost didn't matter. 'For Phoebe Still a Baby', 'Suckling the Mender', 'The Itchy Glowbo Blow': these were just collections of words that were easy on the tongue, needed only because titles were something you had to have. It was unfathomably wonderful; each track a different concoction of delirious haze; nothing jarring, everything masterfully ushered. This is it, I thought; this is what they have been working towards all these years - a fulfilment, an ultimate expression; their entire accumulated craft in one sublime presentation.

A university friend had got a job in a residential home and he was finding it tough. His rota delivered a clear weekend off so I went down there. We took long walks in the neighbouring fields and failed to find any mushrooms, but we had a bag of weed, which we dug into when we got back to his bedsit. The Seoul Olympics were on. We watched the athletics with the sound off, but with *Blue Bell Knoll* on. We listened to it twice straight through. We agreed that if we were ever to hear anything more beautiful, it would kill us.

Elsewhere that autumn however, it began to feel as though the trappings of dull normality were creeping back. Thanks to its use in a beer commercial, 'He Ain't Heavy, He's My Brother' by the Hollies, from 1969, was re-released, inducing a tidal wave of sentimentality that swept it to number one replacing a cover version, 'Groovy Kind of Love' by Phil Collins. In the same chart sat a remix of 'Lovely Day' by Bill Withers from 1978 and 'Easy' by the Commodores from 1977, re-invigorated by a building society advert.

There was something depressing about all this, but 1988 had fight in it yet. 'Desire' by U2 flew to the top of the charts. It was replaced by the full horrors of 'One Moment in Time' by Whitney Houston, but then we were rescued by the best number one of the whole year. It came out of nowhere. It defied categorisation, it wasn't trailing a movie, it wasn't being used in an ad campaign; it had nothing to do with soap operas, or SAW, or house, or acid, or soul, or rap, and it didn't sound like there was a sample or a blary guitar anywhere near it.

Enya was a former member of Irish folk group Clannad, and had spent the half-decade since her departure refining sounds of the ancient past that could only have been made in the technological present: multi-layered vocals and orchestral arrangements that evoked savage nature and the supernatural. 'Orinoco Flow' was about a worldwide pleasure voyage. Indeed, it delivered an experience of riding on restless oceans; with great swells of strings, thundering drums and celestial vocals rising, dipping and bursting all around. It was a while before I learned that there was a coherent lyric - it sounded like a first cousin of the Cocteau Twins. But people rushed to it from all directions. On a golden late October day, it replaced 'One Moment in Time' at number one; as great a moment as when 'Mamma Mia' had seen off 'Bohemian Rhapsody', or when 'Uptown Top Ranking' had put 'Mull of Kintyre' to the sword. It was day to bask in; a day to make you believe – one to crown a special year.

And it even ended well, with various terrific records making it a cool Yule. There was 'Need You Tonight' by INXS and 'Good Life' by Inner City, both good-to-go at parties everywhere. Kim Wilde's 'Four Letter Word' charmed the socks off people. 'Stop!' by Erasure was great jiggly fun. 'Buffalo Stance' by Neneh Cherry caused a real stir, seamlessly blending British beats with US rap attitude and being performed on TV while the singer was heavily pregnant. All of these reached high into the Top 10. Unfortunately, the Christmas number one was 'Mistletoe and Wine' by Cliff Richard - there was, as ever, plenty of dross. But sometimes the most groaned-over records have more to applaud than they're given credit for.

Which brings us back to Kylie. And Jason Donovan. The pair recorded a duet to mark the fact that their respective *Neighbours* characters were getting married. 'Especially for You' was a swaying, likeable ballad that was banging on the door of number one at Christmas. Just below it in the Top 10 was another sentimental single linked to the wedding, 'Suddenly' by Angry Anderson. This wedding was a big deal. 'Especially for You' eventually reached number one, at the start of a new year that would be very different from its predecessor.

It would, however, cost about the same and be packaged about the same. The price of a seven-inch had jumped suddenly in early 1988 to £1.99, but it wouldn't go up again for another four years. In that time, it would be extremely rare to find a copy of a new release without a picture cover – the exceptions were one or two acts who purposely issued releases in plain white paper sleeves with view-holes for novelty value. Some others, such as successful dance label ffpp, included view-holes as part of their branded design.

But every cover came with a chunky little stuck-on label displaying its price and bar-code. These had to be peeled off very carefully. Some of my 1988-89 singles still have them attached because, despite several long minutes of intricate fingernail deployment, it became clear that they were not going to come away without taking patches of the cover with them. And having a laminated cover didn't always help; you might have been starting to meticulously peel up one corner when the thing suddenly just came away, leaving a neat, laminate-free rectangle. This blemish was only visible if you turned it in the light, but you never forgot it was there.

Blue Bell Knoll had an unusual fold-out cover made from textured card rather than laminate, but, as I was painstakingly peeling the label back, it suddenly detached itself, leaving a grainy scar a bit like a bunker on a golf course. Lucky it was on a plain white section. But *Blue Bell Knoll*, though. Even now, I can hardly bear to look at it.

The performance of records in the singles chart, their rate of climbing, peaking and falling, hadn't altered much in years. Neither had designs on the discs' labels. The start of the 80s had seen changes to the corporate design of several majors which had not altered since, for instance the plain satin black of RCA or the plain matt red of CBS. The Warner Bros design had been the same pin-striped faun since 1979 and that of Atlantic had remained unaltered since 1971, apart from the top bit going from blue to green. Bespoke, single-by-single label designs had at one time seemed like being the future, but they turned out to be only of interest to a few: 1989 examples included the Darling Buds, the Primitives and former Frankie front-man Holly Johnson.

Likewise, the migration from printed paper centres to moulded plastic ring centres, which had once seemed a lamentable inevitability, actually went into reverse in 1986-9, judging by the singles I bought in the first six months of each of those years: in 1986, 36% of them had been plastic rings, whereas, in 1989, the figure was down to 23%. This may or may not have had something to do with the fact that bar-codes were now appearing on labels, and this really did piss me off. The bread-heads were invading the turntable, man. Not groovy. Anyway, some labels, such as PWL, Virgin and London, generally preferred plastic rings; others, such as Sire, CBS and Atlantic, generally preferred paper centres. MCA and EMI were among those who seemed to switch back and forth for fun.

Oh yes – fun. 1988 had seen plenty of fun, but everything changed very quickly in the new year. Twelve months exactly after Tiffany's final week at number one, when the places immediately below her had contained Kylie, Bros, Taylor Dayne, Jack 'n' Chill, Debbie Gibson and the Beatmasters featuring the Cookie Crew, the Top 10 was being colonised by well-seasoned purveyors of dull fug and comfy chairs.

Morrissey and Holly Johnson had unremarkable new songs therein, respectively 'The Last of the Famous International Playboys' and 'Love Train'. Above them, Mike and the Mechanics, featuring Mike Rutherford from Genesis, was pedalling 'The Living Years', worthy enough, but for the more senior of citizens to sniffle over. Above him was Michael Ball, barrel-throated star of the West End stage, with 'Love Changes Everything'. Roy Orbison - yes, he of the early 1960s -

was enjoying a revival, with his 'You Got It' now falling from number three. The new entry at two came from old hands Simple Minds, with 'Belfast Child', which would be number one next week - a success which continues to baffle me. The number one was a re-recording of an oldie from the late 60s, 'Something's Gotten Hold of My Heart', by its original performer Gene Pitney plus former lead singer with Soft Cell, Marc Almond.

It was all frightfully earnest and frightfully worthy. It was also old and resolutely male. We were back to the scenario where exciting records would appear regularly enough, but with acres of barren space between them. We were back to normal. I had spent a year and more feasting on pure, energetic pop that didn't reek of exploitation. I wanted more sparkles. So all this "new" stuff was a comedown.

It also happened to coincide with a time of personal hardship and torment for me. It was crappy. I'm not going to talk about it. But at such times, music often proves the only thing capable of taking you by the hand and seeing you through, and it is for such reasons that I will forever love the Darling Buds. In January they breached the Top 30 with 'Hit the Ground', which heralded a forthcoming album. A small gang of us went to see them at The Town & Country Club. Their singer, Andrea Lewis, bopped around energetically, stooping to reach into pots and send clouds of petals flying into the air. The songs were rollicking, breathless and uncompromisingly cute; sometimes sounding like children's counting songs, sometimes like sitcom themes. It was coherent and it worked.

Reviews for their album, *Pop Said*, were enthusiastic. Under the heading 'Blooming marvels', *Melody Maker* called it a "classic". Under the heading 'Make mine a Bud', *NME* exalted the "masterfulness" of many of their songs and awarded 8 out of 10. These reviewers were as willing as I was to step into its sweet world - tracks like the blistering 'Uptight', the swaggering 'Let's Go Round There' and the spellbinding 'When It Feels Good' represented an alternative universe as complete as the one given to me by Sparks when I was eleven.

It proved their peak. They would never get higher than twenty-seven in the singles chart. *Pop Said* managed twenty-five in the album lists. Wasted on an ungrateful public, perhaps. Always an outside bet, probably. But for one deeply unhappy twenty-five-year-old, they were pure and simple salvation. On packed buses and trains heading towards a Central London office, the C90 I had transferred it to was ever-present. While I was listening to that, nothing could get me.

Overall, 1989 was glossy and toned-down; rich in its intrinsic dullness. The landscape was occasionally broken up by things like 'Straight Up' by Paula Abdul or 'Got to Keep On' by the Cookie Crew doing well in the Top 10, or a revitalised We've Got a Fuzzbox and We're Gonna Use It (now shortened to Fuzzbox) enjoying a run of characterful singles including 'International Rescue' from the Top 10 album *Big Bang*.

But such things were relatively rare. SAW reached the absolute pits. Jason Donavan would go straight in at number one in the summer with a pointless cover of 50s teen weepy 'Sealed with a Kiss', into which no effort whatsoever had been put. They then launched Sonia, an icon even more hollow than Jason, who went quickly to number one with the tune-by-numbers 'You'll Never Stop Me from Loving You'. They also launched equally vacuous male vocal troupe Big Fun, via a perfunctory cover of the Jacksons' 'Blame It on the Boogie'. You thought about some of the great records they had been responsible for, then you looked at all this It made you long for the resurrection of a proper star.

Which brings us back to Kylie. She had redeemed herself post-'Loco-motion' with 'Je Ne Sais Pas Pourquoi', a bundle of sweet surprises that held number two for three weeks behind 'Orinoco Flow'. Now, in late spring, she bagged a second solo number one with 'Hand on Your Heart'. On the surface, it was appalling. It had a terrible picture cover and sounded flimsy all the way through. But then, as it began to fade, you were suddenly, somehow, begging to hear one more chorus. How the hell had they done that? It made you simultaneously tear at your hair and sigh with wonder. This piece of utter trash had, despite yourself, made you want to dance.

Now, however, when anyone spoke of dancing, they were probably thinking about the rave scene. With acid fading from the charts, raves had gone properly underground. Imported tunes were still being played at packed clubs; but now also at unlicensed large-scale parties hosted by entrepreneurs happy to flout the law in order to cater for the exploding demand. Every weekend, daring ravers dodged the authorities, contacting each other by phone-box while on the move, waiting for instructions in A-road laybys, until finally converging in warehouses, fields and remote farm buildings to dance till sunrise.

Drugs were integral to the scene. I was still smoking hash and weed but I was curious about acid, especially since I had become such a mushrooms convert. Acid was supposed to be similar, but with a deeper effect. Sounded great. Except that acid was not the big new thing. The big new thing was ecstasy. Over the next few years, I would hear countless homages to these little 'E' pills, how they churned out love like a sausage machine, bringing strangers together in huge waves of warmth.

But it was a pill, made in a laboratory, with all the going-wrong that this might entail. Supply was largely under the control of criminal gangs. Now I'm fully aware that supplying any illegal drug made you a criminal. But these were habitually violent people ruthlessly expanding turf in a new, highly-lucrative market, and facing fewer boundaries than usual when the parties were illegal anyway. Tabloid reports about youngsters taking bad pills and becoming hospitalised did nothing to ease my mind.

The whole thing failed to appeal. The image most easily conjured was of me standing in a muddy field, chomping on a lump of poison, not digging the sounds, and having paid a fistful of tenners for the experience. I wondered whether taking ecstasy was essential for enjoying the music. Long passages of beats and bleeping riffs could certainly sound and feel great, but as *part* of the soundtrack, as a contrast - I wouldn't want a whole night of it. You'd get bored. You'd get fidgety. You might put yourself under pressure to talk to girls. You might end up drifting away feeling rotten, which wouldn't be the point of it. All this might be alright on good ecstasy. But I just didn't fancy pills. I didn't become part of the scene. Nobody close to me did anything more than dabble.

And I therefore couldn't really enjoy it at all, because there was very little of it in a chart dominated by the frightfully earnest and the frightfully worthy. Madonna returned, but with something heavier – the saving or otherwise of your mortal soul. 'Like a Prayer' was all worship, delirium and abandon. It could have been sung to a lover, or it could have been sung to Jesus. The video had a Christ effigy who was black, who came to life, and whose feet she kissed. I didn't love the record, but I bought it and cheered it on. The last week of March was the first of its three at number one.

Before Christmas, I had bought the Bangles' *Everywhere* album, the pseudo-psychedelia of its lead single 'In Your Room' having reached a modest thirty-five in November. The LP had a rich, rounded sound; not greatly exciting. But the next 45 from it would be an extraordinary success. When I first listened to 'Eternal Flame', I was surprised that they'd turned their hand to a proper slushie, even though it suited both their vocal style and the general feel of the album. It was okay. But then it came out as a single. Four weeks after entering the Top 40, it went to number one and stayed there for a month. I was gobsmacked. It was massive. Massive, earnest and worthy.

Soul music was likewise lowering the tempo. London act Soul II Soul were built on the unifying philosophies of lead man Jazzie B, with main vocal duties delegated to bandmate Caron Wheeler. They dropped the bpm to create a cooler, steadier groove for their number four springtime hit 'Keep on Movin''. They kept it there for its follow-up, the sumptuous 'Back to Life (However Do You Want Me)', which was a four-week number one in early summer and, arguably, the single of the year.

Hip hop (or rap, or whatever you called it) was also chilling out. De La Soul appeared from the troubled back yards of New York State with their own positive philosophies, adorned with insider slang and decorative insignia including the peace symbol and crayoned drawings of flowers. The trio gave themselves unconventional hip hop names – Posdnous, Trugoy and Mase. Their sound incorporated laid-back beats, thoughtful vocal delivery and samples that made you smile. Their first two hits, 'Me, Myself and I' and 'Say No Go', saw them firmly established by the summer.

In July, a new Primitives single, 'Sick of It', appeared to enthusiastic reviews. It got to number twenty-four. The album that followed, *Pure*, was a more refined version of its predecessor. Well-constructed jangle 'Lonely Streets' stood out, but the next 45, 'Secrets', failed to make the

Top 40. Neither of the Darling Buds singles since 'Hit the Ground' had made the Top 40, either. Both acts would diminish in stature while continuing to make records that rivalled their previous bests. They perhaps deserved much better, but they had begun to look like a failed experiment. 1989 was a world of superior wisdoms and packaged philosophies, of sober rhythms and sage rhymes, of ruthlessly-marketed teeny icons full of air and revered veterans full of vitamin pills; and all of it subject to a creeping glossification. In such an earnest and worthy world, there was never going to be much demand for these bouncy guitar bands and their sweet little tunes.

Because of the tapes I played in our flat, I occasionally caught mates humming something by the Darling Buds or Fuzzbox. But I had most of my music conversations with people at work and this was now a different crowd. I had taken steps to turn my circumstances around, one of them being to move companies. The new place took its business just as seriously, but had a more relaxed, shop-floor-led approach, giving rise to plenty of flying banter and verbal jousting which could be ruthlessly competitive.

The air was thick with snobbery of all kinds, especially musical. You'd mention something in perfect innocence, and people in far-flung corners of the room would wail in horror, making eye contact with each other and shaking their heads. They were like the clichéd popular kids at school: you kind of wanted them to approve of you, but you kind of wanted them to fuck off; and in the end they didn't do enough of either.

One of these was a Geordie guy, a real alpha male, who had the style, the wit and an impressive string of sexual conquests. He was also more music-obsessed than the others but was alarmed at my pop tastes. Madonna had just released a piece of finger-poppin' confectionary called 'Cherish' as a single and for a while I thought it was here to save the world. When I spoke well of it, he hesitated, then quickly changed the subject. But when I mentioned that I wasn't a particularly big fan of the Smiths, he simply froze, his gaze still towards me but not on me, his jaw moving slowly from side to side, like an action hero whose next move might be his last. Finally, he sighed, paused, drew in breath, paused again, then said: "Listen. I'm going to make you a tape".

This was done out of genuine concern. The tape duly arrived, full of Smiths classics, most of whose titles had some familiarity about them. "Let me know what you think", he said. A few days afterwards, when I could delay my report no longer, I simply mentioned a few as being "good", then enthused about one I had already liked, hoping he had forgotten, before moving on. Actually, I had sat through about a quarter of it before deciding life was too short and turning it off to take gulps of air.

This guy wasn't your full-on sun tan and biceps merchant. He didn't tan easily and he didn't much like U2. But he kept a keen eye on what was hot in the music press - and sustainably hot, as opposed to fleeting fancies for the likes of the Darling Buds. He had respect for the Cocteau Twins; although he was more interested in the comedy value of their track titles than anything else.

He was also interested in any credible mainstream records if a critical mass of his peers, particularly the younger girls, were raving about them. This was therefore an area where we could see eye to eye, especially if it was what we were now beginning to refer to simply as "dance" music, because dancing meant partying and partying meant copping off, so he was right there.

Being a Londoner, one of the things I hadn't understood was that the rave culture, based on the explosion of acid house, had been more of a northern thing (and western, before you Bristol people start): hence my university friends knowing more about it than I did. It was out of the Manchester scene that one of the best records of 1989 came, 'Voodoo Ray' by A Guy Called Gerald, a Hacienda regular who had decided to have a go at this track-making business himself. Its tuneful riffs blended straightforward bleeping with a distinctive effect that was part xylophone, part steel pan, and cool vocal samples to provide as pleasant a trance as you'd ever been in. It fit comfortably alongside the relaxed sounds of Soul II Soul and De La Soul that summer. The Geordie liked it, too.

Dance was becoming ubiquitous. Various subcultures were spreading through Europe's underbelly, and chart hits of every kinds were being made danceable. The hideous Jive Bunny and the Mastermixers revived Starsound's lucrative 1981 idea of splicing together snippets of ancient records over a continuous beat, thereby guaranteeing inclusion at undiscerning parties and clubs. It wasn't earnest and worthy – but they were number one three times in the space of six 1989 months.

The same period saw the emergence of fluid rhythms played on acoustic piano, a step which marked an evolution of house away from the electro part of its heritage; and in doing so, alienated many, including me. It was showcased by 'Ride on Time', from Italian act Black Box. Acoustic piano provided its main riff, while the vocal, sampled for both verse and chorus, consisted of a woman yelling at the top of her voice. All the way through.

Now, I have never taken kindly to being shouted at and I took an instant dislike to this record, both for the yelling and the piano nonsense. But its energy and celebratory ambience pleased plenty of others and it hit number one in early September. It removed 'Swing the Mood' by Jive Bunny and the Mastermixers. Six weeks later, it was finally replaced, by 'That's What I Like' by Jive Bunny and the Mastermixers. These were desperate times.

Morale was somewhat restored by a Belgian group called Technotronic. 'Pump Up the Jam' by Technotronic featuring Felly was my favourite record of the second half of the year. Decidedly dark and tense for a dance-pop hit, its atmosphere was set by heavy, distorted thumps of metallic bass, clicking hi-hat, jagged synth motifs and a female vocal - fresh from a New York street somewhere in Belgium - chanting the lyric as if simultaneously prodding your chest on the beat. The lyric may have boiled down to no more than *let's dance the night away*, but it rocked like a bastard. It was number two for two weeks behind Black Box.

It was good theatre. But it was also fun; and genuine, positive fun began creeping back that autumn. If any other record epitomised this, it was 'Street Tuff' by the Rebel MC and Double Trouble. As Double Trouble and the Rebel MC, they had enjoyed a summer hit with 'Just Keep Rockin'', a light-hearted rap over a vintage reggae bass riff and a modern dance beat. This formula was repeated for 'Street Tuff', but to even finer effect; with catchy slang and a singalong bassline inspiring on-the-spot jiggles in all but the most resolute of grumps. The Rebel MC paused mid-stream to declare it so good that people must be thinking him American: "...and you wonder, *Is he a yankee?* No – I'm a Londoner!" You could only laugh - the Belgians sounded more yankee than he did. Whatever mood you had been in four minutes ago, you were in a better one now. It got to number three.

In the office, the Geordie and I had begun to do the *NME* crossword together. He was expert on most things since punk, but he knew little of important matters such as Mud or the Sweet and his 60s was patchy, so I was more than a match for him. We would take turns going down to the news stand from late Tuesday morning - you never knew exactly when the *NME* would turn up – until returning with the latest copy, whereupon, whatever stage of the day or the sales cycle we were at, we would declare a suspension of business. Everyone else would light a fag or put the kettle on while we hunched over the paper in the corner until it was done.

As this became entrenched habit, something new began inching onto the soundtrack. The *NME* and *Melody Maker* had both been going on about a Manchester group called the Stone Roses. Looking down the indie chart earlier in the year I had noticed a single with the eye-catching title 'She Bangs the Drums', without ever hearing a note of it. The Geordie was now mentioning them, as were other, less music-obsessed people – the group were worth a name-check for those not wanting to be left out. When it was announced that they were going to be on the next *Top of the Pops*, I made a point of watching it for the first time in ages.

Their current single was a double A-side, 'What the World Is Waiting For' / 'Fools Gold' and it was 'Fools Gold' that was performed; a spacey, descending bassline, a warmly funky drum pattern like a becalmed breakbeat, a choppy guitar and breathed tenor vocal occasionally chipping in to do their bit. Their attitude was haughty.

On the same show were the Happy Mondays, also from Manchester, with their *Madchester Rave On* EP, from which they were performing 'Hallelujah', which sounded like a melting fairground: the words were mostly shouted, the sounds were indistinct and they were not the most accomplished of performers. That's no reason to judge anyone negatively, but I looked and listened and felt anxious.

I bought both singles and hoped to start liking them. I played

'Hallelujah' once. Ever. 'Fools Gold' barely more, although I did quite like 'What the World Is Waiting For'. The music papers were giving the Stone Roses extensive coverage. They had something called "it" in spades. There was a moderate hysteria about them. Had I been from Manchester, and especially if I had been to the Hacienda, I might have understood a little more. But I wasn't and I hadn't.

The album *The Stone Roses* had been around since the start of the summer but it was now in serious demand. It had neither side of their latest single on it. Someone played it to me. Bits of it were good. It reminded me most of the Monkees. Two of its tracks would become massive favourites. But the group looked like they would disapprove of me. They sang about wanting to be adored and about being the resurrection. Many people seemed to like this but I couldn't join them. I was also jealous and looking for reasons to pick fault. The Stone Roses were not a snug fit.

But they would provide a bridge to greener pastures. They were an indie band. Indie was a subterranean world. The term referred to the independent status of small record companies existing outside of the dominion of the major labels. The Smiths had been on indie label Rough Trade; the Cocteau Twins were on indie label 4AD; the Stone Roses were on indie label Silvertone.

Being free of the majors meant being free of the pressure to mould and polish your product in the name of appealing to *Smash Hits* readers and cracking the Top 20. Having the Independent Charts in the music papers recognised the importance of this. If you were indie you could be true to your own creative instincts and passions. You could have integrity. You could be credible.

That, of course, didn't necessarily mean you'd be any good, but it did put you in a different place: a world which didn't conform to the smart formality and hard-wired seriousness that the 1980s had trained you to revere. There were no coached smiles and skilfully positive expressions there; none of those moments where you have to straighten up, puff out your well-exercised chest and say: "Yes, I had a brilliant weekend, thank you". In fact, you didn't have to grin at all. Or know any answers. Or have any proofs.

Looking stoned and full of your own attitude was much better.

Wearing looser, un-pressed clothes was, too. Like all scenes, it had its hierarchies and its pressures; but it was a stark contrast with what was above ground. A punter at an indie venue was free to experiment, to develop at their own pace and in their own way, much like the acts they were there to see. To many outsiders, it had spiritual appeal and a certain charm. The youngsters who gathered there seemed to understand something. Indie kids were cool.

At the grand old age of twenty-six, I became one.

Six

For as long as we could remember, social realism and the steady rhythms of popular culture had given us images of disharmony and decay to depict the world we lived in. Television dramas remained under the influence of *Boys from the Blackstuff*, portraying lives crushed under the wheels of economic revolution. Programmes, plays and movies everywhere echoed that tension and repeated those messages. The wounds of the miners' strike had yet to heal and its legacy was lingering gloom. You can protest all you like, but in the end, the only option will be to capitulate and put food on the table however you can in your disintegrating environment. This was the world as routinely presented to us. It was dismal, it was violent, it was heavy with defeat.

The representation of inner-city life, both here and in the US, was just as fatalistic; the pessimism over conflict between youth and police just as engrained. In 1988, rap act NWA (standing for "Niggaz Wit Attitudes") released *Straight Outta Compton*, an influential album delineating the violent lifestyle of the "gangsta", a role presented as the only means of getting anywhere in these places. You joined a gang to belong. You dealt in hard drugs. You dispensed with rivals and assorted nuisances by shooting them dead - including, where necessary, the cops.

Rap had long addressed tough social issues. Back in 1982, 'The Message' had given us pathos-laced depictions of decrepit urban districts. More recently, Public Enemy had decried the racism that these environments represented, while championing black responsibility in handling the problem. *Straight Outta Compton* was different. It was the beating of ghetto chests for the benefit of the ghetto (and anyone else titillated by it). It gave the gangsta rap genre its greatest boost. People related its "truths" to the truths of everything else: *It's a tough world out there – like it and get on with it.* And so it took its place, as a bleak feature of a bleak landscape, putting violence in the winner's enclosure – where it stood alongside Sonia, Jason Donovan and Jive fucking Bunny.

But then: a reaction. De La Soul came from a neighbourhood blighted by drug-related gang wars. Jazzy B, leader of Soul II Soul, came from inner-city streets where mistrust between black youths and the police routinely translated into harassment and violence. These acts took a different turn. Both of them chilled, downed the tempo, embraced positivity and partied. Through their records, they spoke of taking your mind to a higher level, of embracing your neighbours, of being different, of striving for love and peace.

De La Soul rejected the label of hippy, but, in a way, they had asked for it. They made a stand in favour of community and sex. 'Buddy', the single-release version of which was arguably their best moment, was a series of musings on the subject of being a randy youngster, delivered over the most laid-back beat imaginable. It served the cause of harmony: if you're flirting with a sexy teacher, you're not shooting anyone. Hence the peace symbol and the crayon-drawn flowers, the connotations of innocence, the rejection of violence. Make love, not war.

By the end of the year, De La Soul were in the UK Top 10 and using lyrics to name-check members of Native Tongues – their community of like-minded hip hop artists – including Queen Latifah, the Jungle Brothers and A Tribe Called Quest, who would each return the compliment on their records. Soul II Soul were the biggest new act in the UK and looked like a brand – one that preached self-improvement and choosing a better life. It was cool. It was refreshing. Youngsters flocked to them.

That same autumn, the Berlin Wall came down; breached in an act of symbolic liberation. The Cold War was coming to an end, and its inherent threats, real and present for decades, were dissipating.

Wherever you were on the political spectrum, this was a joyous moment. All of us realised how monumental it was; all of us took time to pause and savour it.

Conflict was being defused in still more ways. The use of 'E' continued its spread. Ecstasy induced an exaggerated sense of empathy and warmth towards those around you. Like the breaking of the Wall, it removed barriers. Football hooligans had been going clubbing, taking 'E', and getting well loved-up with their fellow man. Whether persuaded by the prevailing mood, the music or the chemicals, the behaviour of young people in late 1989 was on the move.

As was mine. Things had improved since the summer and, by the autumn, I was looking forward again. So much so, that I was to be found bombing across Clapham Common in a Vauxhall Astra, hunched over the steering wheel, probably red in the face, possibly bug-eyed, making a noise like a piglet with trapped wind.

This warrants an explanation. I was singing. To be precise, I was singing along to the chorus of 'You're History' by Shakespears Sister, which was no mean feat. They were a duo, comprising Siobhan Fahey, formerly of Bananarama, and American singer Marcella Detroit, who had a quite extraordinary voice: a forceful, crafted soprano that could turn a simple line of lyric into an international event. 'You're History' was their first hit and, in its chorus, she powered out the title while Fahey mused in a leering growl beneath. I was doing my best to emulate this as part of my practise for singing backing vocals.

Because I was going to start playing again and be in a band. I had decided to have a proper go at it before I was too old, which, arguably, I already was. There was a widely-held belief that nobody should be in a band beyond the age of twenty-four, because being in a band was rock 'n' roll and rock 'n' roll was for youth. The 16-24 age bracket was the recognised demographic for all things youthful. The primacy of being young, of being one of "the kids", was absolute.

Music press interviews routinely highlighted the age of performers, raising eyebrows at anything chronologically untoward. Excuses would have to be made if they were anywhere near thirty. *It's okay, he's just a big kid* type of thing, possibly followed by some anecdote involving eating flowers, swallowing goldfish or lighting farts. While doing the

NME crossword in the office one day, my spontaneous recollection of early Stranglers releases prompted a guy from a neighbouring team to pause, narrow his eyes and, with a studied shake of the head and an equally studied tone of disgust, declare: "God – that's so *old*".

If you wanted to meet someone and start a band, there was a standard procedure. You placed a lineage ad in the Musicians Wanted section of *Melody Maker*'s classifieds. It cost you around seventeen quid to publish a phone number, a plea, a brief summary of influences and a throwaway mission statement to do with large-scale cultural appropriation, the seriousness of which could be gauged from the rest of the wording.

My wording was sober and sincere. It was responded to by a guitarist from the English north-east who was sharing a basement flat in Shepherd's Bush with a Gibson SG guitar and a pile of un-sleeved albums. He loved the Beatles - John Lennon in particular. He was also big Bob Dylan fan and had a lot of time for David Bowie. We crossed over a bit with the Beatles and my love for Holland-Dozier-Holland sealed the 60s connection. He rolled his eyes a bit at Abba. He remained quiet at Madonna. He didn't know much about the Cocteau Twins.

We jammed 'Apache' and 'Wonderful Land' by the Shadows - him on lead, me on rhythm. We learned Madonna's sentimental but immensely charming Christmas-time hit 'Dear Jessie', which interested him because of the chord changes. We wrote a few songs in an early-Beatles style.

In terms of current music, 1990 started well. My most played single during the festive season had been 'Got to Get' by Rob 'n' Raz featuring Leila K, an intoxicating bundle of energy very much in the spirit of 'Street Tuff'. De La Soul had a double A-side featuring the crisp, radio-friendly 'Magic Number' and the aforementioned 'Buddy'. There was also 'Got to Have Your Love' by Mantronix, a tight, lovingly-polished piece of class built on a bass line you could sing along to, with a female vocal reminiscent of the first two Inner City releases – no party would be taken seriously without it for months. These three Top 10 hits were euphoric and celebratory; they set the scene for what would be a special year for chart music.

And for me. I was now a proper reader of the music papers. I no longer felt like a fraud for being seen with one. I could do the *NME* crossword. I had paid *Melody Maker* advertising money. They occasionally raved about the Cocteau Twins. One February morning, I confidently plonked myself on a commuter train seat with a fresh copy of *Melody Maker.* I began reading about an indie band called Lush.

The article convinced me that I would like them, even though I hadn't heard a note. It probably mentioned the fact that Robin Guthrie of the Cocteau Twins had produced their new EP, *Mad Love.* A four-piece, two of whom were girls, one with a neat mop of flaming red hair, from London, and with enough charm coming off the page to inform me that I was going to buy this EP in the next few days.

They were not the only indie band I had encountered recently. *The Chart Show* was a Saturday morning TV programme which ran down lists of pop hits using video clips, with captions and pop-ups negating the need for presenters and studio audiences who, on *Top of the Pops* at least, had become all but unbearable. It didn't follow the "proper" BBC chart. But it did feature specialist charts, including the Indie Chart.

It was there that I caught a clip of the video for 'Chelsea Girl' by Ride. There were only a few moments of it, but it was just incredible; a buzzing, throbbing, bouncing din of guitars shot through with a shining, heavily-distorted riff and a simple melody delivered by a likeable voice; four guys playing in a dimly-lit space, rocking out, exuding a kind of cool that was intoxicatingly new on me. Lush and Ride. Short, single-word band names that were not plural nouns or literary references. A definite fad. I was in at the beginning of something.

'Chelsea Girl' was not available as a stand-alone single. It was part of the *Ride EP*. Similarly, there was no track called 'Mad Love' on the *Mad Love* EP. These indie bands released three-or-four-track EPs on twelve-inch, with handsomely thick covers in atmospheric designs. I was used to this from buying the Cocteau Twins. Most singles I bought had an image of the performers cut front. These were classier. They cost £3.49 each. Lush were on 4AD. Ride were on the other heavyweight indie label of the day, Creation.

I put them on tapes with a few chart singles. The two tracks on side one of the *Ride* EP were rewound repeatedly. 'Chelsea Girl' lived up to the impact it had made in that *Chart Show* clip, all the way past the final verse, where it took a sudden turn into a new chord sequence and a freak-out so intense that by the end you could barely make anything out - it was like static, you just had to have faith that there was a beat under there somewhere. At the end it simply collapsed in a long, trailing tangle of feedback.

The second track, 'Drive Blind', was even better. It centred on the harmony between two riffs, one a high clang of dirty lead, the other a low grind of granite rhythm, melding into a steady, spacious groove. It was so rich, so loud, so distorted: it was like an exercise in extremity. It changed my drumming overnight.

Mad Love likewise had two great tracks, both swaying and tumbling in cyclones of treated noise and breathed female vocals. 'De-Luxe' opened the EP, with guitar chimes that rose and fell continuously as the vocal melody, chord changes and harmonies emitted a strangeness like a warm blanket. It was in some kind of waltzing time-signature; perhaps 3/4? Perhaps 3/9? Whatever it was, it worked, and they didn't stick to it anyway. There were big moments. There was a jarring freak-out of a middle section. There was a coda of harmonising doo-dee-dos and small percussive explosions. It was bloody lovely. 'Thoughtforms' had the same hurtling 3/*something* time signature thing and the same storm-swirls of guitar noise and triumphant chord changes and bewitching harmonies and another stunning coda. And I thought: *So this is indie - I get it now.*

I played them to the guitarist and he sat up, wide-eyed. We had been all Beatles, Motown and the Shadows. Not anymore. *What was that chord change? How did they do that? How do they count it? How does that harmony work? How did they get that sound? Why does this guitar sound like that, and that one sound like this?* We knew nothing about effects pedals or studio gimmickry; we had only turned up volumes and fiddled with a bit of EQ. But we poured over the chords and the vocal harmonies in the Lush songs until convinced we had worked them out; we experimented with the rhythms of the Ride tracks until going back to the Beatles seemed like surrender.

When I saw a flyer for a Lush gig scheduled for mid-March, I leapt on to the tube at lunchtime and raced to Subterania, a poster-caked club under a flyover at Ladbroke Grove. I banged on the windowless security doors until admitted to the box office by a slightly intimidated man in a jumper who sold me three tickets at £5 each. The guitarist was easily persuaded to go. The third ticket was for a bass player we had rehearsed with a couple of times, but he blew us out, so I had a spare.

By the night of the gig, anticipation had risen further. John Peel was playing 'De-Luxe'. *Mad Love* had been number one in the Independent Chart. Most people I spoke to who had any inkling of indie had heard of Lush. The pavement under the flyover was busy and by the time we got to the doors there was serious congestion. It was like there was no room for an orderly queue so there had to be a crush instead. Security guys were leaning through the doors shouting "It's sold out – tickets only!" over and over again. We pushed along confidently; this wasn't difficult, these weren't the kind of yobs I had attempted to push by in the past. Just before the doors, I turned.

"I've got one spare at face value" was all I said. There was a surge and I was surrounded by yells, including some pretty pitiful pleading. At the first appearance of a reachable fiver, the deal was done. One bloke was almost crying when he didn't get it. We turned and bundled ourselves past the security guys and in.

The air held a residual chemical smell – dry ice. I had been in clubs with mirrors, acrobatic light shows and plastic greenery: I had been to gigs and discos in old concert halls with sprung floors, celestially high ceilings and peeling decor - but this was new. This was smaller, lower, warmer; with rich, lovingly-applied paint on the walls, the columns, and the stage-front.

I felt at home immediately. As the place steadily filled, people checked themselves to let me pass - they got out of *my* way. Assertive guitar music played at sober volumes. Boys trudged along in band T-shirts that seemed way too big for them; those bearing the band name James seemed popular. Some of these guys looked too skinny to pick them up, let alone walk around in them all night.

Many of the girls paraded a particular type of scruffiness; hair slightly unkempt, denim or leather jackets with cuffs gripped beyond the wrist, cotton dresses in floral designs that danced around the knees as they walked; and beneath these, boots – Dr Martens that clasped the ankle, or bigger ones that grasped the shin, or even bigger ones with straps and buckles, that hid them altogether. There were cardigans, jumpers, jeans, blousey tops. All this, and Lush were going to be playing later.

The support band were a wailing, thrashing mob whose music, for me, was a little *too* alternative. The lead singer wore dungarees and tossed her long, heavy hair back and forth as she performed. They were called Th' Faith Healers. Leaning against one of the pillars to the side and studying the performance was a figure that I swore was superstar producer Trevor Horn. There can't have been many people who looked like him. Indie must be getting important, I thought, if he's considering getting involved.

I soon lost the guitarist. He got chatting to a girl and followed her off to the bar. I stood soaking it all up, listening to the records being played, hardly any of which I recognised, and keeping a good spot, watching the stage crew scurrying around getting everything ready.

Then Lush came on, to a roaring, bellowing, whooping cacophony. They began with 'Thoughtforms', at a volume that filled all the available space and blotted everything else out. I loved the volume. I loved the balance of sounds. I loved the asymmetrical hang of the bass player's jumper and his bashful gaze. I loved the way the drummer played with his mouth open and his head turning, as if struggling to explain himself. I loved the lead singer's concentration and her shaped red hair. I loved how, mid-set, a bloke scrambled on stage and placed a careful kiss on her cheek before security got him. I loved how the other girl, on guitar and backing vocals, kept glancing sideways as if expecting a blow. I loved how they all fell back a couple of steps at the grinding, disharmonious bits, like the middle section of 'De-Luxe', to groove it out. I loved how the dry ice swirled and whooshed between and around them and how the lights shone through it in fractured beams as they played. I loved how it kept thumping me. I loved how coolly they delivered everything. I loved how nervous they seemed. I loved how far it was from grinning, dazzle-toothed showbiz. My guitarist friend missed the whole thing.

I went out into the night air afterwards a part of the indie scene. There was no choice in the matter - it was simply what I now *was*. I wished I had found this a decade earlier. But it was fine. I would adopt a look conducive to the more mature end of the scale. I would wear tops in various dark colours, with rounded, high, patterned collars (not turtle necks), and stick to black for jeans and cotton trousers.

Soon, I would be buying two pairs of Dr Martens shoes – Camden clogs - from Holt's next to Camden Town tube station, wearing them on alternate days until they were exhausted, then buying another two pairs. I would add a black leather jacket – plain, stylish, with slim lapels. My hair would settle down as a number one back-and-sides with a slightly waxed, controllable mess on top. I would be going to the gym at least twice a week. There would be a few errors of judgement on the way. But I would look hot.

I got most of the clobber from places in Camden. Camden was southern indie's spiritual home. I would play a lot of gigs there. My metamorphosis was swift. A former work colleague, arriving to see me play at one of its esteemed venues, would exclaim: "I can't believe it. One minute it's all Bangles and Belinda Carlisle, and now... all *this*".

Indie was a distinct world. Yet it was hard to define with precision. For instance, PWL, the label owned by Pete Waterman of SAW, was an independent label, but it certainly didn't make indie music. Very soon, something would be labelled indie simply for (a) not being recognisable Top 10 teenybop pop, (b) not belonging to any recognised genre of dance, or (c) not belonging to any recognised genre of rock. This would leave a lot of grey area, but we're talking generally-expressed perceptions here. In my experience, if you loved a band that were falling short of the Top 20 it was okay if they were indie; loving them wasn't a failure. Especially if they were on an actual indie label and doing well in the actual Indie Chart.

I had found a new way of being. I loved my new way of being. But that didn't mean that I was turning my back on everything else. This was far from the damning zeal of the born-again. The pop charts had been keeping up its good start to the year and, for four weeks from early February, the number one slot had been occupied by one of the best records for a very long time.

'Nothing Compares 2 U' had been written by Prince for his 1985 side-project the Family. Now it had been covered by the shaven-headed Sinead O'Connor, from Ireland, who had first entered the charts two years before, dispensing a blend of posturing and narkiness that was far less alternative in Britain than in her heavily conservative homeland. But this record elevated her beyond all expectations.

Its sound was massive; like towering, ancient stone. Ostensibly, it was a monumental eulogy to sadness: this love cannot be fulfilled; neither can it be denied - all you can do is accept the pain and mourn. She even cried in the video. You could be as cynical as you wanted about this, but she just stared and sang it into you. If you were a sufferer, here was someone who understood.

Having one of the all-time great singles landing here and now added to the growing sense of excitement. The *NME* cover of March 31st featured an image of Shaun Ryder, lead singer of the Happy Mondays, clambering through a giant 'E' shape on top of some building wearing a look of unqualified triumph. Those hippy values were gaining the upper hand. Tolerance and togetherness were going mainstream. De La Soul declared this to be the "daisy age".

Fresh and forward-looking sounds were flooding the Top 40 from all angles. In that last week of March, the chart contained 'Mama Gave Birth to the Soul Children' by Queen Latifah featuring De La Soul, 'What U Waitin' For' by the Jungle Brothers, 'Loaded' by Primal Scream, 'This Is How It Feels' by Inspiral Carpets and the re-released 'She Bangs the Drums' by the Stone Roses. It had 'Everything Starts With an 'E'' by E-Zee Possee shamelessly riding the bandwagon. It had 'Birdhouse in Your Soul' by They Might Be Giants bookishly embodying the untamed spirit of it all.

That week's number three was 'Strawberry Fields Forever' by Candy Flip, a pair of rave-heads from the Potteries covering a hippy classic with a slowed-down breakbeat and a breathed tenor vocal. The number two was 'Love Shack' by the B-52's, a retro-kitsch invitation to a retro-kitsch party venue down the highway, with a retro-kitsch groove and the smell of furniture polish.

At number one was 'The Power' by Snap!, a tinkling, grating, robotic dance smash with bursts of big-voice rapping. The young girls at our office loved it and, when one returned from lunch with a copy of the twelve-inch, she was quickly surrounded by an excited, giggling huddle (and, therefore, also the Geordie). The restless, slightly unsettling effect of this record was echoed soon afterwards by another number one, 'Killer' by Adamski, whose giant, anxious beats, bleeping electronica and sense of mastery perched on top of the chart for four weeks.

It had replaced Madonna, who had also been number one for four weeks, with 'Vogue'; introducing us to a dance style that was apparently taking gay clubs by storm – "voguing" being the habit of freezing, mid-dance, as if posing for a camera in a fashion shoot, framing the face with rectangled fingers. Straight people started voguing in pubs when the record came on. The gimmick was everything; the record was pretty ordinary.

But it was Madonna. I went to see her on the *Blonde Ambition* tour at Wembley Stadium in July. This was a very different experience to Michael Jackson. I got there early and bagged a position close to the front. Technotronic were supporting. They had followed 'Pump Up the Jam' with another number two, the blistering 'Get Up (Before the Night Is Over)', but on stage at Wembley they were useless. Madonna, on the other hand, was fantastic. Later in the summer, she somewhat scuffed the gloss with the silly Burlesque of her 'Hanky Panky' single. But it was Madonna.

Some indie kid, eh? Well in the interim I had seen Lush again. A group of us from work went in May, to see them at the University of London Union – referred to by most simply as ULU (pron. *Yooloo*). It was bigger than Subterania and more boisterous. There was a buzz about Lush. People didn't want to be left out. We were crushed by the surging, swaying throng at the front, which stretched much further back than at Subterania. People all around the place were yapping to each other during the set, rather than losing themselves in the performance as the performance deserved. This was a band on the up; such things were bound to happen.

I had also bought a second Ride record, the *Play* EP, featuring 'Like a Daydream', a blare of slamming rhythms and cascading chord changes that you could dance to. And it was indeed danced to, along with all kinds of other stuff, at parties and gigs in a widening radius. I hadn't been invited to so many parties for a very long time, not ones where I could thrive at like this, ones where togetherness and shared celebration were core business.

The FIFA World Cup was held in Italy. England, with a settled team peppered with world class stars, did better than for a quarter of a century. Their agonising semi-final defeat brought the nation together in glowing, tearful pride. The TV theme was the operatic song 'Nessun Dorma'. But the soundtrack was a number one dance record by an indie band.

Or, at least, an act centred on an indie band. Englandneworder was New Order with a few adornments, such as a lad-almighty comedy actor doing a bit of cheerleading and a superstar member of the World Cup squad delivering a galvanising rap. The song was 'World in Motion': a celebration of unity, of football, and of cheering for your team, which in this case happened to be England, because the band and its audience were English.

Except that it wasn't all English. Everyone was invited. The chorus refrain was "Love's got the world in motion". The *whole* world. The song encouraged us to believe it; the song encouraged us to embrace it. I went to parties where youngsters from Ireland, Australia and elsewhere all joined in to punch the sky and bellow its coda *We're singing for England...Eng-er-land!* in delirious, pupil-dilating huddles. Some heard it as *We sing 'E' for England*. Either applied. Love was on top.

Oh, what a change this was – another break with the all-too-recent past, where the combination of "England" and "football" had meant drunkenness, thuggery and racism, with nothing to balance it out that was visible to the naked eye. Suddenly, the hooligans were all stoned and England had lightened up.

The world noticed. After the third-place playoff match, when the England and Italy teams lined up on podiums, the normally highly-stylish Italians copied the dumb-arsed diddle-dit-dit dance that the England team had started doing, because (a) the world was in motion, and (b) being English was beginning to look like fun.

Partying took centre stage wherever you were. The soundtrack was defined by the classic breakbeats that had formed the backbone of so much electro-funk and hip hop. They had been recycled ruthlessly and versions of them were now popping up all over the place; Candy Flip had slowed one down to stoner speed, while an electronic approximation was used in Chad Jackson's irresistible 'Hear the Drummer (Get Wicked)', a number three while Englandneworder were number one. Now, they were being emulated and approximated by guitar bands. Snare off-beats could be heard everywhere.

It was called the "shuffle beat", because it more often sounded like Candy Flip than Chad Jackson. It was also called "baggy"; originally because the baggy clothes worn by Manchester clubbers in the wake of acid had delivered a metaphor for the whole scene, but subsequently because it provided a label for the looser feel of the music, and gave licence for it to be dance. By the autumn, indie bands, including Lush, were self-consciously introducing new records as being "baggy" before someone else pointed it out. If you weren't making records with that beat, or something like it, you weren't at the races. The shuffle beat would evolve, loosen and morph into new forms; but the point was, bands that would once have used an up-tempo beat were now using a groove.

Soon there was all sorts of media stuff about before-and-after the point where white people learned to dance. We thought: *Hang on a minute – I'm sure I was dancing to the Human League and Blancmange in 1982.* I'm not going to go into this in any depth because it's nonsense. We might have been dancing differently back then, and not always beautifully; but I had never worried about being able to keep a beat. Nothing had really changed. Except that everything had got better.

At the height of the summer, we were invited to a gathering at a big house in St John's Wood, which is dead posh. The house was empty: we were told some story about the estate agent having access to the keys and deciding to hold a party there. This could have been disastrous at any moment other than the summer of 1990. Whatever the truth of the context, it was an incredible night.

It was fine to invite mates who would invite mates. They may have had some beefy security guys that I have forgotten about. I may have forgotten about them because they were so far from being needed. It is possible we were asked to pay for tickets but I don't think we were. We just rolled up. There were ex-public-school people mixing with geezers from South London, equal numbers of boys and girls.

The dancing was in a huge room with polished floors. You entered it from the front by coming down a little flight of stairs, and exited at the back through French windows into the garden, across which the dancing duly spilled, and in the middle of which stood two full-sized bouncy castles. These saw good-natured jousting and formation

149

bouncing in pretty much equal measure throughout the night; but the music was the real winner.

Among the things that got played: 'Dirty Cash' by the Adventures of Stevie V, classy, zinging commercial not-soul for improved times; and 'Naked in the Rain' by Black Pearl - pumping, stomping house. Both of these were big favourites. 'Fools Gold' by the Stone Roses got played, too, its breathed tenor vocal emulated by a new hit from the same north-west: 'The Only One I Know' by the Charlatans.

This was simply massive among the indie crowd. Like many great records, it reminded you of something you had heard before but couldn't quite place – surely that fat bass rhythm and organ riff had come from something in the late 60s, something that had sent hippies wild in underground clubs where projected blobs made their multicoloured way across the walls? Never before had an indie record so firmly said: *Dance. Now.* For those of us trying to form bands, part of the reaction was hot jealousy: even if we did well and got signed, we would never make a record as good as this, or as *now* as this. The Charlatans were bastards. It got to number nine.

But the biggest moment of the night was when 'Step On' by the Happy Mondays fired up. It had long left the singles chart but it was nowhere near done; it epitomised the spirit of the evening, and of many others throughout that year; these tough guys from a Manchester estate, mashed and pissing about, getting the beats and the sound and the mood right for a party, and inviting everyone they knew and everyone they didn't. The boys and girls in St John's Wood stopped talking, they stopped standing in the garden, they stopped looking for a drink, they stopped looking for a quiet corner to organise stuff in, they stopped everything; they squeezed into the big room and danced together like mad.

Sadly, once the summer was properly underway, the number one position got back into its old habits. In the fourteen weeks following 'World in Motion' in June, we had the adult musings of Elton John's double A-side 'Sacrifice/Healing Hands', then 'Turtle Power' by Partners in Kryme, effectively a cinema trailer with the catchy bits surgically removed. Next came the 1960 song 'Itsy Bitsy Teeny Weeny Yellow Polka Dot Bikini' as covered by Bombalurina, featuring the presenter of a kids' telly show where children were encouraged to shout all the time and commit acts of violence with giant inflatables. It used both the "*whooh! Yeeaahh... whooh! Yeeaahh...*" sample and the "Uh, uh... uh yeah!" one, both of which were now beyond cliché. And accounting for the remaining weeks of this Hall of Infamy was a re-release of the Steve Miller Band's so-so 'The Joker' from 1973, occasioned by yet another bloody jeans advert.

But thankfully, not far away, were records that far better represented 1990, blurring distinctions between pop genres, spreading the energy and sharing the fun. Four of them were gathered in the same late-September chart. 'Groove Is in the Heart' by Deee-Lite was a cocktail of retro-groove and positivity-rap as innocent or as drug-enhanced as you wanted it to be, which went all the way to number two and made everybody smile as if they'd just swallowed the first spoonful of the best ice cream ever. 'Fascinating Rhythm' by Bass-O-Matic was a low-slung club grind with hippy-era samples, a whispering growl of a rap and a quite incredible chorus that reached number nine; its main man was a guy called William Orbit, from whom we would hear more. Then there was 'Where Are You Baby?' by Betty Boo, a pouting comic-book action hero who rapped and sang, the cover of the single showing her patrolling an alien planet with a zap gun. It was her second Top 10 hit of the year and, like her first, 'Doin' the Do', it caused anything dull within earshot to shrivel and die.

The fourth was 'What Time Is Love?' by the KLF featuring the Children of the Revolution, a number five of weight and substance, its single edit billed as "Live at Trancentral". It was a modern pop sermon preached at the best rave you'd ever heard, its highpoint riff a four-note siren from deep space. The cover artwork included a brick pyramid with a boombox fixed to the front, bearing the legend "Justified". The whole thing was wrought of legend. Children of the Revolution. Pyramids. Justified. The KLF were the same guys who, as the Timelords, had delivered the execrable 'Doctorin' the Tardis' in 1988. Then, they had been making a point. Now, they were getting serious.

It was a good thing that there were records like these around, because I was about to have one of the biggest music disappointments of my life. The Cocteau Twins reappeared. Out came a single, 'Iceblink Luck'. I listened, waited for it to get going, and was still waiting as it finished. It got to number thirty-eight. It's okay, I thought. There's an album coming out. An album did come out. *Heaven Or Las Vegas* got to number seven, their highest-ever position. I would meet people in years to come who would say: "Oh, the Cocteau Twins; I like them. I've got *Heaven Or Las Vegas*". Ivo Watts-Russell, head of 4AD records, once said something to the effect of it being the fulfilment of what the label had been founded for.

I'm happy for them, I really am. To me, it was the sound of a band who had once reached for the stars putting their slippers on and collapsing onto the sofa. It was all so tame, and tidy, with low ceilings and the heating on not too high and the cat fed. There wasn't one thing on it that excited me or stirred me or sent tingles anywhere.

They toured. I got to see them for the first time, at the Brixton Academy. They stood with monumental stillness as the backing tapes rolled, Robin and the other guy on guitar, Elizabeth singing, moving only her hands and her head, before an ocean of people on the Academy's gently curved floor. I met a few people I knew and couldn't believe how stoned they were. I mean, completely mashed, almost unable to speak. My reverence had seen to it that I was pretty much sober. So at least I saw them. And at least the gig was great.

I never got over the shock of that album. But I had new favourites to coo over now. Ride released a third EP, *Fall*, containing their most commercial-sounding track yet, 'Taste'. Our band's next demo had a song that was very much under its influence, a fact that people were not shy of pointing out. *Fall* got to number thirty-four. Lush also released a new one, 'Sweetness and Light', which incorporated the shuffle beat, initially to my annoyance, but my annoyance didn't last long. In November they filled the Town & Country Club. Miki signed my ticket. 'Sweetness and Light' got to number forty-seven.

But other guitar outfits were swept much higher by indie's new-found danceability. 'I'm Free' by the Soup Dragons and 'Groovy Train' by the Farm, bands who had earned their stripes on the indie circuit, both tasted the big time in the Top 10. Youngsters EMF were more of an overnight success. Their massive, goofy 'Unbelievable', with its dumb-arsed riff, breathed tenor vocal and immeasurable energy, got to number three in December. The following year it would get to number one in the US.

The only thing to rival it that Christmas was by Madonna. 'Justify My Love' was an outstanding, richly atmospheric single written by rising star Lenny Kravitz. The lyric had a woman challenging her man to prove that he deserved all the good stuff she was giving him. It was soaked in sex. She performed it in a rapturous growl - only the backing vocal was sung. On the cover she dressed as a butch gay, cigarette in mouth, glowering. It was built on a drum pattern recognisable from a Public Enemy album. It got to number two. The number one was 'Saviour's Day' by Cliff Richard.

By the start of the following summer, our band finally had a settled line-up and I had quit my job. We tested our cohesion on a pub tour of Cornwall, where the bassist knew people with room for us all to crash. A guitarist friend of the singer tagged along with his own PA, which we used in return for a few acoustic support slots.

We were paid between £30 and £50 a night. The deal was: we do a set of covers, then take a break, then do a set of our own songs, then take another break before a final round of covers. A landlord in Truro, with a clientele consisting mainly of surly-looking bikers, handed over a clutch of notes at the end of the evening with an unsmiling: "Your covers are shit. But some of *your* songs are pretty good". The audiences ranged in size from zero to thirty. We would get used to this.

We left Cornwall intact and started gigging in London. Under the "pay-to-play" system, you handed the venue a deposit, perhaps £25, which was returned if the sum was exceeded by the door takings from people who said they had come specifically to see you. You then got a split of any profit. Losing the deposit was okay if (a) you were doing the gig just for the experience of playing in public, or (b) if it was only two or three times.

This system was manageable if your network of mates, and your mates' networks of mates, were young and had disposable income which they didn't have to save for the weekend. In your 20s, an unscheduled midweek bender was survivable – all you needed the next morning was one coffee, one bacon sandwich and one productive visit to the toilet and you were fine. Someone only had to say "we're going to see a mate

153

in a band tonight", and there'd be a queue of youngsters with beer money at the ready, not wanting to miss out on anything. I calculated that I could get by on such patronage for about a year if I didn't push my luck.

I wasn't the only one with extended networks of friends. The bass player was part of a highly sociable community centred on Acton in West London. I was sofa-hopping for about ten months and often crashed at the house he shared. I got on well with two housemates in particular. One, a real party animal, was enthusiastic about the band and, like us, had no reason to suspect we weren't going to become superstars. He hyped us to all his friends, and to all their friends, and scores of them came.

The other was an avid John Peel listener and music paper scourer. He regularly returned home with a clutch of new twelve-inch EPs, mainly by acts I had heard of but not heard. I occasionally got to listen and catch up. Among the bands he liked were several who had been gathered under the term "shoegazing".

This referred to those who, in stark contrast to look-at-me showbizzy types, stood still in comfortable clothes, heads down and fringes dangling, as they played their atmospheric, dreamy music. It specialised in song titles that evoked qualities of form ('Waves', 'Crimson', 'Breeze') or the barely contextualised ('Colour of the Sky', 'Spanish Air', 'Chlorine Dream'). It could have a mighty beat sometimes. It could be baggy sometimes. It could be seriously good sometimes.

Lush and Ride were shoegazing bands. There were many more. Such as My Bloody Valentine with their noise experiments; such as Slowdive, with their drifty, patter-drummed soundscapes; such as Spirea X, with their vocals like Gregorian chants and huge, rattling beats.

That spring, I got to see what I still maintain was the ultimate shoegazing gig. It was at ULU and the line-up was shoegazing concentrate. The headliners were Chapterhouse, who had burst onto the scene with their single 'Pearl' - grand, echoey drums, big chord changes, jangling effects and a breathed tenor vocal reduced almost to a whisper. It fell short of the Top 40. They had straight hair hanging at perfect shoegazing length, mid-way between jaw and collar. One of them wore a tight little peaked hat. They had been on TV, marching across some open space being interviewed by Miki from Lush, who was distracted by their youth: "...cos you're all about twelve, aren't you?" That age thing again.

Equally preoccupied with age were the second on the bill, Moose. In one interview I read, they referred repeatedly to the fact that they were twenty-eight, which, pleasingly, was even older than I was. I can't remember much about them apart from that. First on were a youthful three-piece called Revolver, who struck heavily stoned shoegazing poses throughout.

This fit with the surroundings. Our band had gone as a gang, and as we made our way towards the stage, we passed several groups of friends sitting quietly on the floor, barely moving. The music from the PA seemed to ooze. The lights were dim. It was all a bit *wilted*. The performances did service to this atmosphere. Part-way into Revolver's set, the singer leant towards the mic, as if doing so made him ache, and with an almighty effort said "This one's called... 'Molasses'".

We pissed ourselves laughing. We felt some affinity with all this, but we also felt superior, an idea for which there was very little evidence. Our demos were okay but we were inconsistent live. After some performances, we wanted to crawl into a hole and hide. But when it went well, it was brilliant. An early appearance at The King's Head in Fulham was such an occasion.

The bass player who had blown us out prior to Lush at Subterania turned up with the band he had settled on. They were following in the footsteps of skinny, young bands playing energetic, punk-tinged electronica to very young audiences – a scene apparently called "grebo". Its leading lights included Carter the Unstoppable Sex Machine (Carter USM for short), the Wonder Stuff, Pop Will Eat Itself and Ned's Atomic Dustbin, whose set favourite 'Kill Your Television' was already a year old.

I can't remember what this guy's band were called, but they all looked like Ned's Atomic Dustbin fans in their skateboarders' garb, multiple wristbands and carefully messed-up hair. They trouped in like they owned the place and he saw us. Instead of a curt smile or a *how ya doin'?* he turned towards us as he passed and, through a newspaper rolled into the shape of a loudhailer, chanted "Kill, kill, kill your television!" The whole lot then set themselves up at the far end of the bar and started smirking.

This was the motivation we needed. We went on first and played with venom. As we finished our set, the stage was invaded, first by the venue guy who had been gruffly off-hand with us earlier – we had to come back again, but next time bring a few more people – and then by a band, even younger than the grebos, who had come to watch on spec and now peppered us with questions about how we wrote this song or got that sound and how could I possibly play drums and sing those backing vocals at the same time and whether we wanted to strike a deal where we would each give the other the support slot if we got a paid headline gig. We felt like stars. Right there, in front of four other bands and another thirty or so people.

This gathering took place amongst all the equipment crowded onto the small stage, and it didn't last long because everything had to be reorganised for the next band. There were no roadies and these venues didn't provide anyone; the sound guy might help here and there if he was behind schedule, but essentially, we had to do it all.

And most of it was done by me because I was the drummer. I had fifteen separate bits of equipment to unscrew, collapse, pack away and remove. The guitarist had four, including his pedals. The bass player had two, although, to be fair, one of these was a valve amp the size of a front door. The singer had none. The tambourine he used was mine.

One of the things we learned was that unsigned bands do get girls. However, it's far easier for a singer to capitalise on this when he has no kit to guard. Some of these stages were very low, allowing a confident girl to hop up easily and lead a cute guy outside. This happened more than once, with me looking on in envy as I stoically loosened my cymbal nuts. Whatever happened, I was always the last to leave the bloody stage. By the time everything was safely in the van, the tides of audience desire had usually ebbed away.

Never mind. With the indie soundtrack as good as it was in 1991, there was plenty of consolation. Records like 'Coast Is Clear' by Curve, 'Easter Dinner' by Tribe and 'Outshine the Sun' by the Belltower contributed to a glorious parade of power, noise and melody that swirled around us week after week. There was a marked variation across these sounds, but for many, the distinct combination of shuffle beat and breathed tenor vocal was *the* sound of indie, providing a template for various hopefuls with guitars in their hands and dollar signs in their eyes.

Late spring hits 'Can You Dig It?' by the Mock Turtles and 'There's No Other Way' by Blur both leapt on this bandwagon as if dismounting from the asymmetric bars in medal positions. The Mock Turtles, in lining up 60s references including a chorus that went "Can you dig it? Oh yeah", made the indie record that Radio 2 listeners could understand. Blur simply made a great-sounding shuffle-beat record. But each got their hit, reaching numbers eighteen and eight respectively. The Top 40 is constantly enlivened by new arrivals and both of these were welcomed. Yet, when its mainstays do their own enlivening, the result can be every bit as riveting.

Which brings us back to Kylie. In February, she had startled everyone with her 'What Do I Have to Do' single which, although peaking at a relatively modest number six, was a piece of sheer class, the SAW sound having undergone tweaks in every department to fashion a more mature, club-essential feel. Kylie was on a new level; comparable in some ways to that of the KLF, who had been number one in the same chart with '3 A.M. Eternal', a record full of KLF slogans and motifs which despite its success was not quite as good as 'What Time Is Love?' or the single that followed it in spring, the fantastic number two 'Last Train to Trancentral'.

That summer saw the reappearance of a few old friends. It began with the last great release by Siouxsie and the Banshees: 'Kiss Them for Me', a tribute to 50s movie star Jayne Mansfield. Many in our band's extended crowd swooned over its dreamy groove and Eastern flavours. It got to number thirty-two. Voice of the Beehive resurfaced, taking the mid-paced 'Monsters and Angels' to a respectable number seventeen, spending eight weeks in the Top 40. But it was a bit flat. And the album that followed it, *Honey Lingers*, was even flatter. The Primitives also returned, with 'You Are the Way'; seemingly surrendering to the fashion for a shuffle-beat but doing it their groovy way and making it work wonderfully. Yet it got nowhere. A further single, 'Lead Me Astray', another glorious expression of what made the Primitives the Primitives, would barely get noticed.

But the season was soon being swept away by Canadian all-purpose rocker Bryan Adams. A new movie, *Robin Hood: Prince of Thieves*, over-sweetened its love interest with the song '(Everything I Do) I Do It for You', which was okay without the movie. And some of the lyrics. And some of Adams' delivery. And the fact that its apocalyptic pledges of devotion were applied by everyone to their own, run-of-the-mill relationships. Oh, and the fact that the fucker was number one for sixteen weeks. *Sixteen weeks.* Some marriages don't last that long.

Almost as remarkable, was that for six of those weeks, 'I'm Too Sexy' by Right Said Fred was number two. This was a cultural phenomenon in its own right. Over a springy dance track, a pair of bald-headed bodybuilders and another bloke ripped the merciless piss out of people who fancied themselves a bit – ostensibly male models but it could have been anybody. It was hilarious. And as cheesy as hell. And if all you wanted to do was prance around to it playing at being sexy, that was fine, because it was what most other people were doing. The lyric was easy to learn, at times surreal, and wide open to interpretation. Nobody had a bad thing to say about it.

In October, one of my university friends married the LSM's oldest sister. The reception was in the upstairs rooms of a renowned South London boozer and the place was packed with happy, excited people. There were soul boys and soul girls, dedicated clubbers and pill-heads, plus a few die-hard prog rockers with bags of weed in their coats. Spirits were high. The dance floor was fairly busy, but groups of guests were chatting and laughing all around the room without noticing what was playing.

Until 'Charly' by the Prodigy came on. Instantly there were whoops and cheers; hands flew into the air; chairs scraped back; drinks were abandoned, left to slop and settle in the glass. Soon, all dance space was taken and the crowd was a single, heads-down entity, lost in homage to churning riffs, to booming bass, to intoxicating samples. 'Charly' was raw, brilliant, and as cool as fuck. It used cartoon voices from an old public information film about keeping parents informed of your whereabouts. It was slipping down the chart now but it had been number three for two weeks, stuck behind Right Said Fred and Bryan Adams.

Other dance hits from the next few months displayed similarly innovative tendencies near the top of the charts. 'Activ 8 (Come with Me)' by Altern 8, 'Insanity' by Oceanic and 'Running Out of Time' by Digital Orgasm were pure electronica: 'Playing with Knives' by Bizarre Inc and 'Is There Anybody Out There?' by Bassheads used the fluid acoustic piano thing, now referred to as "cheesy piano". But these were all eclipsed by a record on the PWL Continental label - 'Get Ready for This' by 2 Unlimited: a worldwide club smash, a clean-cut workout, an undeniably wicked tune. It got to number two and spent fourteen weeks in the Top 40.

Any of these would have been played at parties that Christmas. The ones I went to were mainly in West London with various members of the band's entourage. People who had never danced - shy indie stiffs and former punks who had only ever done the pogo - now had a groove. 'Charly' was usually played. So was 'Black or White', a recent Michael Jackson number one that everybody liked, including me; great guitar riff, great beat. Also 'OPP' by Naughty By Nature, a bouncing blob of hip hop based on a sample of the Jackson 5's 'ABC'. There was an open-mindedness about what could be danced to, and this growing range soon incorporated one particular slab of alternative rock - 'Smells Like Teen Spirit' by Nirvana.

The music papers' coverage of this Seattle trio had been gathering. I had absorbed the name without reading as much as a sentence or hearing as much as a note. But 'Smells Like Teen Spirit' came among us like a hurricane, with guitars growling like none before, in a more danceable rock rhythm than had ever been imagined; one that lent itself to grooving but gave itself to leaping; accompanied by a drum part that broke boulders; and a hoarse, wildly emotional vocal that turned you fifteen in an instant.

The video captured its atmosphere and power brilliantly. It was set in a high school gym, but one cleared of jocks and achievers' gleam, with unsmiling cheerleaders in black outfits calmly going through their routines, until suddenly giving in to possession and tossing their loosened hair in wild thrashes, as the band performed with the same abandon and the dorks headbanged, leapt and writhed in the tar-edged dimension they were claiming as theirs.

Indie kids lost it. Rock fans lost it. Nirvana had emerged from the North American "slacker" culture of grunge, whose bands were already local legends in the Pacific Northwest. They were outsiders and dissenters and, just as punk had once allied with reggae, the scene was finding shared understandings with hip hop. The album *Nevermind* was a monster. Although it never got higher than seven in the UK album chart, it remained on the list for almost four years.

Coincidentally, number seven was where 'Smells Like Teen Spirit' got to on the singles chart. Its structure was echoed throughout the album; a hushed, measured verse and then a blaring, yelling thrash of a chorus. Alternating between quiet and loud would be the standard format for legions of bands in the coming years. Indie and rock had crossed over and the market was huge; the next half-decade would be played out in the shadow of *Nevermind.*

There was little to rival 'Smells Like Teen Spirit' that Christmas, although the KLF had a good go. They were at number two again, with 'Justified and Ancient', a tongue-in-cheek summary of their creed and slogans, for which they recruited Country & Western legend Tammy Wynette to do lead vocals. *Tammy Wynette.* It made your head spin.

It would have been number one if not for 'Bohemian Rhapsody' by Queen. Yes, that. Again. But there was a reason. It had been reported years before that lead singer Freddie Mercury had been tested for AIDS; and although the test was reportedly negative, he had not looked well in public for a long time. He died at the end of November. In Christmas week 'Bohemian Rhapsody' was back at number one, as a double A-side coupled with 'These Are the Days of Our Lives', a song about the passing of time and loss of innocence.

When the Christmas season ends it's normal to suffer a bit of a slump in spirits. But this year I was far too excited about the coming weeks, not least of the reasons for which was the first full-length studio album from Lush. It duly arrived, entitled *Spooky*, with Robin Guthrie again the producer. Lush-heads dived at it. But it was a bit listless. Its best moments all came from recent EPs, sensational tracks including 'Monochrome' and 'For Love', but we already knew those. There was little else to shout about - hugely frustrating. It went in at number seven, staying on the album chart for a mere three weeks.

Yet my disappointment was easily subsumed, because the other reason for my unseasonal early-year excitement was that our band was, in relative terms, on the up. We were part of the scene, playing support to signed bands in places like the Mean Fiddler in Harlesden and the Old Trout in Windsor. We liked to think we had left the real start-up holes behind us now, but there was a cross-over zone between these venues and those where we felt we now belonged.

At the centre of this zone was the Camden Falcon, a pub done out in the same Bohemian manner as Subterania and the Beano's record store. Its stage was in the back room, accessed via a narrow, dingy passage to the side, like the entrance to a fairground haunted house. It was filled with the chatter of music hacks and various other industry people, from sound engineers and producers to members of signed bands who just fancied going somewhere for a drink. But it had charisma, and when we played there for the first time and it went well, we felt special.

It was around this time that our manager became friends with Eddie, the manager of a band called Adorable, who had recently been signed to Creation. As a result, we got good support slots when they toured their single 'Sunshine Smile', a quintessentially early-90s indie record, with a huge, deep sound bookended by a superb intro and trailing screams of guitar feedback.

Eddie was from the Glasgow suburbs which had spawned an impressive list of current music notables, including the Jesus and Mary Chain, Primal Scream, and Creation boss Alan McGee. He himself had been a member of late-80s band the Motorcycle Boy. His girlfriend was press officer for a breaking London band called Suede; a louche, Bowie-influenced group lead by a louche, Bowie-influenced singer called Brett Anderson, who overnight became the hottest ticket in town, releasing their sloping, swooning debut single 'The Drowners' to rapturous applause. Suede, Suede, flipping Suede – nobody on the scene was talking about anything else. Anyway, Adorable played the Falcon – that's where we first saw them and why I started saying all this.

I got on well with Eddie and once he discovered that I was a chart nerd he got me along to the Engine Room pub in Kentish Town, where they held music quizzes among what seemed to be exclusively music industry people. I never pestered any of them to find out exactly what they did, for fear of looking like some desperately networking wannabe; but I heard "he's from Creation, he's Food, he's Rough Trade..." so it felt like salubrious company. And we won more than once, carrying home token but cool prizes, mainly biographies, of people like Mick Fleetwood of Fleetwood Mac and John Densmore of the Doors, all of which proved useful on long van journeys to gigs.

The compère was a willowy guy with a mop of wavy hair, who swanned back and forth among the crowd, mumbling musically into his old-school microphone, deftly reorganising the trailing lead like an old pro in a bow tie. The rounds were quirky and fun: in one extended playoff we had to sit in a row answering quickfire questions with toy xylophones instead of buzzers. But best of all was the lyric round.

I would say that. Because of this story. In the lyric round, you were presented with a few lines from a song. Your team got a point if they could identify it. But you got up to three additional points if one of you was prepared to stand on an upturned beer crate, take the microphone, and perform it acapella. You would be rewarded either for a faithful rendition, or for an imaginative reinterpretation, for example, 'Two Little Boys' by Rolf Harris in the style of 'Purple Haze' by Jimi Hendrix (which would actually one day happen; performed by a band featuring the groom from the 'Charly' wedding).

On this one particular night, the compère unfurled a roll of wallpaper on which was written the first verse of 'I Heard It Through the Grapevine' by Marvin Gaye. When it was time to claim the additional points, I found myself getting to my feet. I have since imagined that I might have performed it in the style of the opening monologue from 'Whispering Grass' by Windsor Davies and Don Estelle. I can do that accent - it might have worked well. But the three pints of export lager I'd drunk were telling me I could be Marvin.

To be fair, in addition to the booze, I did have a thorough knowledge of the song, plus a track record of singing live backing vocals. I took the microphone and went for it, closed-eyed, gravel-voiced and hip-grinding, finishing to a standing, whooping ovation. As it died down, the compère retrieved the mic, put his arm across my shoulders, and breathed: "From now on... I want you all... to refer to this man... as Mr Sex".

So there you have it. The sexiest I have ever been. In a room full of blokes doing a pop quiz.

Yet I did prove reasonably distracting on grander stages than beer crates. Our audiences had the potential to be much bigger now that we were getting good support slots. But they often weren't. I remember talking to Adorable's drummer, a level-headed Scot called Kevin, between our set and theirs, in the Derby Warehouse, which was virtually deserted. In a tone of plain acceptance, he told me that when they had supported Curve, there had been fifteen hundred people in the place. "But this…" he said, gesturing to the emptiness around us, "…is the reality". He said he was going to be a teacher.

There were more paying customers at the Taunton Community Centre where we supported Pulp, a Sheffield band who had been around for ages and had once upon a time received exposure from John Peel (I got talking to their drummer, too; drummers are nice people). The stage was low - little more than a foot above the dance floor. When we played, most of the crowd were at the bar at the back, but a sizeable gang of fourteen-year-olds, all in Carter USM *30 Something* sweatshirts, slam-danced energetically throughout the set which I took to be high praise.

We weren't particularly good that night, but Pulp certainly were. We hadn't been sure what to expect and their soundcheck had provided few clues. I claimed a vantage-point beside the mixing desk. The venue was small, I estimated around three hundred might be able to squeeze in. Along the wall adjacent to the stage ran a ledge that served as a bench. There, guarding his pint between his ankles as he rolled a ciggie, sat a friend of Cathy. We all learned that he was a friend of Cathy because of an incident part-way into the set.

Pulp's lead singer, Jarvis Cocker, was an accomplished showman, his long frame snugly held in a fitted suit, cutting a dash that would one day be widely familiar. He performed beneath an array of silver spheres that hung from the ceiling on wires, which he raised a hand to cradle at various points, his expression distant, his voice moving between deep rumble and emotional outcry. He was transported, and he was taking most of the audience with him. But, at the end of one number, just as the applause faded, Cathy's friend invaded the stage, his pint slopping,

163

and grabbed the mic stand with a grin.

"Now listen", he cried, in as broad a Somerset accent as I had yet heard, "I brought Caaathy here because she saaaid she was gonna daaance, but she ain't been daaancin', so I wanna dedicate the next song to Caaathy, so that she can daaance!" With that, he raised his pint, then hopped off back to the long bench, leaving the singer to blink in quiet disbelief as he recomposed himself. Immediately in front of me, one bloke leant towards his mate and, with a roll of his eyes and in an equally broad local accent said: "Oi bet 'ee Sheffield think we're a roight bunch o' farmers now".

Others, of course, were fully entitled to comment on *my* accent. Few were shy of doing so. "You're a loud-mouthed Cockney yob!" called Piotr, Adorable's front man, ushering me towards a step-ladder. "Get everyone to shut up and listen!"

The occasion was the reception of Eddie's marriage to the press officer, held in the hospitality lounge of the Greenhouse recording studio at Old Street, and it was now time for the speeches. We had been to Greenhouse before, taking advantage of cheap studio time with a junior engineer to record a new demo, while the Wonder Stuff and the Darling Buds were in there. We never saw them, but we did see their food in the fridge: pasta bakes and various, rigorously prepared salads.

Some among us were keen to steal it just for the sake of taking something belonging to a signed band. I resisted, just as I had resisted the idea of assaulting music journalists. We had been in the bar of the Falcon when somebody noticed *Melody Maker* hack Everett True.

"It's Everett True!"

"Is it? Oh. Yeh."

"Let's punch him".

"What?"

"Yeh, come on".

"No. Why?"

"Just fucking do it. Don't even think about it."

"But *why?*"

"Because it's the kind of thing you have to fucking do."

"Well, I'm not fucking doing it."

"God, you're so boring!"

His idea had been to get us some notoriety. But I wasn't into belting or robbing anyone just because they were famous.

There was no belting or robbing at Eddie's wedding. I used my yobbish Cockney voice to gain attention and it was appreciated. I was later introduced to record producer Pat Collier, who was charming. I also had the pleasure of being soundly beaten at pool by William Reid of the Jesus and Mary Chain, who said very little, but was perfectly civil. That was a much better way of being. I never belted or robbed anyone while in that band.

I wonder if any of them remember me now. It was clear that you didn't have to be well-known to be memorable. Among the characters we encountered was the lead singer of a band called Motherload, who wore one of those German helmets with the spikes on as he rocked out on stage. Just the fabulous sight of him, plus the knowledge that his band were called Motherload, was enough to make us giddy with joy. We never learned his name.

But we did learn the name Mick Muscle. He was in a band called Four Degree Crew, who were certainly not indie, and not quite rock, but more of a cabaret distraction. They played a mixture of sincerely-delivered originals and passionate covers, and simply had a blast. They supported us, then we supported them.

Mick Muscle would skip and leap around the stage, as well as among the audience, with his shirt off and his hairless torso bulging, grinning all the way – a less self-conscious performer you couldn't wish to meet. Our singer was convinced he was on E; he himself had just discovered it and declared it to be his religion. I asked Mick straight out and he laughed and gave a shake of the head. Clearly just high on life.

They invited us to see them at the Old Leather Bottle pub in Wimbledon one Sunday lunchtime. I was the only one who made it. They confirmed their cabaret credentials by pleasing the Sunday-lunchtime-in-Wimbledon crowd with their balanced set and accessible visual appeal, including the exposed flesh. Among their covers was David Bowie's 'Suffragette City' and just before they launched into this Mick invited me to come up and share the vocals. I politely declined, not least of the reasons for which was that I was busting for a piss.

Unfortunately, Mick's radio mic gave him full mobility and he bounced after me into the loo, with the result that I sang the end of the second verse and the chorus of 'Suffragette City' to the whole pub, while relieving myself at the urinal beside a half-naked man holding a microphone to my mouth. Never underestimate Sunday lunchtimes in Wimbledon.

Like us, Four Degree Crew would never bother the Top 40. Neither would Adorable, although they probably did okay in the Independent Chart. Pulp would one day be a mainstream sensation, but not for a while yet. We also supported the Railway Children, who had been at number twenty-three two years before with 'Every Beat of the Heart', which I didn't remember. We thought we might have played at the Camden Underworld club on the same bill as Suede, before they were part of our collective consciousness and therefore without knowing who they were. This is now hard to verify and much easier to doubt. Yet we certainly both played there more than once in the weeks leading up to the release of 'The Drowners'.

Their first Top 40 hit was 'Metal Mickey', a bright, stompy crowd-pleaser that reached number seventeen in September, but spent only two weeks in the Top 40, going in at its highest position and then plummeting. This was becoming a familiar pattern of chart performance for cult acts: Suede were music press darlings and the new big indie thing, but the wider population was, for now, less interested.

They were more distracted by the swiftly-diversifying world of dance music. The year before, Mark Summers had enjoyed a number twenty-seven hit with 'Summer's Magic', a programmed freak-out based on the sampled theme from the kids' TV show *Magic Roundabout*, which gave it masses of novelty charm. Now, 'Sesame's Treet' by the Smart E's used the theme from *Sesame Street*; while 'A Trip to Trumpton' by Urban Hype included various samples from episodes of *Trumpton* as a means of dressing up a standard rave beat and bagging a big hit.

But these beats were already evolving away from my comfort zone. Records were appearing with a new uniform drum pattern which, like the James Brown funky drummer break and the indie shuffle beat, just seemed to be plonked on top of stuff. This one was tinny and rickety and cheap-sounding and just too fast to be groovy. Both of these kids' TV records used it, but it was put to all kinds of purposes.

It was even used on slow, smoochy soul songs - well-known smoochy slow songs. Anita Baker's 'Sweet Love' was one such record, an established slow-dancer perfect for swaying to with a partner, or having on in the background as you went about your Sunday chores. When I heard a version where that beat suddenly kicked in, I just burst out laughing. Perhaps that was the point. Perhaps self-appointed pop connoisseurs like me who thought they knew the lot were supposed to be alienated by it. This was the sound known as Drum & Bass.

The Smart E's and Urban Hype records both reached the Top 10 and gave the tabloids something to seethe about, what with innocent childhood being violated by all these explicit drug references. But this trend reached its apogee with 'Ebeneezer Goode' by well-established dance act the Shamen. Its lyric profiled the eponymous character as a dubious, charismatic individual; but its main purpose was to sing the chorus "*Eezer Goode, Eezer Goode – he's Ebeneezer Goode!*" and revel in the *double entendre* therein. Our singer nodded with a smile: "They certainly are". The record was laced with references to drug paraphernalia sweetened by rhyming slang and disarming Cockney charm. 'Ebeneezer Goode' was Britain's number one for four weeks.

It had replaced 'Rhythm Is a Dancer' by Snap!, which had been number one for six. Its spacious, soulful sway had diamond pop quality, enough to cancel out the denouement of the middle-section rap: *I'm as serious as cancer, when I say that rhythm is a dancer.* I was in thrall to it, just as I was to its fellow summer-time travellers 'Let Me Take You There' by Betty Boo, the aforementioned 'Lead Me Astray' by the Primitives and 'I'll Be Your Saint', a second Adorable 45; plus 'Lithium', a third single from Nirvana's *Nevermind* album, which I was listening to on the Walkman several times a week.

So revered were Nirvana, that you would have got away with playing them at almost any gathering. But even more party-popular was 'Jump' by Kriss Kross, a pair of rapping American schoolkids who wore their jeans on backwards for the sake of gimmick. 'Jump' was a sensation, built on a sample snipped from 'I Want You Back' by the Jackson 5 that you quickly forgot was pinched because it was so brilliantly deployed. It reached number two here and was a mega number one in the US. It was a straightforward rap record; but, as we already knew, lots of records that you might once have called soul or house now included passages of rapping. Drawing clear distinctions between genres was becoming more difficult. You might say irrelevant.

It is with this in mind that we should now mention TLC, who reached thirteen in the summer with the infectious frizzy bundle 'Ain't 2 Proud 2 Beg' – very much equal parts soul and rap. They were an Atlanta girl group whose outsized, colourful clothes and outsized, colourful personalities suggested that positivity was becoming entrenched - they grinned and pulled faces instead of gazing moodily from beneath heavy lids. If you were having a party, you would have invited TLC.

The glossier, more elegant girl group tradition was meanwhile embodied by En Vogue, who had been in and out of the charts for two years and had reached number four that spring with the slick chug of 'My Lovin''. In mid-autumn they would be back in the Top 20 courtesy of equality manifesto 'Free Your Mind'. If your dad was having a party, he would have invited En Vogue.

Whoever the party belonged to, you could find plenty of music for it at the top of the charts. 'Please Don't Go' by KWS was a dance version of K.C. and the Sunshine Band's tearful 1979 lament; a cover which somehow managed five weeks at number one, despite undermining the whole point of the song with all its leaping about and grinning.

When finally knocked off, it was by even more bloody covers. Erasure were a duo, one of whom was Vince Clarke, a founder member of Depeche Mode. He had since joined, and written hits for, Yazoo and the Assembly, before pairing up with singer Andy Bell and setting off on a long string of successes as Erasure. Suddenly disembarking from their habitually crisp, lively originals, they made an EP of songs by Abba and called it *Abba-esque*. The songs chosen were 'Lay All Your Love on Me', 'SOS', 'Take a Chance on Me', and the one that got most radio play, 'Voulez-Vous'.

Although disdained and tidied away by most of the population, Abba had residual appeal among gays: they were purveyors of high quality who didn't fit in to the mainstream. At least not now. In the early 80s, they had suddenly found themselves old and out of step, overtaken by newness. And a lot of additional newness had happened since then.

It was with care and timing that I shared my memories of their glories; of the faith-inducing moment when 'Mamma Mia' made it to number one, of having the majesty of 'Eagle' perform a blood transfusion on me when *Abba The Album* came out, of being moved almost to tears by 'Chiquitita' when finally listening to it uninterrupted. There had been other moments, lots of them. I was not just a fan, I was grateful; as if to an inspirational teacher, or an endlessly considerate friend.

Erasure had a back catalogue of sixteen Top 20 hits, eleven of which had been Top 10. But *Abba-esque* became their first number one, sitting there for five weeks. The event made people talk about Abba again. I read an article - either in *NME* or *Melody Maker*, I can't remember – discussing the Erasure EP, which ended: "...but the original is mega-boss and should be thoroughly investigated". After so many years of sneering dismissal, this was a gob-smacking moment. Their rehabilitation would go on from here. The next step was that 'Dancing Queen' (by Abba, not Erasure) re-entered the charts that September and peaked at sixteen.

When I had bought my first Abba single, aged ten, it had cost 50p. The price of singles now, however, had become shocking. In the spring of 1990, they had still been just under £2. It took until February 1992 to edge over that barrier; my copy of 'Two Worlds Collide' by Inspiral Carpets from that month still has the £2.09 sticker on it. But by the summer, when, in an act of naïve trust, I bought movie soundtrack nonsense 'Face to Face' by Siouxsie and the Banshees, the error cost me £2.39.

It was possible to save a bit if you shopped around, especially if you went to some independent stores; but this was the trend in HMV and Virgin. It didn't necessarily signal improvements to other aspects of packaging, either. Increasingly, the chunky white barcoded price labels were being replaced by the little, yellow, clipped-cornered stickers that you were used to seeing slapped on to food tins in your local convenience store. It was a judgement on the status of 7" singles: *We don't need to log them anymore, but if you really want to buy one of these funny little things, go ahead...* They were becoming more of a specialist interest, one for sad traditionalists - those reluctant to move with the times.

Sales had been declining steadily since the high point of 1978-9. Figures for 1992 represented a nadir in that trend. The single would one day re-claim its crown. But it would no longer be made of vinyl.

Seven

It was a warm January afternoon in Bangkok, my third day there. I had been to the temples, slipping through and between clusters of frowningly-focused tourists in bad shorts and pulled-up socks. I had seen the reclining buddha and watched locals at prayer with incense sticks. I'd seen monks in their orange robes. I'd had rides on the river bus that never actually stopped at any port-of-call; it just kind of bounced against the jetty, giving those getting on and those getting off a brief moment to fly through the air in opposite directions before chugging away again. I'd been for early morning walks, far from the tourist areas, as small children walked to school in sailor uniforms that provided spotless contrasts with the grime and traffic fumes all around. They were startled by the sight of a European so far from the bars and the hostels and the hippy shops - they stared and stared. I'd seen floating vegetable markets on narrow waterways between buildings. I had listened to the tuneful chatter, smelled the warm, amber smell - that rich, rounded-off odour, of a place so different I could only marvel at it and know that I would never forget being here.

I was traveling light, with one bag and one Walkman, through which I was rotating four tapes I had made up at home: one of 60s girl group obscurities, two volumes of the best bits of 1992, the year just ended, and a Primitives best-of. But I wasn't listening to anything now. I wanted every one of my senses available for this city.

The food around the tourist epicentre of Khao San Road was a bit dull and nobody ever offered me any with a smile. I was told that the Thais graze, having little snacks on the go rather than sitting down to stuff their faces. I wanted to do the same. I found a cart where griddled squid was being chopped up and put into clear plastic bags, with herby broth and then a spoon or two of chili added, before being given a few stiff shakes and handed to the customer along with a pointed stick. This looked great, but when I got to the front of the queue and the man saw my Caucasian face, he moved his spoon straight past the chili, grinning and shaking his head as I gestured keenly towards it. In the end he gave me a tiny bit and I could have handled a bit more. Perhaps, back at the Khao San Road, they might have catered more readily for the western tendency to eat hot food for a dare.

The cart was stationed on a broad, stone-coloured pavement bordering an expansive area of green, with batteries of new office blocks opposite. The river and all the ancient stuff were far away. Further along, I bought a tin of citrus fizz from a kiosk and sat on a nearby wall to savour it.

For the second time that day, a local guy came over to introduce himself, sat down, and began talking in English. They wanted to practise. They were patient and polite. The one from earlier had left suddenly when a football from the full-blown game on the grass beside us crashed into the side of his face, which I surmised had ignited some decidedly un-Buddhist anger, and he had left rather than deal with it. The second guy was not as chatty, and there were long periods of silence. One of these was broken by me.

"Who are they?" I asked, pointing.

Wrapped around the top of one of the office blocks opposite was a massive hoarding from which a group of young men grinned - wholesome, gleaming smiles to go with their wholesome, gleaming fashions; and the whole image was disinfected, rounded and polished, almost like one of those Communist murals projecting the heroic strength of the proletariat. I thought they might be a pop group. I hoped they wouldn't be. The vision was making me feel slightly sick.

"They are a group", my companion said. "They are famous".

"Music?"

"Yes, yes".

"Blimey".

He told me their name but I was already in denial. It was the grins; the toothy, gleaming, fixed grins; the rehearsed, refined, sharpened grins; the there's-nothing-really-to-grin-about grins. There should be a reason for a grin.

I told myself that this would never happen in Britain. Over-exuberant vocal troupes – reckless and deluded souls made in poor imitation of the Four Tops and the Temptations - often got on the front of teen mags and into the Top 10. In recent years a few had done better, topping the charts in the name of knicker-wetting and little else. But they would never be on a hoarding overlooking a main artery like this. 1992 had been great and my expectations remained high. This was what passed for pop in Asia. This was what the poor bastards here had to distract them from day-to-day tedium. Our rich heritage protected us from such horrors. Or so I told myself.

We would one day call them boy bands.

Just as there should be a reason for a grin, so too should there be a reason for suddenly being on the other side of the world. In my case, it was that the band had split up. Industry people had investigated. The rejections were gently couched, but the changes they said they wanted to see were so fundamental, so time-consuming and so expensive, that it was never going to be worth it; and may have all simply been a euphemism for fuck off.

I was tired of being skint and didn't want to be a thirty-five-year-old still trying to be a pop star. I had gone back to sales work and found that I was in demand. A relative had offered me a rent-free room for a few months, so I saved a lump sum. The choice was: invest it in the band or go travelling. Which was why I was now in East Asia. Just being a fan was going to be fine. In fact, it would one day be brilliant. But first there was 1993.

People talk about 1975 as the worst year ever, because it was not-glam-anymore and not-punk-yet and played out under the dominion of the Bay City Rollers. Well I liked it a whole lot more than 1993. There were barely two handfuls of good records in the whole year. I had spent 1992 dashing excitedly from fresh, startling chart pop to cult indie marvels, with fun-filled soul and nutcase dance records in between. All that suddenly stopped.

Listening to the radio was hard work. I had once rushed to Radio 1 for vivacity, colour and all the new sounds I was going to need to know about. Not now. Radio 1 was different now. It was smug and comfortable and had little interest in vivacity or colour. It was thrilled with 1993, gleefully spooning up worthy adult maturity from the likes of Sting and Annie Lennox. 1993 as presented on Radio 1 and in the Top 40 served an audience who were happy to go on buying records but who, essentially, didn't want to be disturbed.

The charts were increasingly stuffed with covers, re-releases and re-mixes. I returned from travelling to even more of them in 1993, chart detritus congealing into a choking mass of dull fug. Among the number ones was 'Young at Heart' by the Bluebells, a drifty jig with a fiddle on it that needed a good square meal. It had reached the Top 10 in 1984 but now reappeared thanks to another bloody advert. It caught the collective, diseased imagination, as did bright new mainstream stars M People, the very essence of 1993 partying: cleanly pressed evening wear, wafts of potpourri and going "Woo!" on the beat; not one bead of sweat anywhere, and what sounded like Fozzie Bear's sister on lead vocal.

I was of course experiencing something of a come-down from being in a band with prospects, but I still knew a good tune when I heard one. I bought 'Animal Nitrate' by Suede, their first Top 10, entering at seven but getting no higher. 2 Unlimited had their over-urgent 'No Limit' at number one. The record that replaced it there, 'Oh Carolina' by Shaggy, was a clanking, hip-grinding update on a Jamaican oldie, by a Jamaican singer with a distinctive tunnel-growl of a voice.

It showcased "ragga" – short for "ragamuffin", apparently – an emerging genre which added growling and grinding to the Jamaican dancehall sound. Ragga was evident on 'Shout (It Out)' by Louchie Lou and Michie One, and 'Tease Me' by Chaka Demus and Pliers - both good records. You could plonk it on anything you wanted, just as with lovers rock or Drum & Bass. 'Incy Wincy Spider' could be ragga if you sang it in a growl while pretending to dig a ditch with your arse.

Other bearables included the hilarious 'Informer' by Snow - streetwise patois and tough-guy prancing from a white Canadian, which was a seven-week US number one. They also included sparkling dance work-out 'Ain't No Love (Ain't No Use)' by Sub Sub featuring Melanie Williams; and 'Two Princes' by the Spin Doctors, an ultra-catchy slice of US guitar pop-rock with a big indie-style shuffle beat which almost everybody liked. These reached two, three and four respectively.

The best number one of the year was 'Dreams' by Gabrielle, a sweet love song with an infectiously cool arrangement, sung by a girl from East London with an eye patch. It hit the top in July. Otherwise, the finest sound that summer was 'The Key - the Secret' by Urban Cookie Collective, a dreamy dash of stoned, upbeat electronica which - to my ears at least - was utterly wonderful. It was held at number two by 'Living on My Own' by Freddie Mercury, who, sadly, was no longer around to answer for the outrage.

There was some good soul in the Top 10. 'Show Me Love' by Robin S was a riff-blipping club smash whose sound would prove influential; 'Don't Walk Away' by Jade was a deafeningly groovy pop-stomp; 'Right Here' by SWV (standing for Sisters With Voices) was a gentle, melodic drift based around a gentle, melodic Michael Jackson sample.

Despite the expectation raised by 'Two Princes', the Spin Doctors turned out to be a bar-room band with worrying country proclivities. Elsewhere however there was proper indie stuff: good and intriguing indie stuff. I got it in dribs and drabs. I got it despite several grave errors buying singles purely on recommendation. But I got some of the best of it on Danny Baker's radio show.

His pedigree was good - an *NME* staff writer who had made his mark on TV as a voice of slightly irreverent youth. By the time this happened, his youth was also slight. But in the current context, that made him all the more appealing. The sober maturity and dull fug of modern Radio 1 had driven me down the corridor to Radio 5, then a curious hotchpotch of music shows and sports coverage, where he was hosting a breakfast programme called the *Morning Edition* in his distinctive Cockney chirp.

He played great guitar records like 'My Sister' by the Juliana Hatfield Three and 'I Should've Known' by Aimee Mann; both American, both with a female lead. Neither made the Top 40, but another American record with a female lead happened to reach number forty exactly and this one was special. It was the 1993 indie track before which other 1993 indie tracks would kneel and pay homage. It was 'Cannonball' by the Breeders.

Suddenly, 'Two Princes' sounded laboured. 'Cannonball' blared, it grooved, it lilted - it blasted irreparable holes in your boredom. The lead singer, Kim Deal, was bass player in primal-yell-monsters the Pixies, the Breeders being a side-project that had got a bit out of hand. Her voice was a husky, raised hum and sounded like nobody else's. It had been a long time since I had played a record three, four times straight off and still wanted more. The twelve-inch came in a deliciously sturdy cover with a furry crash helmet on the front, and an inner made of reinforced green foil – befittingly stunning. Absolutely everyone I spoke to with indie tendencies was crazy about it.

An increasing number of my friends were meanwhile becoming crazy about cable television, gaining access to all sorts of specialist channels, meaning that radio now had serious competition as a source of new music. MTV was available on cable. So was VH1, a channel for more mature viewers. So also was The Box, a video request channel, a touchstone for what was becoming popular among young people with subscription telly. 'Cannonball' was played on it, so was 'Heart-Shaped Box' a fresh noise-bomb from Nirvana, heralding a new album and reaching number five on the singles chart.

So. 1993. Fewer than twenty good records by my reckoning. Twenty good records largely unrelated, going nowhere, subsumed into the doughy mass of grinning banality surrounding them. In other years you were struggling to edit down a list to fit onto a C90 - I had been forced to have my Best Of 1992 in two volumes. 1993 was rubbish.

And on top of all this was an even bigger development. The CD - or compact disc - was in the process of taking over as the most popular format for recorded music. I was instinctively conservative with regard to this. To my mind, the vinyl single was the proper vehicle for pop and that was that. You could get cassette singles, usually with the main track and its B-side copied onto both sides and coming in various kinds of unimpressive packaging; I had bought a few out of curiosity - only a few. I was still a seven-inch vinyl man.

But CDs were poised to take over. They had originally appeared in 1982 and by 1984 I was noticing them in HMV and Virgin (as well as newcomer Tower Records, which had its main London store at Piccadilly, and whose point I never really got). They were smaller than vinyl records. CD albums were 4.7" in diameter and the singles were tiny, mostly around 3". These looked ridiculous, like the buttons on Great Aunt Dorothy's Sunday coat. You'd lose them down the side of the sofa, and even if you didn't, you'd need a magnifying glass to read the credits. CD singles were not always this small and in time the 3" ones would be discontinued, but sleeve-note point-size would never stop being an issue with CDs. I had first handled them around 1985, in some upstairs area of HMV Oxford Circus - a quiet room that you entered through sliding doors, and which had been specially air-conditioned.

They represented a significant all-round upgrade for music consumption. They were aspirational. CD albums cost around £15; CD singles were over £3 - almost double the price of vinyl. But they didn't jump or get scratched. It was said that they were indestructible. Your CDs were "read" by a laser beam inside your handsomely-priced CD player. A *lazer beam*. We never got interplanetary commuting or jet-packs, but we now had CDs.

Accepting this change was a huge emotional challenge. I didn't want the bloody things. They were rich-arsed, showy bastards' rubbish, like having a sports car on the drive and a full-sized snooker table in the third lounge. And yet I had already bought one. The Cocteau Twins had compiled a Best Of in 1987 called *The Pink Opaque* as part of a launch into the American market. The American market was already convinced by CDs, so *The Pink Opaque* was released on CD only. I got it, not out of blind loyalty to the Cocteau Twins, but out of discovering that it contained 'Millimillenary', my first Cocteau Twins moment, which had never been released on vinyl. So I bought it. And couldn't play it.

CDs had a playing time of 80 minutes, so the idea of CD singles with between two and four songs on them was a bit odd. Even those 3" discs had up to twenty-four minutes of music capacity. Some vinyl EPs had squeezed as many as six tracks onto two sides of a 7", making you wonder about the quality of the pressing, but CD singles had no such problems and would routinely contain five or six re-mixes of the lead track.

It was expected that everyone would replace their vinyl collections with CDs. One of the main selling points was the quality of their sound; the clarity was reputedly stunning. This had been demonstrated to me a couple of years earlier. A friend's parents had invested in a music system with a gleaming new CD player at its core. I was ushered into the lounge by a dad beaming with pride and excitement. "You'll love this" he assured me, "if you love your music", which he knew I claimed to. He positioned me in a special spot in the lounge and put on a CD of Buddy Holly. Familiar tunes filled the air. It was clear. It was clean. It was free of surface noise. He was glowing. "It's just like having them in the room, n' it?"

I decided I would pick fault with it. There was no soul. It was scrubbed and disinfected, its edges smoothed and waxed like a surfboard. There was no bleed between the elements that gave you that rich, indistinct something that made a record more than the sum of its studio parts: Buddy Holly was in front of the armchair; his drummer was partly under the framed abstract and partly beside the fireplace; the guitars were divided between the plant pots and the whisky decanter. I can't remember whether they had a whisky decanter. That's not the point.

That, however, had been a couple of years earlier. Vinyl, that mysterious, alluring vehicle for delivering music to us, which had conveyed the Beatles, Abba, Madonna and everything in between, was on the wane. The industry was revitalising itself and CDs were its means of doing so. Every day I was hearing things like: "I'm getting my new CD player later"; "How's the CD player then?"; "Did you get the Pioneer in the end, or the Aiwa?" They smiled knowing smiles at each other as they stepped over the threshold into that aspirational club, where people got their music on expensive, shiny new discs, instead of those tired, old-fashioned vinyl records that got scratched and sounded hissy and jumped.

To add to which, the condition of new vinyl was becoming an issue. Paper centres on singles now seemed little more than a vehicle for corporate blurb and bar-codes. The plastic rings looked increasingly sorry for themselves – they were shallower, inaccurately pressed, no longer sitting proud. The lettering indents habitually failed to fill with ink to make them readable. Sometimes their shape was not even complete. I had occasionally seen badly-pressed plastic centres with big blotches of black in the wrong place; but I took some singles out of their sleeves now and it looked like someone had just melted a bit of cheese on it.

I sensed that Danny Baker was in a similar place with all this. He was taking the piss out of CDs on the *Morning Edition*. He smeared one with jam to see if it still played. He drilled a hole in another one and waited for the lazer beam to reach it and start panicking. He was checking them out. But only in preparation for bowing to the inevitable. This was going on all over the country.

There was a practical element to my resistance. My records were still at my parents' house: I deposited a stash of recent releases there every time I visited. I had no turntable. But I could play my own stuff if I had a basic CD player. Until my accommodation situation was settled, whatever I got would have to be portable. In February 1994 I went to the beating heart of London's hi-fi consumerism, Tottenham Court Road, and bought a Sony Boombox.

It was black, curved and a little over two feet long. The CD loaded into the top. You opened the lid by pressing down the corner to release it, allowing you to click the CD into place on the circular clasp at the centre of the space thus revealed. You could see the pit where the lazer beam came from. There was a built-in AM/FM radio and a twin cassette deck at the front. A cassette facility was of course essential anyway: I needed to make tapes for the car - only the newest and flashiest of cars had CD players. The Boombox was cool. The sound was good for its size.

I began building a stash of CD singles. I cut up the box that the Boombox had come in, to make an open-top storage crate so I could flick through them just like I had with my 7" vinyl. Among the first were 'Jenny Ondioline' by Stereolab - a cool indie one; 'Visionary', a great lurching thrash by alternative US band Red Kross and curiously-likeable indie oddity 'Diminished Clothes' by Salad.

Owning and handling CDs took some getting used to. A CD album was a chunky tile, essentially a version of the vinyl album cover, but re-shaped and shrunk down. And boy, was it shrunk. The type was so small - I'm back on this subject again and it won't be the last time - that sometimes you struggled to read the track listing and had almost no chance of learning the producer's name or any other important detail without a magnifying glass. Opening the case was a similar challenge, at least at first. One day you would wonder how it had ever been a problem; but those early cases were built to repel. You had to apply your hands in ways that were completely unfamiliar, using hitherto under-deployed muscles and ligaments in long episodes of struggle which threatened minor injury and major loss of temper – and you didn't want to use force; you might snap something.

You did, however, need to hold it flat when you first opened it, since the disc might be loose and could fall out. The reason for the disc perhaps being loose was the bloody teeth. The main component of the inner base was a tray with a little circle of teeth that held the disc in place when you clicked it on. Apart from the size of the type, the biggest pain in the arse were those teeth. They broke with stupid ease, leaving sections of the circle toothless - a broad, gummy curve. Sometimes when I got a new CD album out of its wrapper and opened the case, a whole load of teeth fell out. Like straight away.

The first CD album I bought after getting the Boombox was the one with 'Cannonball' on it: *Last Splash* by the Breeders - an excellent choice. Its other killer moment was 'The Invisible Man', with a guitar groove made of treacle and a deliciously woozy vocal, like a gothic lullaby being murmured into your ear. *Last Splash* maintained my CD momentum. And its teeth stayed in.

By the time I bought another album, a whole stack of singles stretched to the back of the crate. Some had similar casing to the albums. 'Jenny Ondioline' was one. But by far the most common were thinner, what were called "pearl" cases, which opened and closed easily on a hinge that you could click in and out and had its teeth included as part of a single mould. Its artwork and credits were printed on a piece of thin card that folded round inside to form the front cover, the spine and an info sheet at the back, which was obscured by the disc when you closed the case.

Other singles came in simple cardboard sleeves; or had laminated card covers that the tray slid in and out of. Some opened like a birthday card, with the teeth peeping through a port-hole in the design on the right. Sometimes the card was textured instead of laminated. Sometimes the plastic cases were colour-tinted. Soon I had a lovely, rich variety to flick through, pull out and coo over. There had never been quite this diversity with vinyl.

Suddenly I was happy to be moving with the times. And glossy, shiny CDs didn't necessarily mean glossy, shiny musical blandness. The charts were still full of throat-wobbling ballads, four-minute life-coaching courses, horrible covers, re-released oldies and remixes of re-released oldies. But there were a few gems, such as the sweetly aching 'Linger' by the Cranberries which got to number fourteen, and the lurching electro-ragga of 'I Like to Move It' by Reel 2 Real featuring the Mad Stuntman, which reached number five.

The most interesting number one was 'Doop' by Doop, on which the jury remains stubbornly out to this day. An instrumental in the form of a Loony-Tunes Charleston, it arrived in the midst of all this chart dirge like cool spring water on a hot day for some of us, and like an interminable mither for others. It polished its nails on top of the singles chart for three weeks.

The reign of 'Doop' coincided with a particularly important and significant turn, the effect of which would last the whole decade. Finding reliable sources of good indie stuff had proved arduous, but it was now that I stumbled across the solution, in the form of a programme called *The Evening Session* which, remarkably, was on Radio 1.

I would never again be a regular listener of daytime Radio 1. The character it had adopted during the mid-80s had consolidated steadily and, by the early 90s, it was deeply entrenched. The main presenters had been in place for an entire era - in some cases longer. They had massive, adoring audiences filled with maturing parents, office staff and truck drivers, all contributing to a restless tide of corned-beef jollities served up in listener letters, quiz features and telephone pranks.

Precious little of this banter was on the subject of music - indeed, having to play new records seemed an inconvenience. The self-important, middle-aged, establishment DJ disconnected from today's youngster was becoming a recognised species. It was amply lampooned through the characters Smashie and Nicey, portrayed to popular acclaim by Harry Enfield and Paul Whitehouse on TV. Their fictional modus operandi, Radio Fab, was a thinly-veiled mock-up of what dear old Radio 1 had become.

But then, in the autumn of 1993, Matthew Bannister was appointed controller, with the mission of making it a youth station again. This brought him directly into conflict with Radio Fab. He began the systematic removal of the old guard, causing some to resign hastily in order to avoid being sacked. Dave Lee Travis famously did so live on air - his weekend morning slots were quickly filled by the slightly youthful Danny Baker. Simon Bates was gone by the summer. Playlists were adjusted to reflect the changes. Audiences inevitably fell, and quite dramatically, but would in time recover; the mums, dads, office workers and truckers replaced by listeners half their age.

The Evening Session symbolised the revolution. Broadcasting for two hours from Monday to Thursday, it was like John Peel with the weird stuff taken out, emulating alternative regional shows that had popped up all over the country as Radio 1 had stagnated. And the duo presenting it were a long way from the old guard. They talked excitedly, almost breathlessly - and about almost nothing but music.

Steve Lamacq was a former *NME* staffer whose deep, earthy tones made the ornaments rattle along your mantelpiece. Jo Whiley had been a researcher and presenter in various radio and TV contexts and sounded constantly on the verge of laughter and blushing, as if she quite couldn't believe she was doing anything as cool as this. I was used to radio DJs who said things like "Don't think I'll be playing that again", or "Not sure about this one, fellas", but for Jo Whiley, everything was marvellous. She was the first national presenter I had heard who cheer-led her genres unconditionally - if she ever said anything negative about any record, artist or gig, it was on a show I missed. Between them, these two gave legitimacy and high status to a mass of alternative sounds from Britain, America and Europe to listeners nationwide, tying in with the content of the *NME* and *Melody Maker*. Matthew Bannister was presumably pleased.

I certainly was. I had once happily listened to the likes of Simon Bates and Mike Read, enjoying their banter as part of the package while waiting for the good stuff to leap, dolphin-like, from the oceans of dross. But indie had turned my head. This stuff was for real, it was for the kids – the harbingers of energy, positivity, insight, anti-cynicism and all things worthwhile – so to hear these younger voices on the *Evening Session* talking a bit like excitable friends of mine might talk, rather than the mid-Atlantic drones of the carvery-queuing entertainment circuit, was bliss.

The top of the charts at this point was overwhelmingly lamentable. Among the number ones was a cover of Nilsson's yell-ballad standard 'Without You' by Mariah Carey, which added nothing but Mariah to the original; and a granny-friendly cover of the Troggs' soppy 'Love is All Around' by Wet Wet Wet, which we will come back to.

Other chart-toppers included covers in the ragga style: 'Twist and Shout' by Chaka Demus and Pliers and 'Baby Come Back' by Pato Banton, which incorporated Ali Campbell from UB40 to reggae-up and ruin the Equals' stompy and brilliant 1968 number one. None of these would have made Granny want to change channels. Then there were the re-releases and re-mixes. It was like you were continually on the end of a pier in high season; never far from clip-on bow ties or the smell of donuts.

But not on the *Evening Session*. For here were young artists, with their attitude and their authenticity; here were new songs and thrilling boundary-assaults. Most didn't reach the charts, but on the *Evening Session* they felt important. On the *Evening Session* they were *made* important. In this alternative world, they were high art.

And some did reach the charts: Therapy? with the tight, jumpy 'Nowhere'; Beck, with the charismatic, woozy groove 'Loser'; Inspiral Carpets with the joyful 'Saturn 5' - all three got in the Top 20. 'Oblivion' by Terrorvision, a hooky chunk of knockabout fun, got to twenty-one. 'Different Door' by the Posies was played a lot but missed the chart, the discernible influence of 'Smells Like Teen Spirit' perhaps spoiling it for many - but it was terrific. Hole had their own Nirvana link, in that their lead singer, Courtney Love, was Kurt Cobain's girlfriend. Their sound was made of screams and distortions and hammer-blow rhythms. Their new single 'Miss World' peaked outside the Top 40. From Sweden came Whale, whose 'Hobo Humpin' Slobo Babe' made a huge, shouty, lurching impact; from Holland came Bettie Serveert, whose 'Palomine' single was a warmly-distorted guitar hug.

By the end of the spring, I had all these singles to flick through in my makeshift storage crate, along with another good British one, 'Swallow' by Sleeper, whose sound I liked straight away. The single had another good track on it called 'Twisted' and it convinced me to go to see them at the Astoria. Their husky-voiced singer/guitarist was in blue denim from head to toe and loads of people fancied her. The rest of the band looked like they'd just got down off a ladder.

This singer/guitarist was Louise Wener. One publicity shot featured her in a T-shirt with *another female-fronted band* written across it. This was cynical and perhaps unnecessary, but I was already keeping an eye on this issue for my own sake. I naturally gravitated towards female vocals and thoughtful lyrics, including those with a feminist twist (fully understanding that this never helped me get laid). Bands playing catchy, growly-guitar tunes fronted by cute women might become a default template if I let it. I didn't want it leading to a credibility problem. This was commendable caution. But it didn't stop me falling in love with Echobelly.

They, indeed, were a band playing catchy, growly-guitar tunes fronted by a good-looking woman; a good-looking Asian woman at that. We were not seeing many Asian faces in pop. On the video for the new single, she bounced and postured in various get-ups, one of which was a union jack T-shirt with "my country too" scrawled across it. Her voice was powerful - clear and strong.

The single was 'Insomniac' and for at least a week it was the most important thing in the world. I played it to death on the Boombox. I played it loud in the car with the windows down as I drove down busy streets, spreading the good news, as if people were going to be grateful: *All you Mariah Carey and Wet Wet Wet fans, get some of this, for the good of your soul.* The song was typical: its verse was hushed and contained, its chorus a storm of big guitar noise and yelled vocals; the quiet bit and the loud bit, just like 'Smells Like Teen Spirit'. This was now fully-entrenched - how to get a bit of Nirvana to rub off on you.

There was little in the pop charts to compete with 'Insomniac' on my Boombox, but a few things did. Marcella Detroit, let loose from Shakespears Sister, had a stonking single called 'I Believe'; a fine platform for her incredible voice. It reached number eleven. Erasure released 'Always', a tremendous song which, if it hadn't been included in the recent *Hits! The Very Best of Erasure*, might have done better than number four. Above it at two, Canada's Crash Test Dummies had the extraordinary 'Mmm Mmm Mmm Mmm', like a set of modern parables sung by a village simpleton.

But among the quality pop and the indie and the dance and the lazy covers and the remixes, there was another strand. Take That were a group of five scantily-clad young men from the north-west of England who were fit enough to dance gymnastically and at four times the speed of normal people; occasionally doing so in formation, often doing so while singing. They had been bothering the charts for two and a half years, establishing their popularity though videos - all hairdos and teeth and perfectly moulded torsos lingeringly revealed.

Their records were skilfully crafted to minimise the character of unremarkable voices, doused in SAW-type backing and almost overwhelmed by the beat. Two of their first three Top 10 hits were covers, one being Barry Manilow's 'Could It Be Magic', the original of which I had loved on the quiet. Manilow's version had been carefully orchestrated and dramatic. The Take That cover was the mere borrowing of a melody and lyric as a pretext for getting their kit off again. They didn't bother with the right words, but making the lyric coherent was never the point. 1993's 'Pray' was their first chart-topper, beginning a string of four consecutive number ones ending with 'Everything Changes' in April 1994, which replaced 'Doop'.

We weren't yet calling them "boy bands". They were still "male vocal groups", except that now, the vocals were not the leading proposition. Doo-wop, R&B and soul vocal groups from the past represented genres that had marked significant developments in popular music – far more than mere entertainment. This though was a different world, one increasingly in thrall to image and pin-up-ability. Take That were there for you to have pictures of on your wall and dream of being alone with - the music charts and music media were merely the vehicle by which this was all conducted. In Gary Barlow, they did actually have a songwriter whose talents would one day be recognised, but he was the one people fancied least; and he sat dreamily on stools instead of throwing himself about. Until now at least, the quality of the records hadn't mattered one iota. They didn't have to be any good. So they weren't.

There had been other such acts in recent years. The turn of the decade had New Kids on the Block, and a bit later, Colour Me Badd, both of whom had number one singles. But Take That were a sustained success. Their contemporary rivals were East 17, from London, who were moodier, more streetwise, and who in early 1993 had taken 'Deep' to number five, which, despite lyrics such as "I surrender - you're so tender and tanned", was remarkably good.

Most people I knew who liked male vocal groups preferred Take That. Including several grown women I worked with. This I found incredible. I gave a lift to two of them one day, up the motorway to a business exhibition; with, as usual, a collection of recent CD singles taped from the Boombox playing in the car.

"This stuff's boring", one of them suddenly said. "Can't we put something else on? I've brought this." And out came a pre-recorded cassette of *Take That and Party* by Take That; their first album, which had since been superseded. It didn't matter. It wasn't going on. I was horrified that they had even brought it into my car.

Now, I have always been anti-snobbery when it comes to music. But this wasn't music: it was a backdrop to soft porn. And yes, I may, in my time, have sat through hours of radio stomaching the worst the charts had to offer, considering dross to be part of the cultural terrain. But this wasn't radio – this was voluntarily putting *Take That and Party* on in my car. If I let it. Which I wasn't. I swore at her.

"How can you say it's shit? It's just music. It's *fun*. What's your problem with a bit of fun?"

My problem was that, despite appeals to reason, and despite the understanding that I would certainly survive listening to *Take That and Party*, having it play in the car for the rest of the journey would be like driving with an assortment of outsized invertebrates slithering around inside my shirt. A stand was going to have to be made.

The ensuing conversation did not help our relationship. They said I was being childish: I replied that not liking Take That proved I was over the age of sixteen. They claimed that I was jealous of Take That because everybody fancied them: I responded with a promise to listen to the Bay City Rollers on the next journey. They insisted that I was being unfair because they had had to put up with my boring stuff and we were supposed to be sharing a ride: I assured them that, had I known that *Take That and Party* was lurking in one of their bags, I would have opted for monastic silence. They didn't believe for a second that it would actually make me vomit, but I wasn't prepared to run even the slightest risk; the invertebrates were all too real. It soured the atmosphere. The rest of the journey was tense.

I was genuinely struggling with this. People have the right to just-a-bit-of-fun. That's how I often approached choosing a movie to see, or somewhere to go for a drink. But this was music. There was a difference between liking a performer first and foremost and liking the records first and foremost. It's natural to warm to someone if they make a good record, but fancying a singer or admiring their voice doesn't make their records any better.

Pop was being cheapened, in this and other ways. Karaoke had recently arrived from Japan, as a vehicle for a night out, often a preferred choice for groups of office workers. The pair in my car loved karaoke. It involved singing a selected song through a PA, with the lyrics being rolled on a screen before you. You had a mic, a backing track, an audience, a stage and lights. You could have almost any big hit from history - any of it taken off its gallery mounting, removed from its frame and tossed across the pub so that members of the public could indulge their star-performer fantasies.

Walking into a bar to find a karaoke all set up and ready to go could be utterly deflating. But if circumstances made avoidance impossible – I worked in an office, remember, and needed to keep my job – I usually chose Manfred Mann's 1966 number one 'Pretty Flamingo'. Most people had a song that was their karaoke song. If you got up there, you wanted to be good. Some took it extremely seriously; especially if they were singing something like 'Wind Beneath My Wings', one of those tissue-scrunching mega ballads that is always depressing when done by someone under the age of thirty. The pair in my car loved 'Wind Beneath My Wings'.

XfM wouldn't have played 'Wind Beneath My Wings'. XfM was a new independent radio station, billed as an alternative playground where indie hogged the playlist. This had to be good news. I had made a few attempts to tune in and had always found it hard to get a good signal; but one March morning, on the way back from a meeting, I decided today would be the day.

I stopped alongside the green at Highbury Fields, in order to visit the box office of a nearby venue called the Garage and get a ticket to see (another female fronted band called) Tiny Monroe. Having parked, I fiddled resolutely with the tuner until successful, then sat back and fund myself listening to Blur.

Their shuffle-beat hit 'There's No Other Way' was three years old now. They hadn't really followed it up, but they were still around, putting out records to critical attention and achieving so-so chart positions. It looked a bit sad. They had probably had their moment.

Now, here was their new single, 'Girls and Boys'. A goofy, pseudo-disco beat and playroom effects, a chanted chorus about boys liking girls and girls liking boys and girls and boys digging each other while on holiday, and a lead vocal that slurred and drifted in bargain-bucket Saahf-East. I interpreted it as: *This is all you lot are doing, you sad fuckers, just copping off with each other – we thought you were into serious music. Go on, have this and piss off.* It seemed like the sound of a band giving up in a strop. Surely nobody was going to actually like it.

But like it they did. It got to number five. It was on the radio endlessly, on station after station, not just XfM. An album soon followed, *Parklife*, presenting us with plenty more of this Gawd Blimey Guv'nor stuff. It went in at number one and would spend a total of 106 weeks on the chart.

I never became a regular XfM listener. I never heard enough that I liked - maybe I was just unlucky when I tuned in. There were the bloody adverts as well. The *Evening Session* seemed livelier and more colourful. But the best alternative music had made everything seem livelier and more colourful. New stuff was coming in from everywhere. Because of Nirvana, a huge chunk was American. Pearl Jam and

Soundgarden were among the other well-known exponents of grunge, their music characterised by punk-influenced, heavily distorted guitar sounds, by vocals made of growls and wails and by themes of alienation and outsider-ism.

Their badly-fitting, colour-deprived clothes and lank hair were visual manifestations of slacker culture, a riposte to showing up in the office early, perfectly groomed, energetic and keen. Each of these positions were just fashion, each as phoney as the other. But they represented available tribes in the new social spectrum. You could join either. If you were lucky enough to have the choice. As I was. Or, you could mix 'n' match. As I did. Which is how I had my sales job and my suit and my company car, in which I drove to get tickets for alternative rock bands while listening to XfM, or while listening to tapes of singles reviewed by the *NME* and *Melody Maker* and broadcast on the *Evening Session*.

But this was comfortable, because increasingly, I was doing it on my terms. Day-to-day behavioural convention was changing. You could dilute corporate stiffness with as much slacker as you fancied squeezing in. I was already saying "man" in most of my verbal sentences, using it almost like punctuation. But it wasn't the long, considered, American "man", it was the clipped, Brixto-Jamaican "mun", rivalled in frequency only with "wicked". As in: *That sandwich was wicked, mun.* If the slip into the vernacular was well-timed, it could be accepted anywhere. Nobody judged you for it now.

In coming to the fore, Nirvana's Kurt Cobain was, in many ways, the perfect figurehead for all this. He was the genuine article; talented and distinctive, with pain and despair integral to his expression – the epitome of the tortured artist. His heavy drug habit was well-known. The fractious nature of his relationship with Courtney Love, with whom he now had a daughter, was regularly alluded to. He was tormented and fucked-up. He was the real thing. The public loved him. Then, one day in early April, we learned that he had been found dead at his home. The gunshot wound to his head was reported as self-inflicted.

There was a lot of mourning. There was also a lot of soul-searching over the exploitative nature of wanting anyone to live up to the image of the great bona fide rock star that we carry around in our heads, and about what that lifestyle does to people - real people. Talk time in the media was given to it. Talk time among friends was given to it. Cobain, racked with depression and drug dependency, had died aged twenty-seven, the same age that Jimi Hendrix, Janis Joplin, Brian Jones and Jim Morrison had all been at their premature deaths. His mum was reported as having warned him not to "join that stupid club".

DJs paid tribute, they shared thoughts, and played his songs, in among the new releases and current sounds. We had been celebrating a rock hero; now there was a vacuum. But very soon we were listening to the first charting single from a Manchester band that would fill much of it; a band about whom there was more fuss and excitement than even the Stone Roses and Suede had generated.

They would soon come to represent an equally significant but different kind of hero. Alan McGee had apparently signed them to Creation on the spot, having seen them by chance in Glasgow. This is the very stuff of legend and, with a few tweaks to detail, it turned out to be a true story. So, Oasis were already legends. Now they were going to be the biggest band in the world.

'Supersonic' went in at number thirty-one and was gone from the Top 40 a week later. But that didn't matter. There was something different about it from the first play. Its beat was steady, relaxed, spacious; underpinned by a growling guitar that began groovy and got groovier. The lyrics were hedonistic collages, scattered musings and anecdotes about doing whatever makes you feel Supersonic. But you didn't have to go even that deep on it – you just had to groove.

It stood out from the playlist on the *Evening Session*: it made other things seem a little pretentious, a little hurried, a little *strained*. And it was authentic. Kurt Cobain had been authentic. If something was authentic, it was moved to the front of the queue. Such things didn't impress me generally, because it had little to do with what was on the record. But this authenticity thing was something over which I found myself making an exception with Oasis.

One of the biggest alternative acts at that point were Manic Street Preachers, who had appeared early in the decade as glammed-up punks; and although their conspicuous efforts to gain notoriety had divided audiences, most people recognised that they were extremely good at being glammed-up punks, and they began gathering a following that would swell handsomely. But the cynicism had frustrated them; they sensed the widespread perception that they were in role rather than authentic. In 1991, their guitarist Richey Edwards had responded to this by shockingly carving "4 real" deep into his forearm with a razor for the benefit of his *NME* interviewer, who happened to be Steve Lamacq.

It was easy to judge a group of punk fans dressing up in white blouses, leopard skins and make-up when they came from post-industrial South Wales in 1991. But a gang of mates from modern, working-class Manchester who wore the same clothes as everyone else in their neighbourhood, on and off stage, made a different impression. Much was made of the credibility of Oasis and I accepted it as important.

Others around me recognised it as important, too, even if they shrugged it off. My social circles were shifting again. I had quickly lost touch with everybody from the band. My closest work colleagues were types who whooped when 'Y.M.C.A' came on at parties and did the dance. But other atmospheres were available.

Around the corner from the office was a small pub, where a live DJ got busy on Fridays as soon as the suits started appearing. Sunlight was still streaming in through the windows and there was this full-blown disco going on - it was hilarious. They played pop hits from the mid-70s, including Mud, Suzi Quatro and the Sweet, and some were as pleased to hear this as I was – dancing with the same enthusiasm, playing air drums in the right places. One of these was a section manager who had recently joined. I had already bonded with him a bit over football, but we gradually found we had similar taste in music.

He lived to the west of London and we went to see Echobelly at the Old Trout at Windsor, a small club on the indie circuit where I had once played a support slot. 'Insomniac' was still current and they played a good gig, making a strong impression, especially the singer, who I now knew was called Sonya. The section manager made a strong impression on me in the bar beforehand by sucking a spliff so hard that it turned into a glowing blade several inches long. I saw this as a manifest "bollocks to all this" attitude, a feeling I felt I could identify with. It was later echoed by Sonya's yelled frustrations in the closing song, 'Scream'. I leapt to all sorts of comforting conclusions about the kindred spirits now surrounding me.

He and I were among the few hundred who saw Oasis at the Marquee in early June. We already knew they were from Manchester. They were formed around two brothers: Liam, the younger one who sang, and Noel, the older one who played guitar and wrote songs. They put on no airs or graces whatsoever in interviews. They scowled and swore and gobbed off. The extent to which you warmed to this depended on how much you already liked the idea of them. In the pub beforehand, we bumped into a mate of the LSM, also from Manchester, with a small gang of Manchester mates he was working with in London. They were, of course, going to see Oasis too. It was a very Manchester thing.

Oasis were a striking spectacle. What surprised me about the performance was that despite the groove and energy in their music, they all stood very still, concentrating with unadorned seriousness on making this great big sound. Liam had his hands clasped behind his back, his mic positioned just a bit too high, so that he had to turn his head to the side and up in order to sing into it. He held a large tambourine, which he played intermittently and without ceremony. There were no histrionics, no leaping about, no retreating half a yard to gurn and writhe through instrumental sections – by their faces alone you might think that they were each doing a crossword.

The only disturbance to this was when some pissed-up twats at the front started chanting "you dirty northern bastards", an occurrence which resulted in Noel stepping forward to the mic and asking "dirty northern what?" in a way suggesting that he was prepared for full engagement on the point. The stony cast of his face, plus a few variations on *shut up* from around the auditorium, caused the twats to re-think and they piped down.

They should have concentrated on dancing. The section manager did. He danced while clasping the briefcase he had gruffly refused to leave in the cloakroom. He danced with a striding, knees-bent lurch, looking at various points as if he was disappearing into a hole in the floor. For now, and for another couple of weeks, there was room at Oasis gigs to dance in such a way. We plotted future excursions.

The very next night, it was Lush at the Astoria 2, which was also on Charing Cross Road, between the Marquee and the much bigger Astoria. They released two singles on the same day – 'Hypocrite', a sharp, punky belter, and 'Desire Lines' a flawed epic (and I do love flawed epics) reminiscent of the *Lawrence of Arabia* soundtrack. The album which followed, *Split*, revealed a darker, harder turn. It charted at nineteen and spent three weeks in the album chart. It remains one of the very few albums that I can listen to right through without getting bored or annoyed. Neither of its singles got in the Top 40.

These days, I was rarely more than a few days away from the next gig. I went with a mate to the Fleadh at Finsbury Park, a day-long Irish music festival with a range of rock and folk acts (some of whom needed their Celtic credentials explained). We saw Kirsty MacColl, Suzanne Vega and Sultans of Ping FC. We may have seen some others worth mentioning, but the smoking and drinking kind of overtook us a bit.

At Water Rats, a small club on Gray's Inn Road, I saw, on different nights, Tiny Monroe for the second time and Sleeper for the second time. Each of these had good new singles out: Tiny Monroe had the classy, drifting 'Cream Bun', and Sleeper had 'Delicious', a wild, bouncing flail all about joycus shagging.

Echobelly also now had a new single, slipping into the Top 40 with 'I Can't Imagine the World Without Me'; a thrashy, high-octane stomp which included a trumpet part perhaps influenced by the Beatles' 'Penny Lane' and a rhythm guitar part perhaps influenced by the Sweet's 'Blockbuster'. At their next reachable gig, I bought a T-shirt with "Echobelly" on the front and "I Can't Imagine the World Without Me" on the back, which I was still wearing twelve years later; and a pin badge bearing the same title, now mounted on a magnet in my kitchen.

It was a tremendous single. But it wasn't quite the best indie single of the summer. That honour was claimed by another female fronted band, this one with two female guitarist-vocalists. They were from Chicago. They were called Veruca Salt. Their single came out on the Scared Hitless label and was called 'Seether'. All this makes it brilliant before you've even heard it.

It was about a headcase who might have been an imaginary friend or an alter ego. It started *DUR NUR NUR NUR NUR – OW!* and got better from there, with the best rhythm guitar you'd heard for years - riffing, then chugging, then thrashing; in lean, mean balance with a lean, mean vocal. The *Evening Session* supported it with fists raised.

It got nowhere near the charts, but it was an instant classic anyway. If you knew it, you loved it. They came to the UK in July and played at the Garage. It was packed and the stifling heat gave the atmosphere a tense edge, even before the crowd-surfing started. This phenomenon was by now well-established. It was where a youngster would stand on the edge of the stage and hurl themselves off, get caught by the crowd, then be passed back and forth above their heads - sometimes they might be hoisted in the middle of the crowd and passed forward instead. The abandon of Veruca Salt's sound made this gig a tantalising crowd-surfing prospect. There was no kind of protective moat at the Garage. The security staff prowled the stage continuously and repelled anyone that came within clambering distance.

But instead of deterring them, this only roused them further. By the time the headliners took the stage, a solid wall of security guys stood facing the jam-packed crowd, so that for a lot of the gig, you couldn't see the band apart from the hair of the lanky bass player. Up to five youngsters at a time were being passed forward, in sitting positions, until just out of reach, goading staff with come-on-then expressions and hand gestures, before being withdrawn to make way for the next one. The security guys occasionally swiped at them, like bears vainly trying to catch dive-bombing birds.

This strained stand-off continued, with tensions rising in step with the heat, and the band stoically making their way through the set behind this human wall; until, suddenly: *DUR NUR NUR NUR NUR – OW!* and the whole place – I mean, the *whole place* – went mental; leaping, flying bodies, limbs at every conceivable angle; blotchy faces matted with sweat-soaked hair and contorted in the act of screaming the words. If any moment ever crystallised why indie gigs in the 90s could be so brilliant, that was it.

The Oasis star was meanwhile rising further. The next time we saw them was at the Astoria; not Astoria 2 - the big one. It was mid-August and they had another single out: 'Shakermaker', which was not as good as 'Supersonic' and had a verse that reminded everyone of 'I'd Like to Teach the World to Sing (in Perfect Harmony)' by the New Seekers. Not that it seemed to matter – it went straight in at number eleven. And it dropped out of the Top 40 three weeks later.

At the Astoria they were supported by a band from the midlands called Ocean Colour Scene, who had appeared a few years before with a single called 'Yesterday Today', a piece of pure 1991 shuffle-beat which I had quite liked but which missed the Top 40. Having done little since, they were now somehow important enough to have their name printed on the ticket, rather than it simply reading "plus support". The section manager was unimpressed. At one between-songs moment he bellowed: "I saw you three years ago - you were fucking shit then and you're fucking shit now!" The lead singer found his face in the crowd and just grinned at him.

"It begs the question," came a voice close to us, "why did you come to see them?"

"I didn't come to see them – I came to see Oasis" went the growling reply; and he stared the protester down.

This was going to be an interesting guy to go to the Reading Festival with. It was him that suggested it. He had been before – I hadn't. Reading was one of only two established music festivals of this size: the other being Glastonbury. The bill over the weekend was going to include Lush, Echobelly, Hole, Manic Street Preachers, Terrorvision, Pulp, Sleeper, Salad and Tiny Monroe, plus loads of others that I had varying levels of enthusiasm for. The main stage compère was going to be Steve Lamacq.

Oasis weren't there. But their new single 'Live Forever' was on a two-week peak at number ten and the festival was heady with it. The melody and feel of this record, its blending of power and tenderness, seemed proof that they really were something special: not just authentic working-class lads who could put phoneyism in its place and cobble a few hits together, but purveyors of true, all-time-great quality. Jaws dropped. Its lyric was a bid for immortality. Its spirit wafted around the festival site; a reminder that we were all in the right place, doing the right thing – that this scene was a gathering power.

Reading always happened over the August Bank Holiday weekend. It had been a hairy-arsed rock festival back in the days when rock had been the rebellious genre: but it was now colonised by indie. The section manager's mum lived nearby and was going to provide the camping gear. I was going to my first proper festival. I was thirty.

We arrived mid-afternoon on Thursday, thinking this was early enough to have the pick of camping pitches, but the queues were already telling us it wasn't. We found a spot about half-way between the furthest fields and the arena, close to one of the main paths which, initially, we thought a good idea. We met a girl from work, who was the first person I ever met with a pierced belly-button. We put up our little dome tents next to each other. She was tense and didn't seem to want to talk about bands. She had other people she was going to meet and be with. She was perhaps nervous about having two guys close by after dark. I planned to be too stoned to be a threat to anyone.

I wasn't familiar with festival culture to any extent yet. A torch was one of the things we hadn't thought to bring, although we each had a lighter. We had brought a small stove, a couple of pans, some dry food, a water-carrier and a bag of tins. We had brought a tin-opener but it broke immediately. The tins were successfully ruptured with a Swiss army knife, but then we couldn't light the stove and ended up spooning cold food from battered containers which constantly threatened to lacerate our fingers.

I eventually learned that most festival-goers were well-off kids who got most of their food from the vans and field cafes. There were a few tarpaulin-covered areas serving breakfasts, which never seemed to have any available seats. We had not brought camping chairs. I don't remember it raining but I do remember paths becoming increasingly churned with mud in the course of the weekend. We hadn't brought waterproof footwear. You just had to grin and bear the portable toilets. We *had* brought loo roll.

The crowd was largely good-spirited and largely there for a laugh. Among the negatives was the girl from work having to clamber out of her tent in the middle of the night to scream at two guys who were pissing on it. Elsewhere there was the usual pushing-in problems when waiting to be served beer; and also, the pushing-in problems when waiting for a band to come on: or often, just as they were launching into their first number. This is worst when someone gets hoisted up to sit on someone else's shoulders and completely obscures the view you have been nurturing for the last hour. I have, in my time, taken direct action in response to this, but you've got to be properly angry.

Anyway, back to more pleasant aspects. People were wandering around in all kinds of clothing. I had my Echobelly T-shirt on and there were myriad others. My favourites were the Terrorvision ones that had "fuck you and fuck your tent" on the back. We were standing behind one of these as we watched Hole, which was only their third appearance since Kurt Cobain's death. They were good – I liked their *Live Through This* album, its title now being something into which you could read increasing amounts. Courtney Love was fascinating.

That was on the main stage. On the indoor Melody Maker Stage, Echobelly were again impressive and I spotted Asian girls edging their way to the front. Sonya radiated such authority, had such a fantastic voice and looked good enough to eat – I was becoming convinced she would be a monumental star, marking some kind of ethnic breakthrough as well as rocketing her band to the top of the charts. We were one week away from the release of their debut album, *Everyone's Got One*. It would reach number eight.

Lush were good, despite technical problems. I can't remember seeing Sleeper but I imagine we did. Ditto Tiny Monroe and Salad. Salad had released the single 'Your Ma' earlier in the summer, which was mad and brilliant. It would have been on the same *Evening Session* order sheets as airplay favourite 'Mall Monarchy' by Compulsion, who were also there. Compulsion sounded like they'd listened to 'Staring at the Rude Boys' by the Ruts so often that they could no longer conceive of rock sounding like anything else. Since I loved 'Staring at the Rude Boys', this was not a problem. 'Mall Monarchy' was bloody great. Almost everything else in their set sounded like it.

At the end of each night, when the last of the headliners left their respective stages, as the bars and food vans in the arena all closed and security began gathering in conspicuous gangs, another world materialised. It was a world of small bonfires, wrapped-up huddles and small-scale fringe activity, each generating their own island of light in the gloom. Here and there mini speakers blasted out dance music, with huddles perhaps nodding their heads sagely to it, or just staring blankly into the flames. Many others were up and dancing. The section manager was wont to throw himself into these situations, doing his striding, lurching dance and introducing himself in his

197

characteristically forthright way. I sensed that he thought less of me for holding back. Other distractions helped us bond better.

Among noticeable developments in crowd behaviour at gigs was the evolution of the mosh pit in line with the quiet bit/loud bit thing. Kids would sway and jostle through the verse and then go totally wild at the chorus – slam-dancing, pogoing, crowd-surfing and leaping about as far as their hormones could carry them. If you were watching this from behind, the stage lights would turn it into a silhouette show and, since many of them had long hair, it really did look like something from the Muppets. Nothing at Reading '94 brought the hilarity of this home to me more than the Crap Stage.

There might have been as many as thirty performers involved in the Crap Stage, or as few as eight; it was hard to tell. All of it or none of it might have been rehearsed. Close to a perimeter fence stood a truck that folded open at the side to reveal a stage, a PA and a sign that said "The Crap Stage".

Two bands played there while we watched; young guys in jeans and t-shirts, gurning and growling away amid a sound limited and distorted by their cheap PA, doing the quiet bit/loud bit thing so that they could rock out with hair flying, while a gaggle of muppets got into the spirit at the front.

It felt like a parody, but we weren't sure - until the second band, who began a song which my memory has since referred to as 'Front Loader'. This was clearly going to be a special moment. Tension was allowed to mount. The bare-chested lead singer stood at the edge of the stage with wild staring eyes. The verse alternated between a growling, grinding guitar riff and a repeated single line of lyric, while a guy who was possibly the owner – he was older, with a beer belly, goatee beard and a plain cap - leant out over the audience, one hand gripping the truck and the other conducting the crowd with a stick.

The verse went:

Front loader – no way!
Front loader – no way!
Front loader – no way!
Front loader... baaastaaard!

At which, the band, and the muppets at the front, exploded into an instrumental "chorus" comprising sustained bouts of thrashing and leaping, that eventually calmed down so that the verse could be repeated. It was one of the most incredible things I had ever seen. Our eyes and cheeks were soaked from laughing. All in a dimly-lit corner of the Reading Festival at midnight.

The extent of our hysterics may have been influenced by intoxicants. We had certainly been drinking and smoking, but not that much. At one point, a small piece of decorated cardboard, which I was assured was an acid tab, was passed to me and I ate it. But it was obviously just a bit of decorated cardboard. I was kind of glad, really. The gear had given me some uncomfortable moments all by itself. One of these had been when Beavis and Butt-Head appeared on the big screen beside the Main Stage.

For me and a few slightly deranged others, the *Beavis and Butt-Head* TV show was among the very best things about the 1990s. From its beginnings on MTV it had become a Friday night fixture on Channel 4, broadcasting just before alternative magazine programme *The Word*.

Beavis and Butt-Head was an animation featuring two messily-drawn suburban teenagers with the lowest of aspirations, who shared the preoccupations of the least mature of every age from six onwards: explosions, toilets, junk food, tough guys and naked chicks. Anything in these categories was "cool" and everything else "sucked". Double-entendres were manna from heaven. All someone would have to do was say, for example, "wood", and they would abandon whatever they were doing for a prolonged snigger, instantly reminding the viewer of the joys of being fourteen. Or thirteen. Or whenever it was when this could still trump anything else.

Each episode found them in a new situation through which these credentials could be further secured. They began on a dilapidated sofa in a dilapidated room watching something on TV that would become the stimulus for a half-baked scheme for making easy money, becoming instantly cool, or getting chicks. None would work, but something somewhere would occasion their trademark sniggering. If you impersonated either snigger in public, peers instantly recognised it - they either moved away with a groan or danced towards you in elation.

For loved it was. There was enough craft in its brutality to delight the mind. But, most of all, and best of all, when sitting on their sofa they would critique music videos. At this they were brilliant, taking pretentiousness and over-exuberance down several pegs just by being themselves, and passing comments that made you howl even though you would never have said them out loud yourself. Generally speaking, a video was in one of two categories: either it ruled or it sucked. Their favourite genres were hardcore rap and heavy metal. Beavis always wore a Metallica t-shirt; Butt-Head always an AC/DC one. They had pet targets: Bono of U2 was "Boner"; British bands were "from that country where everything sucks". When some naff acts appeared, they simply screamed in terror. If not verbally attacking performers they were verbally and physically attacking each other. It captured a particular mind-set of a particular stage of life, with additional detail thrown in. Most of the time I giggled at it like a kid.

So, it was while I was being a bit affected by weed that we were standing close to the Main Stage in between acts, and MTV insignia was being flashed up on the screens at either side, and Beavis and Butt-Head were suddenly introduced and encouraged to give a message to the good people of the Reading Festival, at which point they froze, as they always did when they were put on the spot and unprepared, sniggering under their breath while looking deeply anxious; and this went on for ages, while I myself began looking deeply anxious. I was relieved when it ended.

It's unlikely that they ever approved of the kind of poppy dance music that UK audiences were increasingly lapping up; unless, that is, there was a cool chick on the video. They probably liked the Prodigy. The Prodigy were more theatrical and a bit dirtier than most boppy house stuff. Their 1993 album, *Music for the Jilted Generation*, had been full of impressive, state-of-the-art sounds and its singles charted highly, albeit without coming close to the wonders of 'Charly'.

Dance music took a range of forms in the 1994 charts. 'Son of a Gun' by JX and 'Get-a-Way' by Maxx took the chanting, riff-laden house form; 'Rhythm of the Night' by Corona and 'Another Night' by (MC Sar &) the Real McCoy took the proper-song house form. For lovers of the slightly aggravating novelty dance form there was 'Swamp Thing' by the Grid, with its banjo, fiddle 'n' barn sound, almost immediately emulated by 'Everybody Gonfi Gone' by 2 Cowboys, which I mention just because of its close similarity to 'Swamp Thing' - it only ever annoyed me.

Other dance hits used new Drum & Bass rhythms: 'Incredible' by M-Beat featuring General Levy, which lived up to its title; and a record where Drum & Bass met cheesy piano and enough other stuff to ensure popularity among club-goers and those still a bit too young to be club-goers – 'Let Me Be Your Fantasy' by Baby D. This surprised everyone by sweeping to number one at the end of the autumn.

All of these records were big hits: a number thirteen, an eight, a seven, a four, a three, two twos and a number one. Dance in 1994 was more interesting than dance in 1993. By the autumn, things generally were changing for the better. Usually when this happens, it is because of new acts who hit that precise interfacing-point between the underground and the mainstream; that sweet spot where almost all the best pop is to be found. Yet occasionally, an established artist gets caught up in the spirit of changing times and proves able to reinvent themselves so as to be a readily-accepted part of it.

Which brings us back to Kylie. She had now ditched SAW and PWL for the production team Brothers in Rhythm and the label Deconstruction. She was presenting a more mature image – the term "SexKylie" had been coined and the media soaked it up. Her re-launch single, 'Confide in Me', was a clear departure; synth-pop exotica with Eastern mysticism in its beats and in its epic riff; the vocal hovering somewhere between Madonna and Donna Summer. The artwork inside the sleeve presented her as a mixed-race teenage club-goer with tight ringlets.

In the week that it reached its peak of number two, the debut album by Oasis, *Definitely Maybe*, went straight in at number one. It would spend 187 weeks on the album chart. We were entering an exciting new era. But there would be resistance from dark forces. Many of those now buying CDs by Oasis, Echobelly and others would fail in their duty to resist the spread of evil. I myself would not be entirely guilt-free. Almost two years previously, I had gazed in horror at hoardings on a Bangkok office building, at a pop band who were spray-cleaned, hand-polished, and no-reason gleeful. One who, I was assured, were massively popular because of it.

That image was somewhere in my consciousness as I hungrily anticipated the coming year, but it wasn't at the forefront. It didn't need to be. How could anyone in Britain opt for that when they had all this real, *proper* stuff? The freshness, the energy, the noise that ruffled all the right feathers, the sweeping away of all that rotten old-ness; the promise.

Those were the things that would constitute our future. Surely.

Eight

For a generation whose cultural attic was piled high with idealised impressions of the sixties, 1994 was special. Peace and love, so long dismissed, so long sniggered at and embodied only in visitor shop souvenirs, history documentaries and stoner sitcom characters, had somehow survived the 80s: a disparate alliance of dissenters, party loons and trendies now carried it forward, each nurturing their own precious parts of it. Much of its old insignia was retained, but new vocabulary had been added: positivity. tolerance, inclusion. It had enjoyed a Second Summer. It had a new drug; one whose effects directly served its cause. Unity and the primacy of youth were once again at the heart of popular culture.

A new cohort of guitar bands echoed the inherent idealism, just by virtue of being guitar bands; regardless of whether they welcomed it, regardless of whether their detail was Beatles-like, Velvet-Underground-like or even Herman's Hermits-like. Expectation rode on their shoulders. Everyone knew the sixties couldn't come back. But, equally, people understood that it had unfinished business.

Having been in a guitar band, I already considered myself involved. But that November, our company moved to Camden, indie's southern heartland. This was the proper bollocks – much better than the West End or the outskirts of the City. I could wander its streets at lunchtime, wearing the Doc Martens I had bought from Holt's next to Camden Town tube, wondering whether any pop stars were at that moment sitting in Holt's trying on a new pair. I would pass the occasional pop star on the pavement. Miki from Lush would avoid my smile. Ian from the Stone Roses would think I looked sharp in my new mod-cut suit. I was in Camden now.

Indie's enhanced status was a key component in the gathering excitement, in the overtaking of cynicism and of conservatism – with both a small and a large 'C'. Whether or not they had been overtly allied to the Thatcherite revolution, the fashion, attitude and sounds of the 80s were associated with its intransigence and triumphalism. But house, acid, soulful positivity, pop innocence and the return of guitars had laid siege to all that. Youth was winning. Partying was its faith, and ecstasy was part of the belief system - its 1990 heyday had proved to a generation that conflict could be dismantled as surely as any old Berlin wall.

And this generation was increasingly on the right side of arguments. Conservative legislation had been clashing with the alternative for half a decade. The Entertainments (Increased Penalties) Act 1990 had formally criminalised the staging of unlicensed outdoor raves and warehouse parties. In 1994, a new piece of Conservative legislation, the Criminal Justice and Public Order Act, changed the law regarding certain "anti-social" behaviours, which directly affected various aspects of youth lifestyle and culture, with the staging of raves chief among them. The wording of the Act referred specifically to music with "repetitive beats". If this phrase is new to you, please reach your own conclusions: they are likely to be similar to those at the time.

It was criticised way beyond the congregation of usual suspects. The ruling political party had declared itself in opposition to the groovier, more tolerant country that Britain had become. John Major was their leader. It had been two years since his general election victory, the Conservatives' fourth in a row. Events had almost immediately damaged their economic credibility. Now there was this Act.

Change was a sweet scent that wafted through every window, day after day. Those not particularly well-appointed with social and political detail drank it in just the same. We had never thought much of scowling and glaring as a means by which to prove your adulthood. We were into harmony and togetherness; into being *nice*. Our spiritual heritage was moving into the light. Nobody was contradicting us anymore. Positivity; tolerance and inclusion; love and peace, man; this is cool and does not suck - take your pick. These things might win after all. Rock 'n' roll might actually win.

The autumn soundtrack had a particular fizz and sizzle to it. September echoed endlessly with 'Live Forever' by Oasis; and then their album came out, seeming to encapsulate everything freshly legitimised and championed - getting' down, spliffin' up, rockin' out. There seemed to be little room for anything other than *Definitely Maybe*.

But plenty managed to squeeze in. There was 'Confide in Me' by Kylie at number two, 'Incredible' by M-Beat featuring General Levy blipping and morphing away at number eight, and 'Love is All Around' by Wet Wet Wet at number one. Still. It had proved difficult to shift, crossing over into market after market, accessing various realms of the barely functional and the decidedly undead; until it had been top for eight weeks, then ten weeks, then twelve weeks - and *still* counting. In mid-September, after fifteen interminable weeks, just after Kylie crashed in at two, it was finally removed. But not by Kylie.

'Saturday Night' by Danish performer Whigfield was a formation dance with a meaningless lyric. It was a hit throughout Europe, particularly at holiday resorts where it fit the bill perfectly, pleasing everyone from those able to leap and spin to those needing a hand to get up from their seat. It had something of 'Chirpy Chirpy Cheep Cheep' about it. When it was finally released in the UK, every segment of the holiday market raced to the shops. It dethroned Wet Wet Wet, for the first of four weeks at number one, spending a total of seventeen in the Top 40.

Another single that remained in the charts to the end of the autumn came from another bloody soap star. Michelle Gayle had once been on kids' drama series *Grange Hill*, before going on to become one of the first significant black characters in *Eastenders*. Now she was launching a chart career. Weary sighs may have ensued, but her 'Sweetness' single had more charm than a punnet of puppies, with *shoop-sh'doo* backing vocals and gossamer keyboards draped across a candied slice of radio-friendly pop-soul. It took seven weeks to climb to its peak of number four. Clearly, too many people had spent too long pretending they didn't like it.

Worthy indie that fell short of the charts included 'Shining Road' by the Cranes, 'I Don't Know Where It Comes From' by Ride and 'Caught by the Fuzz' by Supergrass. But 'Welcome to Paradise' by Green Day got to number twenty. And Oasis then got to number seven.

'Cigarettes and Alcohol' was a piece of secular revelation. It told you not to bother waiting for those best-things-in-life that may never come, but instead to take responsibility for your own fulfilment; drink this, smoke that, swallow those and snort the rest. "You gotta make it happen!" rang the chorus. Such a lyric would never have floated in the 80s; but this was now. Believers were still dancing and yelling to it long after its three-week chart run was over.

Perhaps the best indie moment of all that autumn came from London band Elastica, fronted by the enigmatic Justine Frischmann, who had been a founder member of Suede and was now dating Blur's lead singer Damon Albarn, a fact significant only inasmuch as it brought indie into the orbit of the tabloids. Their new one was 'Connection' and it was an immediate stand-out; its clownish lurch and goofy hooks topped with a snooty, scathing vocal. It went in at seventeen and was gone two weeks later, but posterity has bestowed fitting recognition.

I never saw Elastica live, but that autumn I saw Echobelly twice more, the second time just before the release of another single, 'Close... But', which did nothing. I went without the section manager, who had by now run out of patience with my lack of enthusiasm for announcing myself to a crowd of strangers like I had just fallen from the ceiling.

In December, 'Let Me Be Your Fantasy' by Baby D went to number one. Then the Stone Roses finally returned, now on the super-major Geffen label, heralding an album modestly entitled *Second Coming* with the single 'Love Spreads' – a recognisable Stone Roses noise, but mushy and formless. It went in at number two and it took security four weeks to march it from the charts. We needed an antidote.

Which brings us back to Kylie. She released 'Put Yourself in My Place', whose peak of eleven did it no justice. Its video was no more or less than a striptease performed by the singer in the weightlessness of a space vessel, with "gratuitous titillation" stamped on it with a branding iron and no link at all to the lyric. Whether keen to see Kylie's kit come off, or repelled by the idea of something so crass, many people will have taken investigations no further, when they might otherwise have basked in the full wonder of this stunning record and, perhaps, played their part in taking it to a more fitting chart position. I fucking hate videos sometimes.

Close to Christmas, I went with my flatmate to see Oasis at the Hammersmith Palais. The crowd was energetically excitable, no doubt due in large part to chemical intervention, but also due to the promise of new material, including the next single 'Whatever', which wasn't on the album. It would go in at three in Christmas week and spend a creditable seven weeks in the Top 40. It was a relatively tiresome plod, but it was a new relatively tiresome plod by Oasis and that was what counted. People drew comparisons with *Magical Mystery Tour*-era Beatles, few thinking it a bad thing. Liam Gallagher wore shades with small lenses, like John Lennon had.

Later that week I was in a checkout queue at HMV, waiting to pay for my copy of 'Whatever' on CD. The line was fifteen or so long and, as I peered around, I realised that every person in the line was holding a copy of the same single. These were not fey youths in outsized band T-shirts, they were older, smarter, serious-looking adults in business suits. Just like I was. How many of these, I wondered, had once been part of a band, like I had? How many of these, I wondered, already knew about Lush and Echobelly and Sleeper and Salad and Veruca Salt, like I did? How many, I wondered, would be going home tonight to buil' up if there was any gear around, like I would be? How many, I might also have wondered, felt that their time was about to arrive?

As 'Whatever' delivered Oasis a new personal best of number three and the *Evening Session* declared 'Seether' by Veruca Salt to be their Single of the Year, it was hard not to anticipate 1995 with excitement. For many of the dissenters, party loons and trendies, the next few years would indeed deliver. But they wouldn't for everybody. The thing is, none of us can ever be totally satisfied with any scene, or genre, or phenomenon; or conversely, disapprove of one in quite the same way as those around us because, essentially, our set of tastes is unique.

Around the turn of the 80s, sexologist John Money coined the phrase "lovemap". This states that, as a result of early sensual experience, your sexual preferences are set and are difficult to alter in adulthood. I think that there's a musical equivalent of this; that our early musical loves serve to determine whether we will like this sound or that sound when we're older. Creation boss Alan McGee would one day be accused of only signing bands that reminded him of his favourites from his youth in the punk era. Most of us will have heard interviews on the radio where artists play something influential from their formative years which they claim will surprise listeners, but which makes us think: "Yep - that explains a lot".

We could perhaps all trace the lineage of our own tastes. My personal preference for girl-fronted bands with melodic tunes is almost certainly due to a childhood love of the Seekers. Add the growly thrashes of new wave to mirror the fury and frustrations of a late-70s adolescence, and you get Blondie. No surprise then, that I would later love the Primitives so much.

Continue that thread and you get to Echobelly, Sleeper, Salad and the rest of the current line-up. Salad had a slight but discernible perversity about them that reminded me of the Sparks records I had worshipped aged eleven. My lovemap also has important threads beginning with the Supremes, but we'll come to those. For me, it was the new-found success of melodic tunes coated in growly, thrashy guitar noise that most flavoured the mid-90s.

The buzzword "Britpop" had been doing the rounds for a while. Monthly music mag *Select* had famously run a cover in April 1993 which said "Yanks Go Home", beside an image of Brett Anderson of Suede standing in front of a union jack, accompanied by a list of British bands that were apparently going to see off those pesky Americans. This had its appeal – I was one of those wanting the British flag to be put to more positive uses than had often been the case. Suede were properly massive and I liked a couple of the other bands mentioned.

But there was no unifying musical style among them – all these acts sounded different. People call the mid-90s the Britpop era. I call it the melodic, thrashy guitar era – the era of the quiet bit/loud bit post-Nirvana settlement, because that's what I happened to like best; and it was far from exclusively British since so many of the acts providing it came from America, or Holland, or wherever else they happened to have been born.

Nevertheless, it was all put under the heading of indie, and the statistics show how well the category was doing. In 1994, there were 45 indie records that breached the Top 40, nine of which got into the Top 10, including from Suede, Blur and Oasis. In 1995, that number increased to 67, fifteen of which made the Top 10, with two going all the way to number one. Given that in 1995 there were 143 Top 10 hits and eighteen number ones *per se*, this was no mean feat.

However, there's one big, fundamental problem with this analysis. It's the question of what indie actually was. Because in these years, with guitar music now re-established, definitions became blurred and less meaningful. As I was going through chart listings in the course of assembling these figures, I found myself including some acts and not others. And, the more I thought about it, the harder it became to justify. I resolved the issue and completed the task, but only by stretching the net to cover things I really didn't want included.

There was enormous diversity inside this stretched net. Many had that melodic, thrashy guitar sound. But some bands had violins. Some had gospelly backing vocals. Bands like these may have retained an aching authenticity: but others stopped giving a damn about conforming to anyone else's expectations – they found they had a bunch of fans and just got on with pleasing them by the shortest route. Some were rock bands who weren't metal and just wore sweatshirts and jeans to perform commercial songs in. Some were on major labels, not independent ones. Some of those on major labels sounded more indie than others on independent labels. Some on indie labels were beginning to sound like regional theatre pit orchestras. It was no longer "indie". It was just "stuff".

In the pub, in the office smoking room, or at our desks when we should have been working, we argued about which bands were indie or not indie, sometimes even whether a band had forfeited their right to be indie as a result of their last record. These squabbles were fun, often passionate, occasionally bad-tempered, but ultimately pointless, our respective positions each dictated by an individual lovemap.

It did at least prove that indie was something we cared about. It was also something we could now revel in. 1994 saw a build-up and a breakthrough, but 1995 was a year for just basking in it, for leaving all the doors and windows open so that more could float in. For many fans of our generation, 1995 is a year of satisfying music memories. It was the first year that the chart, as well as the general soundtrack, seemed *flooded* with it.

Melodic, thrashy guitar noise gave us Top 40 hits like 'Inbetweener' and 'What Do I Do Now?' by Sleeper, 'Great Things' and 'King of the Kerb' by Echobelly, 'Basket Case' and 'Longview' by Green Day, 'Waking Up' by Elastica and 'Violet' by Hole. There was Cast, fronted by former La's bassist John Power, with 'Finetime' and 'Alright' (the Supergrass song with the same title is mentioned later). We also got 'This is a Call' and 'I'll Stick Around', the opening salvoes from a band fronted by the drummer from Nirvana, Dave Grohl, who were called Foo Fighters, which I thought was a dreadful name, but which I, along with everyone else, would get used to.

Some of these acts got to perform live on *The Word* surrounded by prancing twonks who would have pranced to anything as long as the camera was on them. Sleeper did 'Inbetweener' there in January and a month later Veruca Salt appeared with 'Number One Blind', a down-tempo, grungy delight which missed the chart while being better than almost everything in it.

Other great guitar records falling short of chart success but loved by tens of thousands included 'Drink the Elixir' and 'Motorbike to Heaven' by Salad, 'Something So Wild' and 'Ray Ray Rain' by Bettie Serveert, 'Universal Heart-Beat' by Juliana Hatfield, 'Sweet 69' by Babes in Toyland and another mad thrash from Veruca Salt, 'Victrola'. There was no room in the Top 40 either for the Amps, a Breeders side-project, whose fantastic 'Tipp City' sounded like a Breeders track that had been axed for being both far too catchy and far too drunk.

But then there were those that everybody remembers, because they were massive and unavoidable and made it normal for indie to be at the top of the charts. 'Wake Up, Boo!' from Creation signings the Boo Radleys could scarcely have been more radio-friendly, its bouncing, bubblegum feel and refrain of "Wake up, it's a beautiful morning!"

being hailed as brilliant indie by those suddenly aware of indie who didn't really understand indie (I was developing this snobbery effortlessly and, in wielding it, may only have been demonstrating that I didn't really understand the Boo Radleys). It got to number eight and, given its lyrical hook, it was kind of inevitable that it would end up either on a cereal advert or as a jingle on a mainstream radio breakfast show. In the event, it was the latter.

Then, in May, there was a new single from Oasis, and this time expectations were at fever pitch. 'Some Might Say' was more than a match for the pressure. It had a similar pace to 'Supersonic' but with a different groove and *louder*, its lyrics a mix of wisdom and simple rhyming convenience. The verses put arms across the shoulders of those to whom life had dealt a poor hand: *Some might say they don't believe in Heaven/Go and tell that to the man who lives in Hell.* Yes, indeed. But then, words of hope: *Some might say, we will find a brighter day.*

Was this an update on 'Streets of London', inspired by scenes from the streets of Manchester? Was it a call to finally and fully reject the 80s ethos? Was it a metaphor for the whole country? It was hard to resist these lines of thought (and, therefore, easy to simply ignore the baffling lyric in the chorus). The tune was great. The tune was more than great. It was stupendous. And it went straight in at number one. It was only there for a week, but for one whole week, the world was conquered. It spent six weeks in the Top 40.

They kept coming. Next: 'Common People' by Pulp, one of the acts listed on that *Select* Britpop cover. It was about a rich-kid college girl with a romanticised idea of working-class life; excitedly wanting to slum it despite her true place being with Daddy's wealth. The narrator is her increasingly uneasy lover, perhaps thinking about the reality of Oasis's *man who lives in Hell.*

Lots of Heaven, Hell and social comment going on. It lent gravitas to the indie attack and was an area that mainstream pop rarely if ever touched. Hole's songs were full of feminist anger (see 'Violet'); Juliana Hatfield was scathing about modern glamour (see 'Supermodel'); Lush sheltered themes of childhood mistreatment beneath the most glorious of tunes (see 'Kiss Chase').

'Common People' spent two weeks at number two in June and was in the Top 20 for six weeks. Legions of university-educated professionals would be bouncing joyfully to this for years to come, while being sneered at for missing the point by me – also a university-educated professional. I felt that the point was the song and the changing times. The point for many of them was simply Britpop.

If any record was integral to that summer holiday it was 'Alright' by Supergrass, a tankard-clanking anthem built on a saloon-bar piano jangle that fit the prevailing mood. It was number two for a fortnight, spending two months in the Top 40 and getting played everywhere for week after week.

But in the last week of August came the episode which highlighted 1995 indie more than any other. Blur, with their mega number-one album *Parklife*, and Oasis, with their mega number-one album *Definitely Maybe*, had been squaring up to each other as the big rivals of that ill-defined Britpop thing. Well, they hadn't actually, just a few digs in the papers, a few snide comments, a few assertions of the "my album is better than your album" type. But rivalry makes good copy and it was easy to amplify this one, since (a) the albums were so different and (b) it was a band of blokes from the north against a band of blokes from the south. Then it was announced that each could be releasing a new single on the same day.

This was it. The heavyweight clash of Britpop. That is exactly how it was billed on a mid-August *NME* cover and echoed everywhere else in the media. People took sides. I thought *Parklife* was lightweight drivel that pranced around with a fixed grin, while *Definitely Maybe* was substantial authenticity that rocked; plus, I was still blissing out to 'Some Might Say'. So I came straight off the fence. It was inevitable that one of them would be number one after the first week of release – most number one singles were going straight in now – it was just a matter of which. There seemed to be a lot at stake.

In the event, Blur put out their least annoying thing for ages in 'Country House', while the Oasis' release, 'Roll with It' was disappointing. Blur took the heavyweight title – they got the number one spot and held it for a further week. The best of a pair of not-that-good singles had won. At least 'Country House' was catchy and had a bit of life in it, while people were quick to draw comparisons between

'Roll with It' and the trudging core output of denim dinosaurs Status Quo, dubbing the culprits "Status Quoasis". But I was gutted. I sulked and sulked. I angrily wanted to know why, given the stakes, Oasis hadn't bothered to put out something brilliant. Maybe they thought they had.

Honours, however, were pretty even. They had one number one single each and one number one album each. Pulp, the Boo Radleys, Elastica, Supergrass and the Charlatans also had number one albums in 1995. So did Shaun Ryder's new fuckabout outfit Black Grape, whose number eight single 'In the Name of the Father' was a late summer treat.

But that autumn, one new album towered above all others. Oasis, who had waved defeat away with an up-sweep of the finger, released *(What's the Story) Morning Glory?* and the public fell upon it like ravenous dogs. It was grandly creamy, with less room for the edgy and groovy and far more for the spacious anthemic stuff, of which, on first listen, 'Champagne Supernova' was the best. The next single, however, was 'Wonderwall'; and this quickly began carving its name into the tree-bark of British pop culture.

It seems that any major alternative act is obliged to produce a signature anthem; one that is dull, worthy and revered; something far too important to bother entertaining or energising anybody. R.E M. had 'Losing my Religion' featuring a mandolin and Oasis had 'Wonderwall' featuring a cello. It went to number two in November. An ultra-cheesy "lounge" cover of it by Mike Flowers Pops went to number two at Christmas. Indie was *that* well-established.

I wonder how indie appeared to onlookers. We must have seemed a funny bunch. A tribe of grumpy weirdos revelling in an outsiderism that we could always choose to leave. We didn't dress smart when we went out. We didn't always mind out p's and q's. We had our weird obsessions. We weren't into "fun" like Take That fans. Imagine not wanting to have fun?

But the scene was also sexless. There were loads of people to fancy, but it wasn't sexy. Getting away from sexualised environments was part of the point and often sweet relief; but this was one of the reasons why, in addition to indie and straight pop, I often veered towards R&B.

When I was a teenager and the mod revival was on, R&B stood squarely for Rhythm and Blues, meaning the un-polished black

American music that the original mods had danced to. Now, the term meant something different. Soul was kind of old hat. Performers and vocal groups gathered around terms like "swing", "new jack swing", "swingbeat" and "swingalong". Actually, I made that last one up, but you can see how flighty these sub-headings were.

Suddenly, top-selling compilation albums were appearing with these phrases flavouring their titles. They featured male and female artists performing in those sequences of vocal gymnastics that were standard fare given the music's gospel ancestry. But alongside these were groups and solo performers that sang plainly and cleanly and, in order to grab the attention, sang about sex. Since the early 70s, the focus of mainstream soul had been explicit in its shift from championing social justice to getting things right in the bedroom - but explicit was now given a new brief.

Adina Howard had 'Freak Like Me', a "freak" being someone who would happily lose any vestige of Nice Girl once she got between the sheets. Adina was going to freak in the morning and freak in the evening for the right kind of roughneck nigga; on a single that had sneaked up to number thirty-three in the spring. There were also Nuttin' Nyce, who had 'Down 4 Whateva', a statement of intent indicative of what the Jamaican girls I worked with referred to as "slackness". In its lyric, they promised to consider anything as long as the guy brings his own condoms. It got nowhere near the charts. But people knew about it.

Among the male performers was R. Kelly, who, as I write, is still in the shadow of decades-old allegations regarding relationships with underage girls. His early-1995 Top 10 hit was steamy smoocher 'Bump 'n' Grind'. His vocal delivery was straightforward compared to the likes of Boys II Men and Jodeci, two acts notorious on this scene. There was no shortage of opinions on them from R&B fans I knew - how each of their members performed, how they dressed and how ugly they were (Jodeci, by general consensus, were not the prettiest of guys).

Boys II Men, whose rather good 1992 UK number one 'End of the Road' was still their swayin', finger-poppin' trademark, were - like Jodeci and plenty of others - into the kind of virtuoso warbling that had been delighting audiences for ages. As a given intro tinkled into life, off would go the *woh-woh-yeah-yeahs*, twisting and spiralling, over and over, before any discernible lyric appeared. This often continued in the choruses, where backing vocalists were routinely left to sing the chorus melody while the lead dropped behind for more voice box acrobatics. When what you wanted first and foremost was a good record, this could be a pain in the arse.

But in carrying it off, a singer (a) confirmed their right to be on a platform of such stature, and (b) stamped their membership of a community, one with a proud identity, one that had mainstream superstars Whitney Houston and Mariah Carey for heroes and plenty of room for more. Meanwhile it alienated many: like me, sitting there going: *Yes, yes; all very impressive, but where's the tune?*

Anyway, this was acceptable as part of the swingbeat package – cool, sexy tunes with cool, sexy beats, all about grown-up love, or else on the newly-liberated subject of gratuitous shagging. To me, in the hot, hot summer of 1995, it made a lot of sense, especially since my own personal life had livened up a bit. I got a couple of these compilations and went quickly on to albums by their standout artists. I got *The Show, the After-Party, the Hotel* by Jodeci, featuring the hit single 'Freek 'n You', in which it was declared he intended to freek his tight-bodied girl in every freekin' way, all freekin' night and all freekin' day. I only ever played the album a couple of times. Ditto *Do You Wanna Ride?* by Adina Howard.

I played the Aaliyah album more. This was *Age Ain't Nothing but a Number*, from a performer whose tender years I was then unaware of. She was under the wing of R. Kelly, which now implies certain things; indeed, they were apparently "married" in some arrangement which only lasted a year but she was fifteen then. *Fifteen.* You know what? I'm not even going there. Anyway, the album was fine, with a range of sounds from the mellow-swingin' 'The Thing I Like' to the twinklingly pretty 'At Your Best (You Are Love)'. I liked her voice.

R&B left room for rappers to drop in and do a guest spot, a phenomenon that was set to grow and one day become common practise. It would habitually annoy the hell out of me, but it didn't always have to. Guest rappers appeared on another album I got that summer, but there they performed integrated bit-parts, adding something to the content rather than simply intruding. And it remains one of my favourite albums ever - *CrazySexyCool* by TLC. It, too, pushed the sex angle; but by comparison, all other sexy R&B albums seemed a bit, well, *grubby*.

Yes, they were cute, possibly the most visually-appealing girl group since the Ronettes, and with cute nicknames: T-Boz, Left-Eye and Chilli. But they were modern, savvy and bursting with personality - it wasn't just hard stares and smouldering looks and sticking your bum out. Left-Eye burned her boyfriend's house down when he pissed her off. I had loved 'Ain't 2 Proud 2 Beg' in 1992 as well as another track on that first album called 'Hats 2 da Back'; but *CrazySexyCool* was funny and horny and sheer class. Its first two singles, 'Creep' and 'Red light Special', were among the highlights of the year. I played it more than any other LP for months.

Its next single, 'Waterfalls', got to number four in September, embodying the positive, unhurried flavours of the summer and enhancing the group's standing. The song was serious and sage - a plea for young people to reject the gang culture and take a more virtuous path; choose a life that was safer; choose a life that was longer. It was an island of sobriety in a sea of sex.

In the contemporary world of R&B, TLC had achieved a damn-near-perfect balance. Yet I rarely heard them played at parties I went to - R&B was standard fare but my peers were older than most TLC fans; it was mainly R. Kelly, Boys II Men and En Vogue. Or Michael Jackson, who had the new album *HIStory: Past, Present and Future, Book 1*, but whose older stuff was usually chosen. Perhaps you'd get Montell Jordan, whose laddish swagger 'This Is How We Do It' got to eleven in the UK and number one in the US; perhaps Bobby Brown, whose stonking 'Two Can Play That Game' was a mainstream dance monster, its cheesy-piano sound flying high at every party and every club for months, and which got to number three in the charts.

Just like my favourite indie, my favourite R&B didn't quite conquer the hit parade. Most of the singles I liked peaked somewhere between twenty and forty. Among that year's number ones, you only found Michael Jackson, if that counts, and the set-piece street drama of 'Gangsta's Paradise' by Coolio, if that counts. But you also got the

Outhere Brothers. Twice. You have to mention the Outhere Brothers if you're talking about 1995.

They were extraordinary. Here, among all this smooth, swaying, slow-burning sexiness, were two boys getting giggly and over-excited about bums and tits, like a pair of black Benny Hills in basketball vests. Some of the suggestions R Kelly or Jodeci made on record might have won a girl over under certain circumstances, but the Outhere Brothers' intentions were only ever shared between lads behind sheds.

Nevertheless, 'Don't Stop (Wiggle Wiggle)' made its way deliriously to the top of the charts for a week in the spring, on the back of its prurient 'OHB Club Version', the third of six mixes on the CD single. The follow up, 'Boom Boom Boom', topped the chart for four weeks in July, and you can take the pick of its mixes for lyrics about tasting nunnies, having a booty on your face and slipping peters inside folders. And in case you think I was above all this, I'm afraid I wasn't. I laughed out loud. And bought both singles. You'll have to take my word about the irony involved. And no, I didn't tell girls about it.

I could always talk to girls about indie, though. Chart statistics suggest that 1996 was an even greater success for the genre. There were 81 Top 40 hits, of which 29 got in the Top 10 and three of which went to number one. But that's only if you include the Prodigy, which you probably can. They had two number ones, 'Firestarter' in March and 'Breathe' in November.

'Firestarter' was just incredible. It didn't explain itself; it made no apologies; it fit alongside nothing; it just kicked the door down and flew through the room, ripping things off the walls as it went. It had one of those intros that disorientate; full of sounds that interweave but don't let you get a proper measure of the rhythm until the beat kicks in, when suddenly that and everything else makes massive, intoxicating sense. The lead vocal was delivered by the title character elucidating in the first person: he was a twisted, dangerous firestarter – like a deranged sibling of Ebeneezer Goode. The 90s produced nothing better. It was number one for three weeks and in the Top 40 for nine.

The other indie chart-topper came from Oasis. Their next release from (What's the Story) Morning Glory? was 'Don't Look Back in Anger', a song ostensibly about accepting your fate without bitterness;

a good-old communal sway of a singalong rendered more meaningful with every pint. It became their second number one in March and swelled their audience further.

Other charting indie records included - excitingly - three from Lush, who started the year by getting to number twenty-one and on *Top of the Pops* with the mop-shaking 'Single Girl'. Their next two singles, 'Ladykillers' and '500 (Shake Baby Shake)' got to twenty-two and twenty-one respectively; between them spending a typical indie total of five weeks in the Top 40.

'Dark Therapy' by Echobelly pipped these by reaching twenty. Sleeper had what would prove their best placings, with 'Sale of the Century' and 'Nice Guy Eddie' both getting to number ten. Cast breached the Top 10 three times, the best of which was the first, 'Sandstorm', number eight in January. Garbage, a bunch of older people including *Nevermind* producer Butch Vig and ultra-cool vocalist Shirley Manson, made their first Top 10 appearance with the big-hitting sneer 'Stupid Girl'. Blur were in the Top 10 twice more, with 'Stereotypes' and 'Charmless Man'.

But Suede deserve special recognition. In July they re-surfaced with 'Trash', at number three; the first of what would be five excellent Top 10 hits from the number one album *Coming Up*. You would expect the leading single from a top guitar act to do well, but the fact that four others went Top 10 from a best-selling album is testimony to how good 'Beautiful Ones', 'Saturday Night', 'Lazy' and 'Film Star' were. They spent thirteen weeks all-up in the Top 40.

Then there were the new arrivals. The Bluetones hit number two in February with the clean, polite 'Slight Return'; they would have other clean, polite hits in the coming years. Ash went to number four in April with the far noisier 'Goldfinger'. Welsh band Super Furry Animals began their absorbing, idiosyncratic chart career by reaching eighteen in July with 'Something 4 the Weekend'. September saw the number twelve hit 'On a Rope' by San Diego band Rocket from the Crypt; a rock 'n' roll circus resplendent with tattoos, quiffs and horn players – and an album entitled *Scream, Dracula, Scream!* for which alone they deserve a mention. They would one day release a single bearing the title 'When in Rome (Do the Jerk)', for which they deserve another.

Non-charting notables that year included Fuzzy - two girls and two guys from Boston, Massachusetts - whose late spring single 'Glad Again' was a stomping, jangling explosion of delirium, and whose next one was as good a cover as the era produced, transforming the Beach Boys' plaintive 'Girl Don't Tell Me' into a magnificent, blaring rock-out.

There was also Kenickie - three girls and one guy from Sunderland, Tyne and Wear - whose early summer *Skrillex EP* contained the track 'Come Out 2 Nite'; its blaring garage-groove and tales of teenage frivolity catching the ear of John Peel listeners to the extent that it was made number one in that year's Festive Fifty.

I read that they were aged seventeen and, as I was entering my thirty-fourth year, I decided that going to see a band half my age would be a fitting birthday gesture. So, I did. At the Union Bar in Maidstone. Wearing leather shoes and smart trousers, and hanging back by the bar, so that people would think I was from the record company. I wasn't the oldest one there. I think the others were possibly their parents. Kenickie were cool, and they were on the up. Unlike Fuzzy, they would one day make the charts and be on *Top of the Pops*.

Yet despite these statistics, my morale was deflated in 1996. It had started with Oasis losing to Blur in the heavyweight clash – yes, I know I should just let it go, but it was fucked up – and continued when the next Oasis number one was a long way from my preferred Oasis type of sound. There was also the fact that my very favourite acts, Lush and Echobelly for instance, were nowhere near the Top 10 while all this was going on. It had become something I was buying into with less enthusiasm.

But there was a natural process at work here. It was usually safe to assume that, in continuing to develop their sound, any act was trying to broaden their appeal. It's even safer to assume that their record company wanted this to happen. The life story of acts had always been a pattern of building steadily to a peak of commercial success and then, if they were fortunate, maintaining it.

Given our individual musical lovemaps, however, it follows that there will have come a point where this development crossed over with our particular taste before moving away again. This point could have been an act's first EP, their first chart entry, or that adored mega-hit that didn't quite make it to number one - it depends. This makes sense of my reaction to *Heaven or Las Vegas* by the Cocteau Twins, for example. My judging it a betrayal when so many others adored it, was only a reflection of where our respective cross-over points happened to be.

If this applies to the evolution of individual acts, it also applies to that of scenes. The drive to appeal to wider and wider audiences would dramatically alter the nature of indie bands in the 90s. Some had to adapt as the mid-decade explosion happened - jostled away from their narky underground roots towards those smoothly-planed forms necessary for mass approval, maybe losing their way in the process.

For those who had been transformed by indie's alternative universe at the start of the decade, there was now a growing sense of loss. Bands that made it after the explosion defaulted to being more agreeable and family-friendly than the bunch that had led the charge. That's not to say we went from Siouxsie Sioux to Doris Day overnight. But the general drift was real and discernible. The breadth of the audience meant that the new bands were not like the old bands.

Kula Shaker appeared at the beginning of this change. They were retro; Eastern-mystical; a fantasy of the alternative in the same way that the Mock Turtles had been, operating as a living museum without actually indulging in costumed re-enactment. The strange, distorted chant 'Tattva' reached number four in the summer, standing out but somehow also conforming; arguably joining Oasis in having a late-Beatles fixation. Those who had *(What's the Story) Morning Glory?* certainly dived headlong towards Kula Shaker. Copies of their CDs sat in BMW glove compartments and lay strewn across glass-topped coffee tables. If you looked along someone's CD stack and their album *K* wasn't there, you just assumed it had fallen under the sofa or something. With the fast-grooving 'Hey Dude' getting to number two in September, they became a fixture in the entertainment firmament, a few indie points for your cred rating.

And people wanted indie points, all sorts of people, not just the dissenters, party loons and trendies. It was what made the ambiguous 'You're Gorgeous' by Babybird such a big hit, a number three that spent a whopping six weeks in the Top 10. Same goes for the number four 'Good Enough' by Dodgy, a feelgood ditty with a jazz trumpet that wanted you to dance in a cocked trilby. Both were good records, but they lived in a different universe to 'Firestarter'.

The occasion that underscored this came in August, at the event which, for many, encapsulated the pre-eminence of Britpop in 1996. Over two nights, at Knebworth, an outdoor rock venue in Hertfordshire, Oasis tasted omnipotence in front of a quarter of a million people. The Prodigy provided support, as did Cast, the Charlatans, Manic Street Preachers, Kula Shaker and electronic dance act the Chemical Brothers. Ticket applications outstripped availability several times over. It was mad. Just look at that line-up. But Oasis at the top of it all and supreme.

So, in the final analysis, there was huge singles chart success for indie in 1996. Oasis, Ash and Suede had number one albums, too. Again, these figures come from my own definitions of what indie is and isn't, and this very fact, as has already been explained, renders the whole exercise full of holes. So, in one way, it means little. But in others it means plenty. It means a lot more, for instance, when you look at those acts who were number one more often in 1995-96, and whose singles did not plummet out of the charts after two or three weeks.

There was Celine Dion, a meticulously polished tune-belter with vocal affectations slightly more Jennifer Rush than Whitney Houston, whose break-up ballad 'Think Twice' was simply monstrous. And I'm only here referring to its stats. It was number one for seven weeks. It was in the Top 40 for twenty-five. Perhaps most incredibly, it had taken thirteen weeks to climb to number one.

Then there was Robson & Jerome, a pair of high-street-fitted uncles taken off some peak-time TV show or other, who were suddenly releasing records; standards like 'Unchained Melody' and well-worn covers like the Frankie Laine classic 'I Believe', as well as – get this – '(There'll Be Bluebirds Over) The White Cliffs of Dover'. They crammed these onto three singles which between them spent thirteen weeks at number one. They were their only three singles. They would one day put out a Best Of album without releasing any more.

There was also Simply Red, who, on their initial mid-80s appearance, had shown the potential to be a funky soul outfit but who ultimately chose instead to entertain Auntie without waking up Grandma. Their single 'Fairground' was number one for a month. There were others, less annoying. You may think that, in isolation, any of the above might be considered okay, even if you need a stiff drink first. But when 'Dark Therapy' by Echobelly could only get to twenty and Salad couldn't even get in the charts, the scale of their success made some of us concerned for the state of humanity.

But then of course there was Take That. They would have eight number ones in total. In 1995-6 they had the final three, starting with 'Back for Good', which, one had to admit, was a decent song, the first to raise them above the status of mere tit-flashers, although the celebration when 'Some Might Say' by Oasis removed it from the top was still especially raucous. The next one, 'Never Forget' was a return to normal; and the last one, put out following the tabloid-quake of losing their golden cheeky-boy Robbie Williams to the lure of solo stardom, was an uninspiring cover of the Bee Gees' 'How Deep Is Your Love'. They then split up, flooding column inches in even the most serious of newspapers. But by then there was Boyzone.

Boyzone were another male vocal group, a kind of Take That Jr. They were about to have their sixth consecutive hit, the least successful of which had reached number four. Half of these hits were cover versions. But this new release would be their first number one, an uninspiring cover of the Bee Gees' 'Words'. It is the most downbeat ballad you can imagine, but in the video, they managed to get gyrating girls involved. When they did it on *Top of the Pops*, all but the lead singer sat on stools until near the end, so that the most exciting moment in the whole thing was when they stood up.

Boyzone echoed Take That, twirling and swirling with their big dance moves and their white teeth and their smouldering; even though they made a point of keeping their clothes on. It was just so pointless. I tried to ignore it. But their very existence felt like an insult. Once again, the upper echelons of the chart were being effortlessly assailed by spinning, grinning, prancing pretty-boys without a song worth performing. Boyzone didn't have a 'Back for Good'. What they had was an air of entitlement, summed up by the utterly doubt-free smile of their leader, Ronan Keating, who would soon begin taking various presenter positions in TV and radio, spreading blandness like a virus.

Vocal groups had a chequered history. They had been a fixture of the rock 'n' roll era right up to the Beatles, continuing through soul and popping up in the odd teenybop situation since. But most other teenybop sensations had played instruments, or at least had the decency to appear on stage holding instruments.

Some hadn't. One act from 1982 had stuck in my mind. They were a girl group, except that they weren't really girls - they were women, with big early-80s hair for which they appeared too chronologically advanced; they looked like teachers doing a staff turn at the end of the school concert. They were called Toto Coelo and their song was a cod-exotic chant called 'I Eat Cannibals' which went Top 10, and they pranced embarrassingly on *Top of the Pops* in customised bin liners, making theatrical faces with big eyes and exaggerated body shapes fit for a detergent advert.

One day in the early summer of 1996, I was watching a music channel on cable, when on came a new video. There were five girls, moving through some lavishly-decorated venue or other, with theatrical faces and big eyes and exaggerated body shapes, performing a song that sounded like it had been composed by girl guides beside the camp-fire after one giant marshmallow too many. The verse was someone trying to say what she wanted, but never quite managing it: first she wanted to huh, huh, huh; then she wanted to zig-a-zig or some such bollocks. The chorus threw the words "lover" and "friends" into a bowl and mixed them with sentiment about things everlasting, spooned from a pink packet with a unicorn on it.

My first thought was: *Oh God, Toto Coelo gave birth.* My eyes and ears hurt; my toes were curling. I was mortified for them. How could they possibly think this was going to do anything but get laughed at? I remembered some of the mad, obscure videos from *The Max Headroom Show.* This was going to be one of those. Years from now, I thought, it will be dug up and paraded before an audience by a chortling host shifting excitedly in his seat clutching a bunch of cue cards, and the audience will roar and do impressions and appreciate the researchers' efforts.

Oh, how fucking wrong I was. The act was the Spice Girls. The song was 'Wannabe'. It was shown again and again and, despite my feeling that we should take to the streets over its gathering threat, it went in at number three and, by September, would have celebrated its seventh week at number one.

In a matter of days, the Spice Girls were everywhere. It was Spice this and Spice that; as many connotations of the word as could be found, fully endorsed and performed on the spot by members of the group in interviews, using theatrical faces and big eyes and exaggerated body shapes. They had names, actual names, which we were at liberty to learn if we wanted, but we didn't have to because they each had their own persona. There was Baby Spice with a dimpled smile, Scary Spice with frizzy hair, Posh Spice with a well-heeled hauteur, Sporty Spice in a tracksuit, and another one who looked like a 50s movie star – but because she had red hair, she was Ginger Spice.

This, in the main, is how they were known and how they were referred to; in every newspaper and every magazine and everywhere else. Like a collectable set. They weren't particularly good singers or great dancers; they didn't have grace or poise. They had energy and attitude, which, seemingly was all you now needed. You yourself could be like this if you'd been to drama club a few times. You too could form part of a collectable set.

I remembered when I was little, impatiently sorting through newly-opened box of my favourite breakfast cereal, looking for a Crater Critter. Crater Critters were little model aliens with their own characteristics. There was one given away with each packet. The box displayed a line-up of them, making you want to be an expert on the lot and own the set. This is what the Spice Girls made me think of. They were Crater Critters come to life; dinky moulded moppets to collect and cherish.

Which was almost certainly the point. This was family entertainment, something that everyone could join in with. And they did. Everyone. Whether they had children or not. People I worked with, too old to openly approve of Boyzone, voiced enthusiastic opinions, saying which their favourite one was and why they liked them, chuckling deliriously as they un-critically ran through their characteristics like someone playing a memory game, and usually getting the same kind of applause for it.

Plus, of course, the cry of "Girl power!", which, so the marketing messages went, were what the Spice Girls were all about. The revolutionary new idea of girl power. The game-changing notion that girls could do exciting stuff. Did people ever ask: "Girl power? But what about Elastica and Lush and Sleeper and all those others?" No. They did that knees-bent, fist-in-the-air thing and went "Yeeeaaah! Girl power!" Because of the Spice Girls.

It was an anaesthetic. You didn't have to deal with the real world if you were discussing the Spice Girls. It was like a horror movie where I was the only sane one. If I raised objections I was snapped at, or sneered at, or simply pitied. Just a bit of fun. That phrase again. It was now given such vindication as to be invincible. One of the guys I used to talk to about indie bands - who had been so indie as to like the Pixies, for fuck's sake - one day started telling me what he liked about Sporty Spice. The facial expression with which I responded to this made him simply glide along to someone else: seamlessly; and without the merest adjustment to his tranquil smile.

With all this, it was inevitable that there would be a follow up single and an album. The next single, 'Say You'll Be There', smooth, cosy and unremarkable, went straight in at number one in October. A month later, *Spice* went straight in at number one in the album chart. Another single, '2 Become 1', dreamy, lyrically-challenged and slightly less unremarkable than 'Say You'll Be There', went straight in at the top just in time to be the Christmas number one. There were Spice Girls calendars under the tree. And Spice Girls pencil cases. And Spice Girls lunch boxes and drinking bottles. There would soon be Spice Girls dolls. The moulded moppets had taken over and the country was content. And 'Sale of the Century' by Sleeper had only got to number ten.

These weeks were a come-down. Indie had been successful, spreading far beyond the status of underground; but its advance had now been halted, its next wave of converts swept away by vocal groups whose relentless marketing rendered the need for good music obsolete. Also, it was being adopted by people who annoyed me, and who were buying CDs by acts I hated, thinking they were being well indie, just because they played guitars and stood at the edge of the stage like they owned the place.

Suddenly, the fact that our company had moved to Camden, and that I was now swanning up and down those pavements in my suit, jangling the keys of my company car, was something that told a story about what had happened to indie. The alternative was no longer alternative. It was the Spice Girls in the role of the revolutionaries. Until the summer of 1996, "wannabe" had been a term of derision.

While 'Wannabe' was at number one, our company had an outdoor barbecue for staff, with bosses flipping burgers and the rest of us kicking back with beers. Among its attractions was a karaoke, run by two geezers with the sleeves of their chunky cardigans hoisted up to reveal tattoos, roll-ups hanging from the corners of their mouths and the remnants of what had once been quiffs flopping around above their foreheads. They had all the old 50s and 60s stuff lined up and ready to go, along with 'Wind Beneath My Wings' and, probably, 'Back for Good'. I did 'Pretty Flamingo' again. They took breaks during the proceedings, at the end of which they would warm us back up by doing a couple of numbers themselves. The second time, they did 'Firestarter'.

My spirit broke. This was only a few months old. It was an unassailable monument to alternative greatness, to youthful energy and nonconformity, to the right to party *our* way. It was untouchable. But now, here it was being touched. A pair of sixty-something Elvis fans had incorporated it into the same repertoire as 'Wind Beneath My Wings'. I watched the one performing, mic held to his lips, bouncing with knees bent, grinning, telling us he was the twisted firestarter. For him it was just a laugh. I thought: *Rock 'n' roll – it's all been for nothing.*

Within two months, a girl I knew at work would come all the way from the far end of the building to crouch down beside my desk and tell me that Chris Acland, the drummer with Lush, had committed suicide. The band split up. Six and a half years previously, Lush had altered my course in the space of one *Melody Maker* article, one EP and one gig. Now there was this. The autumn of 1996 felt as desolate as the spring of 1990 had been exhilarating.

I was thirty-three now. Everyone thought I was younger but I wasn't. *Thirty-three.* We were hurtling towards the end of the century. In the year 2000, I would be thirty-six. That fact had been popping into my head since childhood. My image of the year 2000 me hadn't altered since it was first conjured: tame, grey hair moulded to the contours of my head, a plain, beige coat and a pleasant smile. A figure getting gently on with the business of being older. That would be me in three years.

Traditionally, those outside the revered 16-24 age group no longer went to clubs or gigs. But they still liked music; old stuff, from their time. The acts that catered for them, either with new releases or with covers, were not meant for the charts – with the exception, that is, of the occasional Perry Como hit or something in the 'Chirpy Chirpy Cheep Cheep' vein. They made albums advertised on TV in the dead of night, ones boasting about not being available in the shops. Except that they would be in shops one day, destined as they were to languish in the racks of charity outlets. That was the extent of their visibility. Older people just sank into the background.

And listened to Radio 2. Terry Wogan did the breakfast show on Radio 2. Terry Wogan was insanely popular. His warm, reassuring presence was tinged with dry humour, a gentle appreciation of the double-entendre and the slight whiff of mischief. As a mainstream music radio presenter, he was almost perfect. He had been doing the show for ages and, since the late 70s, had additionally established himself as a context-variable TV host. Friends of mine had listened to him way back in the new wave era, perhaps finding more common ground than with Dave Lee Travis or Mike Read on Radio 1.

Early-morning Radio 2 was a mixture of inoffensive old hits, family-friendly new hits and an assortment of curiosities, all taking average-listener blood pressure into account by being flatly unprovocative. It was the personality of the DJ you tuned in for and this was low-hanging fruit for piss-takers. Wogan had his own *Spitting Image* puppet. The greatest fear for the Smashie and Nicey TV characters was being hived off to "Radio Quiet".

As a child on camping holidays, I had often woken up long before the adults stirred, with only the transistor radio and a single earpiece for company. Radio 1 didn't start until 8.30. Radio 2 had an early Sunday show where listeners requested tunes which were then played on a Hammond organ – hymns, classical ditties and 'Oh, I Do Like to Be Beside the Seaside.' When it was too early for *Junior Choice*, this was all there was. It had informed my perceptions of Radio 2 ever since. With the exception of the odd Terry Wogan fit of giggles, why would you ever bother? If Radio 1 was too annoying, just play a compilation tape or something.

So I wasn't going to switch to Radio 2. I still wanted new stuff. I had this vision of myself as some kind of cross between John Peel and Gandalf: a warrior out amongst all this human normality, steeped in pop as an art form and having the experience and insight to know what was good and what wasn't, while holding lazy snobbery to account.

I would be an outsider who *really* got it, unlike these part-timers who strapped on bits of pop as decoration, who thought Ocean Colour Scene were indie, who pointed at the sky and went *wohh-wohh!* I would be an authority. A Wise One. People would come to me for advice, and I'd reverentially trot out a Sleeper lyric like I was quoting Keats. I could see ways of making this Wise One role work.

Little did I know, however, that in doing so, I wouldn't necessarily be standing out from the crowd. In fact, it's more accurate to say that I would be a mere speck in a swollen, swirling demographic.

Nine

Jonathan Ross was and is a class act. His twinkling enthusiasm and slight speech impediment defined his early television appearances and to these he soon added the debonair manner that would become his longer-term signature. He was fashionable. He was funny. He didn't take himself too seriously. By the end of the 90s, he was fully-established on TV and radio, an anchor on chat shows and a compère at awards ceremonies, upholding the requisite conventions of these roles while adding his own touches; connecting with the mighty and the modest, loved by young and old.

In 1999, he was handed the prestigious mid-morning Saturday slot on Radio 2. His previous wins had been all very impressive, but in the world of entertainment this appointment really meant something. I liked him. I had met him once. I found myself tuning in to cheer him on. He declared his love for David Bowie, which, as an expression of his colourful flamboyance, seemed as alternative as things were going to get in this context.

But one hot summer's morning – I remember exactly where I was (in a parked car at the coast) and what I was doing (waiting for mates who were failing to get their shit together) – I tuned in for the start of the show and he opened with 'Pretty Vacant' by the Sex Pistols.

Blimey. That unnerving lead riff of rusting, jagged iron, that primal blare of rhythm guitar and drums, that snarling vocal; the safety pins through the flesh, the outrage, the filth and fury, the blood and the hate – he was really, actually playing it, here, in arguably the most important slot of the schedule. At a time when the sound of pop was being smoothed-off and calmed, it flew from the speakers to shock and de-stabilise, opening the primetime Saturday morning show on Radio 2 – *Radio 2* – while Grandpa was making the sandwiches and Mum was folding the washing.

Radio 2 wasn't like this. If it wanted to start a big show with a bang, it would use something from a nice act with a bigger beat than usual. 'Dancing Queen' by Abba would be close to over-doing it. But 'Pretty Vacant' was playing. Jonathan Ross was giving us pure dissent and raw rebellion in a world busily banishing such things to the margins. He was momentarily some kind of god.

The Sex Pistols had re-formed in 1996. Re-forming was still taboo then. Groups split up because they could no longer stand each other, or had grown apart musically, or had simply run out of steam. They had only one reason to get back together: money. The Sex Pistols called their caper the *Filthy Lucre Tour*, something which, along with their confrontational, foul-mouthed stage-craft, at least afforded them some dignity. They went away afterwards and we didn't begrudge them a payday. They would have further reunions, becoming increasingly cuddly each time.

But the material needs of ageing men were one thing. This sudden popping-up of their original music was quite another, especially on *that* playlist. I had tuned in dutifully, as a guest-listener; hoping for, at best, a bit of warmth, a modicum of amusement, perhaps a touch of seaside-postcard titillation. Instead, here I was, feeling energised, joyful, triumphant; here I was, a sworn enemy of the dull and the mediocre, listening to Radio 2 and being thoroughly catered for.

Over the next ten years, post-youth pop fans would begin to find themselves being catered for handsomely. They would have an abundance of facilities thrown at them: magazines, cable TV channels, radio stations; and festivals - loads and loads of festivals; not to mention what would happen when the internet got properly up and running. Providing for this demographic would segment music entertainment to the point of constriction. Every niche would become its own little universe, each with its own sensibility, each with its own mythology. Each would contain acts formed specifically to serve it, to be played on its radio stations and perform at its festivals.

And, whatever your age, if you wanted nostalgia, you would get it. Reforming would quickly lose its stigma: chart acts from your day would get back together, make themselves stage-fit and do their stuff like they were young and cute. Their sound would be better than ever and closer to that of their records; which it would have to be, since satisfying live audiences would soon be their only way of making money.

This chapter is the story of the journey from the mainstream's taming and assimilation of indie to that Sex Pistols Saturday. The time between would be largely prone to disappointment, discomfort and disgust.

I was already hacked off at the end of 1996. The charts were ruled by the Spice Girls and Boyzone, rather than by the likes of Echobelly and Veruca Salt. Oasis were mega, but their most popular songs were all slippers and cocoa: 'Wonderwall' and 'Don't Look Back in Anger', rather than 'Supersonic' and 'Some Might Say'. I sighingly accepted, as 1997 got underway, that this was how things were going to be.

Yet I remained as involved as ever. That year I would buy chart singles featuring electronic pop, glossy pop, US R&B, British R&B, European dance, British dance, hip hop, country rock, bouncy British rock, things that I would call indie, things that other people would call indie in the teeth of my ire, male vocal groups, female vocal groups and various oddities that defied description. I drew the line at Boyzone.

I still poured over CD packaging: the click-opens, the fold-shuts, those that were nice to run your fingers across, those you worried might stain from a grubby smudge, those that seemed to fray at the spine through mere use - those which, in the end, had to go into protective plastic wallets for the sake of longevity. As ever, I wallowed in the variety of designs on the covers and on the discs. As ever, I strained my eyes trying to read the credits.

There were other things about CD singles. For example, there was CD1 and CD2. You got CD1, with the main song and a couple of bonus tracks, but then you were invited to also buy CD2, with the main track again, but perhaps in the form of an extended album version, along with different bonus tracks, perhaps old hits played live; or, more alluringly if you were devoted to the act, different new songs not on any previous release.

Different new songs were cool; I had always loved getting something fresh on a B-side. Indie bands were good at having different new songs. Most other genres just slapped on live versions, or successions of remixes under ever more contrived names - I've just made up 'Clean Out the Guinea Pigs Mix' and 'Sciatica Limp Mix' but I can't be completely certain that these weren't used somewhere in the 90s.

CD1 came with the primary packaging, perhaps with its teeth-tray on a hinge, opening to reveal another tray on which you were invited to store CD2, which had perhaps come in a simple cardboard wallet which you were presumably expected to trash. No doubt the sale of each one counted for chart purposes.

And there were freebies. You might get stickers. You might get sets of cards, with photos of the act on one side and excerpts from lyrics on the reverse. Occasionally you got a poster, one from which you could never quite expunge the folds; some were comically small, but they were free. Perhaps CD1 had colourful cards and CD2 had a poster. It might set you back five or six quid for both. I bought both only a handful of times. CD singles generally cost between £1.99 and £3.99. Prices changed during a chart run: they were cheapest on release, so that you would buy them in the first week and make them a high new entry.

The other thing that CD singles usually provided was a postcard, pre-paid and addressed, often to somewhere in Leamington Spa. You were invited to fill these out with your details and send them off. Some were merchandise promotions, but often they were just questionnaires, your incentive being to get more information on the artist, or other artists on the same label, by return of post. They wanted to know which age bracket you fit into, plus other things like the music magazines you preferred and where you first heard the tune you had just forked out for.

Sometimes these cards were circular and you discovered them beneath the disc as you lifted it away. Some folded out with the inlay, to be torn off at the perforations. But most were rectangles sitting loose inside the casing. They weren't all pre-paid; some had the temerity to say "affix stamp here". 1997 was still too early for email addresses and mobile numbers, not to mention data protection. These things went off in Her Majesty's mail as an unconcealed display of your name, address, age and, depending on the artist, some significant clues as to your vulnerability. I've kept my annoying cards. And my comical posters.

In terms of how I got to hear new releases or made decisions on what to buy, nothing had changed much since I had bought my first CDs. The breathless chippering that Radio 1 was steadily defaulting to meant I could listen to it only in short bursts, but I still had time for *The Evening Session* and the Sunday teatime Top 40 rundown. There were some artists whose singles I bought automatically and unquestioningly, at least until they did two shit ones on the trot. I still bought some purely on the strength of press reviews.

But mostly, I got new music from *The Chart Show* on Saturday morning ITV, the same programme on which I had first seen and heard bands like Ride all those years ago. *The Chart Show* had one year left to run in its uniquely useful format. It would be replaced by *CD:UK*, launched as a rival to the live studio set-up that was proving so popular with the Saturday morning hoards on BBC 1.

This was another small sign that things were slipping away from me a little. My feelings and perspectives were changing. The cynicism that comes with deep experience was beginning to tell. *Oh, that's just like so-and-so; I heard that idea when I was still squeezing my bloody spots.* Never mind the fact that, to any fourteen-year-old (for whom, lest we forget, these things were intended), the sound in question was shiny-new and possibly marked the first day of the rest of their lives. Never mind that.

It was bothersome. I was having to go down avenues that didn't interest me. My peer group, meanwhile, had various new priorities. I myself now had a proper regular girlfriend and, with a little support, was being more mature more often. It was getting harder to be a pop picker in the classic mould. And for now, that mould was all I knew.

A good job, then, that mainstream pop was at that point in reasonable nick. The number ones included the sample-based novelty of 'Your Woman' by White Town, sounding like R2D2 being punted down the Cam sipping Pimms; the electronic emanations of 'You're Not Alone' by Olive, whose restless shuffle took a few attempts to get to grips with if you wanted to dance to it; and the exquisite Californian swoosh of 'Don't Speak' by No Doubt, possibly the best chart-topper of the year.

Other high points that year included the jazzy electronic intimacy of 'Remember Me' by Blue Boy, a number eight; and the edgy groove of 'Naked Eye' by Luscious Jackson, an under-achiever at twenty-five. Republica did a bit better with their ear-battering singalong 'Ready to Go', which made a big impression but reached a puzzlingly low thirteen. Higher, at eight: 'A Change Would Do You Good' by Sheryl Crow, who for three years had been successfully peddling various homages to less-than-virtuous adulthood; the spaced-out stomp of this one perhaps making it her best of all.

Sheryl was the enigmatic party girl across the street. But Natalie Imbruglia was the girl next door doing her homework in a snuggly cardigan. She was first seen on Aussie soap *Neighbours*. Then, suddenly, she released a single called 'Torn', which, in its own uniquely modest way, became impossible not to love - you just closed your eyes and let it carry you away on its undulating bed of sparkles. Anyone who genuinely didn't like 'Torn' was floated in a tank with electrodes connected to their nerve clusters while scientists made observations. It was massive. It is one of the top 100 best-selling UK singles of all time. It was in the Top 40 for sixteen weeks. But it didn't get to number one. It was held for three weeks at number two.

The villain of this tale is 'Barbie Girl' by Aqua, a first-person personification of the toy whose ultimate effect it to make girls hate themselves. Both the record and the band were dumb, plastic and tongue-in-cheek, which gave us the excuse to relax. We perhaps relaxed too much. Everybody remembers where they were and what they were doing when they first caught themselves humming it. A moment of shock. It made you want to delete your humming history. The next two Aqua singles would likewise go to number one.

There was also great indie music; except that I wasn't calling it indie anymore, but let's not go there again. It's indie. 1997 had a particularly fine crop. The most interesting and impactful of them included 'Nancy Boy' by Placebo, a blast of gay defiance which reached number four; 'Love is the Law' by the Seahorses, featuring former Stone Roses guitarist John Squire, which reached three and spent a creditable seven weeks in the Top 40; 'Step into My World' by Hurricane #1, featuring former Ride guitarist Andy Bell, which peaked at number twenty-nine, doing no justice whatsoever to its wonders; 'Monkey Wrench', a number nineteen from Foo Fighters, who I had been persuaded to get into and boy was I now into them; 'All You Good Good People', a number eight from Embrace, whose big-sky megasounds would adorn the soundtrack for years to come; and 'Monday Morning 5:19' by Rialto, which only got to thirty-seven despite extensive airplay, but which came from one of the best albums of the decade. All of these are worth investigating and may lead you towards follow-up singles and album tracks that will fold your shirts and massage your feet.

The remarkable thing about this clutch was that, given the best guitar music of the middle of the decade, they all had male vocals. But there was little else to link them. Great records through they were, they weren't knitted together into any kind of scene. Indie had no momentum; it simply was. It had peaked. It had failed to conquer. That's how I felt about it. But that now seems odd, because 1997 was the absolute zenith of "Cool Britannia".

Britpop was in excellent health. What had begun as a defence of "repetitive beats" had turned into a celebration of any kind of beat. If you had a guitar and were on the radio, you were part of the movement. Those gladdened by the sight of anything with the union jack on it were joined by those whose palate was being refreshed by the uses the flag was now being put to. In the lead-up to the 1997 general election, the leader of the opposition - younger, un-tarnished, scornful of those government incumbents and their Victorian values - was making much of having played guitar in a band as a youth. He was part of the movement, too. Britain danced. Britain rocked. Britain was top of its charts.

In March, fashion magazine *Vanity Fair* published a "Cool Britannia" edition, with Liam Gallagher and his celebrity girlfriend lying on union jack bedclothes on the cover. The pages behind it featured young British artists, writers and publishers, all of whom were top of the world. Its headline was 'London swings again!' Echoes of the 60s were all too clear and present. The union jack was once again fashionable.

Britain's sense of love, its modern art and its gorgeous rock 'n' roll were sweeping the board.

In May, this young, untarnished leader of the opposition, Tony Blair, swept the board at the general election. Soon afterwards he held a reception at 10 Downing Street for the UK's artistic elite, inviting headline actors, leading writers, top comedians and others to share their magic with his new administration. Creation label boss Alan McGee was there, along with one of his leading lights, Noel Gallagher of Oasis. The best-remembered image from the occasion was Noel holding a glass of bubbly and sharing a laugh with Tony. Two top boys together. Rock 'n' roll in the heart of the establishment. Cool Britannia indeed.

It's easy to conclude that indie had properly won. In thirteen of the fifty-two weeks of 1997, the number one position in the album chart was held by the Spice Girls. But for way over half of the reminder, it was either Oasis, the Charlatans, the Verve, Reef, Mansun, Ocean Colour Scene, Radiohead or Blur. For another six on top of these, it was *The Fat of the Land* by the Prodigy. Radiohead, with their sophisticated, heavy, despairing fragility, were considered to be some kind of pinnacle of western culture. But it was precisely that kind of dourness than most characterised the peak of Cool Britannia. The dissenters, party loons and trendies were no longer in the foreground.

Oasis were making downbeat pseudo-epics whose groove and sparkle were heavily supressed. The Verve had the dull fug anthem to end all dull fug anthems in 'Bitter Sweet Symphony', a record presented as a high point before which we all had to bow and scrape. I entered into the spirit, buying CD1 and CD2 and playing them a few times before admitting that this endlessly repeating sample with bits of droning vocal attached was actually boring the shit out of me. Other things on their *Urban Hymns* album, particularly the number one single 'The Drugs Don't Work' and its follow-up 'Lucky Man', were good; but it all took itself far too seriously. Symphony. Hymns.

On the last day of August, Princess Diana was killed in a Parisian underpass. The nation plunged into abject mourning. Tony Blair had a new platform from which to exude statesmanship and connect with the people. Elton John re-wrote 'Candle in the Wind' in tribute to the people's princess and it was number one for five weeks, becoming the top-selling single of all time in the UK. This, following the six-week stay at the top for 'I'll Be Missing You' by Puff Daddy and Faith Evans featuring 112, a record made in response to the killing of rap hero Biggie Smalls - a token of how drug-riddled and violent black US neighbourhoods remained.

It was non-stop pallbearing. Will Smith had the more up-tempo 'Men in Black' at number one for four weeks between these two, but check that title out. Everyone was at a funeral. The new sounds of Oasis and the Verve blended in seamlessly, wiping away the people's tears with a bar towel. Having a copy of *Urban Hymns* was a sign that you understood and belonged. Its sales gathered pace throughout the autumn. People had once fitted in by having a trio of ceramic ducks flying across their wall, or a print of a big-eyed Spanish kid above the fireplace; now they had a CD of *Urban Hymns*.

The odd bit of Spice Girls merchandise would have helped, too. Perhaps *Urban Hymns* was propped up against a Spice Girls candelabra atop a Spice Girls doily. Possibly not. But you talk about Cool Britannia in 1997 – Ginger Spice had led the charge in February by wearing a sparkly union jack outfit at the televised Brit Awards. They had their collective fingers even in that topical pie.

The Spectator, a right-leaning cultural and political weekly, had already interviewed them on the grounds that, it was asserted, they were too important not to have their political views sought. The interview gave them the opportunity to, among other things, parade their Eurosceptic credentials and declare their love for Margaret Thatcher as the "first Spice Girl". Mainly just showbiz, of course; provocative tittle-tattle to go with the wide eyes and exaggerated body shapes and keep the cameras pointing the right way. But it was in *The Spectator*.

If you were the kind who turned their back on anything that was just a bit of fun, who didn't like moulded moppet pop performers, gratuitous merchandising or Margaret Thatcher, the Spice Girls were the epitome of wrongness. And hard to escape. Everywhere you looked they were pissing you off. That autumn, they met Nelson Mandela, the global embodiment of the struggle against oppression, and he would declare the encounter to have been one of the high points of his life.

Nelson Mandela. It was almost unbearable. Then, they did the most despicable thing of all. They released a single I liked.

The very title 'Spice Up Your Life' made you want to hate it. It was Latin. Actually, it was cod-Latin and it made no bones about it. But it rattled along with frenetic intensity, its every nut and bolt straining in the cause of rhythm, like Gloria Estefan on eight pints of rocket fuel. The lyrics were as useless as ever, but they were simply brushed aside by this welter of noise - any longer than three minutes and it might have hurt someone. I couldn't believe I was enjoying a Spice Girls record so much. It was number one for a week, removed by 'Barbie Girl'.

Maybe they had pulled their socks up a bit because they now had rivals. At the end of the summer there appeared All Saints, a four-girl singing combo who were moodier, more smouldering, more urban - wide eyes and exaggerated body shapes just weren't their thing. Indeed, they were billed as a street-wise Spice Girls, but probably only because, for now at least, you could only talk about female vocal groups in the context of the Spice Girls. So far, they had only 'I Know Where It's At' to their credit, a cool-groove number four, but they were destined for great heights, and liking All Saints would always be okay. Their first chart-topper, the lament 'Never Ever', reached number one in the first weeks of 1998, its urban tinge providing a bridge to a year whose flavour was more urban all round. Because R&B was beginning a process of dramatic reconfiguration.

Missy 'Misdemeanor' Elliott was a name exciting to those music papers that liked their hip hop far more than they liked their soul. But she wasn't really hip hop, she was *urban*. Her first Top 20 hit, 'The Rain (Supa Dupa Fly)', incorporated an oldie I liked and this put me off it a bit; but her second, 'Beep Me 911', I loved. I found myself buying the *Supa Dupa Fly* album and there was something about it; plenty of recognisable 90s R&B reference-points but with harmonies and melody lines that raised it above the norm. It was ruthlessly de-cluttered, so that any new element had a big effect. Tinny guitar loops, horn riffs and restless hi-hat tinkles all took turns in breaking up the smooth drift.

Collaborators on the album included Busta Rhymes, a relative newcomer, a rapper with his own distinctive rasp who, by the time I bought *Supa Dupa Fly*, had registered two extraordinary hit singles including the number two 'Turn It Up / Fire It Up'. Missy's producer, Tim Mosley, was known simply as Timbaland, a name uttered in a snaking haze of reverence. The pair promoted a series of protégés, the most recent one being Nicole, on whose number twenty-two hit 'Make It Hot' Missy had appeared. But Timbaland had another young performer to push. Because he now provided the guiding hand for Aaliyah.

I had bought her 1996 album *One in a Million* because it was a new album by Aaliyah. It had a sparse, hard-boned atmosphere, but was otherwise the kind of R&B album I was used to: there was a good single - 'If Your Girl Only Knew' - but the mind kind of drifted after that. I didn't register the production credits; probably didn't have time to read the whole list - it was longer than the first piss on a big night out. But Missy and Timbaland featured prominently.

They were now featuring all over the place. The pair were synonymous with each other and collaborated on project after project. Generally speaking, Missy was an artist who also wrote and produced, whereas Timbaland was a producer who also performed. 'If Your Girl Only Knew' was his work. It would come to be seen as his breakthrough.

By the middle of 1998, he was taking the opportunity that this represented supa dupa seriously. He produced an Aaliyah single called 'Are You That Somebody?', the sound on which was simply incredible. Its arrangement was stripped right down to the barest of bones, its rhythms playful, sounding like cartoon characters sneaking between hiding-places on tiptoe. The vocal melody followed these rhythms precisely, the only contrast being Timbaland's not-altogether-necessary backing vocal, the odd hi-hat tinkle and the intermittent sample of a chortling baby. Here and there, the beat, sometimes the whole backline, was suspended, for just a moment, before kicking back in. This would come to be called "stop-start", and branded a Timbaland trademark.

On the day I bought it, I marched onto our open-plan office floor and, standing before my sales team with the single held aloft in its pearl case, launched into a breathless, passionate speech about it being the most important and innovative thing to happen to pop music in years. They smiled and nodded, muttering polite receipts, while others sitting within earshot silently waited for me to calm down or go away. I'm sorry, but it just burst out of me; I couldn't stop it. Soon enough, I was blushing over the incident. But not because I had been wrong about the record.

New sounds are often labelled revolutionary if all they do is spawn a tiny sub-genre. But this was a convincing vision of the future projected before an entire culture. Half a decade before, R&B had been in the grip of Boys II Men and Jodeci and all that Whitney Houston / Mariah Carey noodling. Suddenly, these things looked unequivocally antiquated. 'Are You That Somebody?' only got to number eleven. But that didn't matter. R&B was un-tethering itself.

Hip hop was more interesting in 1998, too. There were characterful, discrete pleasures like 'Zoom' by Dr Dre and LL Cool J, a laid-back shuffle that got to number fifteen. Busta Rhymes appeared in the line-up of the Flipmode Sqaud for the frivolous 'Cha Cha Cha' which I played a lot but got nowhere. One of the year's big number ones was 'It's Like That', an early Run-D.M.C. track re-framed by producer Jason Nevins, which came out of the blue to top the UK charts for six weeks. Its sound was as bleak and hard as its lyrics. The video depicted gangs of youngsters out-bad-assing each other with their scowls and their moves in a multi-storey car park. It was something different for a number one.

Indeed, the 1998 number ones made an interesting, if not always sparkling, list. Oasis reached top spot for the fourth time with 'All Around the World', another mid-paced trudge that went on for an unforgivable 9:38 of gratuitous section addition, drawn-out *lalala* passages and repeated modulation, a strategy which has always been a refuge of the slightly desperate. Its lyric made a bad start ("It's a bit early in the midnight hour for me") and amongst the rest of its tiresome plod, the phrase most often repeated was "it's gonna be okay", which, as the key rose further and the vocal became increasingly strained, made it seem as if Liam was trying to convince himself.

The Spice Girls had two more, both of which had laughable lyrics but sounded gorgeous: 'Viva Forever' in the summer and 'Goodbye' at Christmas, the latter presenting them as a four-piece, now that Ginger had become important enough to go solo. It was ironic that, with such moulded moppet considerations having nothing whatever to do with the quality of the records, the drama (for drama it was, believe me) should be played out against a backdrop of such delicious Spice Girls sounds - these releases were a treat for the ears.

Further irony lay in the fact that All Saints had annoyingly followed 'Never Ever' with a single consisting of twinned covers, which we insisted on calling a "double A-side" even though it was on CD. The pairing of Red Hot Chili Peppers' 'Under the Bridge' and Labelle's sassy 'Lady Marmalade' seemed like cold calculation, whizzing blue-collar poetry and overt sexiness into a cred-smoothie; but it worked and was number one for two weeks.

Their other 1998 chart-topper, 'Bootie Call', was much better; a piece of wonderfully-crafted nonsense that came with a set of postcards tucked into the casing, each one with an All Saint giving you a smouldering look that was yours to keep. For young men in 1998, All Saints were the epitome of feminine allure. I, of course, being older, was above this. I noticed marketing effort being put into the smouldering looks; I saw comedy in trousers that were hanging off the hip in the name of fashion; I recognised seaside postcard elements in the idea of a bootie call, which I assumed was a telephoned invitation to visit with your overnight bag. It was just frivolity and I was fine with that. So were the *NME*, who made its release a cover story.

I was fine with plenty of other things about 1998, among them a convincing comeback by Madonna, who roared back with the album *Ray of Light*, exhibiting a mature energy that completely re-galvanised longstanding fans. 'Frozen' was her first number one single in eight years; its wind-blown exotica coming courtesy of producer William Orbit. The next few years would be the William Orbit era - his swirling, gravity-free sounds with their outer-space whooshes and bleeps would characterise an impressive chunk of its best pop. *Ray of Light* produced five Top 10 hits, including 'Frozen', and also the title track, which got to number two. There was a confidence and purpose not heard in Madonna for a very long time. Madonnadom was fully re-established.

From the many others we could examine in 1998, let's pick Garbage and Hole. Garbage, because they were now the epitome of pristine modern pop. Their second album, *Version 2.0*, was full of mini-classics, peppered with scraps of melody and lyric that you were certain you must have heard somewhere before, and in some cases actually had: they even pinched classic song titles, one of its highlights being called 'Push It'. This and 'I Think I'm Paranoid' were obvious choices for singles. Both got to number nine. But *Version 2.0* was a number one album and for a while became as essential a piece of lounge accessory as a lamp.

Hole, because they released a single called 'Celebrity Skin', with lyrics made from rusted razors and noise-settings capable of flattening buildings. Somehow it got no higher than nineteen. In a world of space-like whooshes and bleeps, pared-back R&B and electronic sounds whose depths were unfathomable, here was a demonstration of how possible it still was to lose your mind and body in the primal detonations of rock 'n' roll. Why had nobody thought of that guitar riff before? How come no one had ever thought of making such sleaze so celebratory? Anyone with longstanding growly guitar sympathies was blown away. I wanted to buy a piece of land and build a temple to worship it in.

So there was plenty to be fine about. Yet it all risked being overshadowed. Despite many big positives, there were things that increasingly bothered me. I mean, *really* bothered me. To be precise, three things. The first was the matter of performance patterns in the singles chart.

Let me explain. Whether or not you had ever liked it, the UK's number one was something you saw as a big deal. You looked up to it. Even if you hated it, you had some sullen, glowering reverence for its status. Many number ones had shot up the charts, reaching the top spot in a few short weeks; but others had taken their time getting there, their appeal steadily gathering until the moment when they were finally out-selling everything else. Records had to battle, whatever position they were destined to reach, struggling and heaving to get to that number by which history would classify them. It was all part of the noble rhythms of the chart; the heroics of pop.

In April 1969, 'Get Back' by the Beatles had gone straight in at number one. No other record did this until 1973, when four records did, three of them by Slade (the other by a certain glam superstar who fell from grace dramatically in the late 90s). The next straight-in wasn't until March 1980: 'Going Underground'/'Dreams of Children' by the Jam. With some acts, there was such a build-up of excitement about new releases that extraordinary things occasionally happened. But in almost every case, even with teen idols on the scale of Donny Osmond or the Bay City Rollers, a new single would take two or three weeks to get to the top. A straight-in was extraordinary. Between March 1980 and June 1987 when I graduated, there were another eight. Just eight.

Within a decade, it was very different. Of the seventeen singles that went to number one in 1995, eleven were straight-ins. In 1996, twenty out of twenty-four went straight in. By 1999, it was thirty-three of the thirty-six. Twenty-one of those 1999 chart-toppers were number one for one week only. The marketing and publicity people had done their job of bagging the number one slot and that was all they were bothered about.

Once upon a time, you could hear a first-play on the radio at breakfast and be down at the shops buying it by lunchtime. Not anymore. Nowadays, a record was on the radio weeks before its arrival in the stores, preparing its audience like so many coiled springs. Adverts gave prominence to its release date; DJs told listeners how many days there were to go before they could buy it.

The result was that almost every record now went in at its highest position and then slid down the chart with as much dignity as it could muster. There were exceptions: 'Think Twice' by Celine Dion, as already mentioned, took thirteen weeks to get to the top and 'Never Ever' by All Saints took nine; but they were a tiny percentage. The rhythms of the Top 40 had changed; they were now tightly controlled by people who neither made the records nor - we couldn't help but imagine - enjoyed them.

It felt cheap. It felt as if all the mystery and intrigue had been removed. The tension-build on the chart countdown was phoney: you almost always knew who would be number one that week. Presenters' uncertainty was all but scripted. The whole thing was a sham. In 2000, thirty-nine of the forty-one number ones went straight in; only seven of them were number one for more than a week. *Forty-one number ones.* I imagined pop quizzes in years to come – how the hell was I going to remember them all? You have to think about things like this.

The second thing that bothered me was dance music. In the world of pop, "dance music" was now a discrete phrase with new, chiselled meaning. Almost every type of music since the dawn of time had got people dancing, either with a partner, or in formation, or sometimes individually. In the years following rock 'n' roll, jazz fans and mods made individual dancing the norm, and this quickly evolved into the free expression and delirium of the psychedelic era which, in its own way, echoed the abandon of evangelical church congregations. Skinheads had their own dance styles. So did soul fans. So did punks. You could, clearly, dance to anything.

By the 90s, however, we had come to understand "dance music" as electronic sounds with those mythologised repetitive beats. Radio presenters were using the phrase to describe a more distinct, removed world. *Tonight: dance.* And if you said you were into dance, you were declaring yourself modern. You could still dance to music from the 70s/80s soul tradition, but a hit soul song would now be given a "dance mix", perhaps a few beats per-minute faster, almost certainly with a house rhythm slid underneath.

When olden-days disco was reborn as house, its "four-to-the-floor" beats pattern was standardised. They had become house beats. Now, in the late-90s, they were simply called dance beats, the implication being that these were the only beats you were now entitled to dance to.

The classic disco drum and hi-hat line had gone *dom-tiss, dat-tiss, dom-tiss, dat-tiss.* Now, the *dat* had largely been removed. By 1999, your common-or-garden dance hit was going *doom-tiss doom-tiss doom-tiss doom-tiss* (occasionally *docca-tiss ducca-tiss docca-tiss ducca-tiss),* often with additional off-beats scattered across the top, but sometimes not. It was a bedrock for almost anything electronically-generated or sampled, like a pizza base to which you could add whatever toppings suited your palate. But however it was flavoured, it was called, resoundingly, "dance".

These records could be bland to the point of corroding your living spirit. In the summer of 1999 came 'Better Off Alone' by DJ Jurgen presents Alice Deejay, on Positiva, a dance specialist label, whose distinctive blue, white and black symmetry had become part of the landscape. Here, 'Better Off Alone' had a comfortable home - its formula was *doom-tiss doom-tiss,* plus a painfully plain electronic riff, plus a characterless vocal repeating the title.

It got to number two, spending three weeks there, with a total of thirteen in the Top 40. *And it had climbed*, entering the chart in its first week at four. It was a big, big hit and a flagship for what dance music had become. To cement its club credentials, this - as did any other dance record worth its salt - opened and ended with long, winding stretches of *doom-tiss doom-tiss* so that the next record could be seamlessly blended into the mix. This of course did not apply when hearing it on the radio or playing your CD single. Which is how most of us heard it most of the time.

But it wasn't all like this. Recent dance tracks had often been charismatic, characterful and exuberant. A common feature of these records was a gradual climb towards a chorus where the main rhythms, riffs and vocal refrains could all come together, sweeping you along on a wave of euphoria, two or three times in the course of the song. It became a recognised template. The last chorus was habitually extended into a grand finale and it was held back, tantalisingly, the beat suspended in long, climbing percussive patterns, building and building, beyond the point where you thought it must surely give, then past another point where you thought the same thing, before finally breaking in an explosion of energy and joy.

The king of this kind of record was Fatboy Slim, the stage name for a DJ who had once been Norman Cook of the Housemartins. He took niche tunes and re-fashioned them into some of the best-remembered dance records of the late 90s, including 'Renegade Master 98' by Wildchild (Fatboy Slim Old Skool Edit), 'I See You Baby' by Groove Armada (Fatboy Slim Remix) and 'Brimful of Asha' by Cornershop (Norman Cook Remix Single Version)', which went to number one. For one week, obviously.

To add to which, he had hits in his own right. Big hits. Epoch-defining hits. 'The Rockerfella Skank' was almost, all by itself, the sound of the airwaves in 1998, with its power-driving vocal sample "Right about now, the funk soul brother" and its tempo changes which controlled the listener as firmly as any held-back final chorus. Later he had 'Praise You', a low-temperature, modern-fitted, surface-wipeable dance single; an almost perfect pop record for the beginning of 1999. And it went to number one. For one week, obviously. Fatboy Slim was a superstar. A superstar DJ.

Superstar DJs were as important as recording artists. DJs made records. Artists wanted increasingly to DJ. Dance was where it was at. By 1999, there was a dance stage at the Reading Festival. By Reading 2001, DJs would have their own tent to do their sets in, while dance acts who still wanted to sing and dance in the old way pranced and bounced on bigger stages elsewhere, so that punters might wander around the site and not see a guitar for hours.

I, meanwhile, wanted to dance to Hurricane #1 as much as to any Fatboy Slim Remix. So why was that word being applied in such a narrow way? Why did a soul hit have to be given a dance remix in order to be taken seriously in a club? Was the latest soul hit, or groovy indie-type record, not rhythmic or galvanising enough? This whole dance thing was winding me up good and proper.

There was, however, also an aspirational aspect to it. Top clubs were exclusive haunts. Each major city in the UK had its top-dog dance venue, like The Ministry of Sound in London or Cream in Liverpool, both of which quickly evolved into brands, with sweat-tops and baseball caps bearing their logos available at premium prices and CDs of its star-turn mixes being stacked up in the shops.

And there was Ibiza, a Spanish island that had come to be seen as an epicentre of hedonism and escape, and to which brand-conscious dance-sceners now headed in droves. The names of its venues, Amnesia, Space and Privilege among them, were soon known to the general public. Ibiza became something people felt they had to do at least once; an expected pilgrimage for with-it youth. That is, those among the with-it youth who had the money.

A more affordable dance music scene was the gym. Going to the gym was now essential for anyone who took their status and self-esteem seriously. Increasingly, TV sets fixed above the exercise bikes and running machines pumped out videos from cable channels. At the peak of my own mid-90s gym-going, these had been mainly MTV, VH1 and The Box, with playlists that were relatively general. By the end of the decade, it was much more streamlined, with long stretches of music at precisely the right tempo for cruising to at optimum burn while your mind was elsewhere. Anything charismatic, characterful and exuberant - in other words distracting - would undermine its purpose.

The act which epitomised this development were Vengaboys, a multi-national but predominantly Dutch affair, also on Positiva. Their records were dippy and vacuous, with lyrics which, had they been in Dutch instead of English, may have carried the promise of possible meaning, thereby avoiding having an effect on the discerning listener similar to hot needles being slowly driven through the temples. But they were perfect for the gym. Their debut hit was even called 'Up and Down'.

The first seven of their singles went high in the Top 10. Two of these were number one. The first they titled 'Boom, Boom, Boom, Boom!!', apparently not considering the fact that there had been a number one only a few years ago called 'Boom Boom Boom' to be a problem. In this title, you may have noticed they included not one, but two exclamation marks. Maybe they didn't realise that merely having one exclamation mark in a song title was almost always shit. Perhaps they held the UK Top 40 in such contempt that they didn't care.

Vengaboys were almost unfathomably horrible - but in these months of lax quality control they went down a treat, their pumping, peep-peeping electronica matching the commercial landscape of video games like Mario Kart, incidental music on slapstick kids' TV and clownish ad-break product placement. And, of course, the gym. Yet they were positioned as dance; their album was called *Up and Down – the Party Album!* With another exclamation mark.

But the worst was yet to come. In September 1999 they had their second number one. This was 'We're Going to Ibiza!', an adaptation of the 1975 chart-topper 'Barbados' by Typically Tropical. As per Vengaboys usual, it was a load of brainless workout sky-punching that made food-smeared toddlers clap excitedly in their high chairs. And they pronounced "Ibiza" as "Ih-bits-ah". And when I disgustedly pointed this out to people, they just shrugged, which meant either that (a) pronouncing it that way was fine (b) the way in which anything was expressed was immaterial within the context of a pop record, or (c) that the chart didn't matter anymore and therefore neither did anything that happened in it. The Vengaboys were the logical conclusion to a particularly unfortunate turn taken by that thing we now called dance.

Dance music, by its very nature, should be inspirational. But there was very little that inspired anything beyond wanting to be seen as a cool-arse in a club. It made my visits to clubs in that time flatly unremarkable. Okay, so I had never been mad about clubs and I had a steady girlfriend now so there was a dimension of going out that no longer applied to me, but still.

If dancey pop or the Radio Mix of given dance tunes filled most of the chart, then the bulk of the remainder was taken up by the third thing that bothered me: the continuing proliferation and spread of moulded moppets.

In 1998 and 1999 they seemed to be taking over completely, their presence seeping through our culture like toxic waste on litmus paper. There was a new launch everywhere you turned. Sure, there had been no-frills heartthrobs before; there had been heartthrobs who had exposed their chests and gyrated so as to excite teenagers before; there had been entertainment-for-kids acts before; there had been acts trading solely on attitude before. But this had always been diluted by the other things in the charts. In 1998-9, conditions were different.

Distinctions between zones of showbiz were now thoroughly blurred. The phenomenon of whirlwind TV successes entering the Top 40 had been normalised. TV stars were recording artists. Recording artists were being DJs. DJs were making dance records. Dancers were being organised into singing groups.

And then there were the grins. As far back as I could remember, cynicism and sneering had been an integral part of pop presentation, mirroring the tendencies and struggles of adolescence. But realism was being swept away by something truly cynical and sinister: the gratuitous, uncompromising, corporate grin. These days, there was no difference between a grin you would give in a pop performance and one you'd give in the final, packet-thrusting frieze of a detergent advert.

The embodiment of this horror was a London group called Steps. If you were unfortunate enough to catch them whilst forgetting yourself and tuning into a late-90s edition of *Top of the Pops*, for instance, you'd get oh-so-simple formation dance moves and those fucking grins in spades. It was like someone was hissing into their ear: *Grin or the kitten loses a paw.* It was family-friendly. It was *oh, cheer up.* It was just a bit of fun. Their videos were empty expressions of everyday aspiration. Their records echoed the SAW sound, but a polished and tamed version, making the days of 'I Should Be So Lucky' seem like savage nature. Their success stood as an illustration of how the company execs and marketing people were strangling our charts to death. Because their record label, Jive, was an independent, they got to the top of the Indie Chart, too.

They were a huge live draw, filling arenas with fun-chasing families hungry for the easy-to-copy dance moves and the loud tunes and the flashing lights and the factory-produced grins. Fourteen of their sixteen singles were Top 5 hits and included two number ones. This was no big deal compared to the Spice Girls or Boyzone, but it sure outdid anything worthwhile. And there was worse to come.

Standard-issue pretty people were popping up everywhere. Where, now, were the ugly but interesting-looking fuckers of rock and punk and reggae and soul? Gone was the world of sexy by deed. This new lot were all shiny-faced, symmetrical bastards with white teeth and slim hips, all doing the same, brain-numbing thing.

Five, whose branding insisted their name was presented as "5ive", were aimed at girls who liked the bad boys - guys who did their formation prancing on the darker side of town, who threw off-the-peg hip hop shapes like they were fending off seagulls. They were from London. They had eleven Top 10 hits between 1997 and 2001, including three number twos and three number ones. They had original songs by various teams of songwriters. They were formed by the same team that hatched the Spice Girls.

911 were granny-pleasers with a neat line in covers: their first chart appearance had been with a version of Shalamar's wonderful 'A Night to Remember' which they rendered utterly pointless - not an inconsiderable feat. They had eight Top 10 hits between that and their only number one, a 1999 cover of Dr Hook's smoochy 'A Little Bit More'. In June 1998 there arrived the all-girl B'witched, from Ireland, one of whom had a brother in Boyzone. They had original songs, with group members listed among the songwriting credits. Four of these were UK number ones.

Having mentioned Boyzone, it should be noted that their rate of success had not slowed; they had their third number one in May

'98 and their sixth in May '99, a cover of Ann Murray's 'You Needed Me'. That month of May represented a new peak of moulded moppet dominance. It ended with 'You Needed Me' being number one, having replaced relatively veteran US prancers the Backstreet Boys' only UK chart-topper 'I Want It That Way'. For the two weeks before that, the number one had been 'Swear It Again' by Westlife.

Westlife, from Ireland, were the acme of moulded moppetism and the nadir of the singles chart. Assembled by Boyzone manager Louis Walsh and entertainment entrepreneur Simon Cowell - and co-managed by Ronan Keating - they would denigrate the UK Top 40 whilst breaking almost every conceivable performance record pertaining to it.

They went to number one with their first seven singles, just a decade and a half after we were wetting our pants over Frankie Goes to Hollywood being only the second band to top the charts with their first three. Of their first thirteen chart entries, eleven went straight in at number one. There are other glittering stats, to do with the number of number ones in a single year, or to do with accolades for individual songs. They did it all with singles which, by broad consensus, are hard to recall any detail from. I could remember nothing between 2006 and swotting up to write this. I mean it.

If a Westlife song or video came on, I would, without fail, either leave the room or switch stations, whichever was quickest. Everything about their sound, look and performance was engineered to be bland enough to hurt. Their repertoire of hand gestures and facial expressions covered everything from slightly roused to fairly comfortable; peppered, in big moments, with singing-properly grimaces. The actions included reaching out (warmth), open arms (honesty) and tapping the chest (sincerity); with the group shifting from one to the next individually, so that the choreography was less about synchronicity of movement than about the marshalling of committee-endorsed emotion, enabling virtue to be redefined in their numbed image.

The songs were, in the main, mid-and-downtempo affairs, recycling family-entertainment themes - letting go, you and I, evermore, sharing lives, saying goodbye – in records that began with lingering thaw-drips of piano or acoustic guitar, trowelling the serenity smooth before the first quivering vocal. I've never taken heroin but I imagine the effect is similar. Being a Westlife consumer was a decision to opt out, to reject the messy realities of existence, to deny the possibility of progress, or the necessity of fresh air and fresh vegetables. As you perused the chart, a position occupied by Westlife was like an ugly void: there were indeed words printed, with a song and visual allocated to it, but it was a black hole, into which any vitality, energy, invention, brightness or hope nearby was dragged screaming, to be swallowed and forever lost.

Their appearance didn't prevent the arrival of other moulded moppets. In the summer of '99 came A1, from London, with the same manager as Steps, who were so similar to 911 that they might have been made from a phial of 911 D.N.A., but who had a band member who wrote songs, and another one who was Norwegian, and eight Top 10 hits, two of which were number ones.

The same summer also saw the appearance of S Club 7, the final act in this round up. There are more that could be mentioned; some in the time-honoured girl group design and others in a genuine R&B tradition; but S Club 7 were moulded moppets par excellence, like Steps but younger – mixed gender, mixed race. There had been a TV series apparently, where they all had characters, I suppose a bit like the Monkees but, I imagined, shorn of any vestige of rebellion or dissent in a world that loved Westlife. I may watch an episode one day and be pleasantly surprised, one day when I no longer believe life to be short.

Anyway, their records were teenybop life-coaching sessions: all friends forever, keep going 'till you reach the top, aim high and you'll get there; that kind of mulch. In the world of S Club, life is lovely with clean clothes and a smile - if you only believe enough, you'll achieve your heart's desire. In the meanwhile, you can get into formation with six of your friends and do one of these dance routines.

This new chart landscape felt like a deliberate attempt to sap my spirit and wound my soul. I saw all kinds of political and economic conspiracy in S Club 7. People I knew, grown men and women who I worked with, were actually enjoying them; and ironic though some of it may have been, actual it remained. Between the middle of 1999 and the end of 2001, they had four number ones, three number twos and a number three from eight singles. The plan was working; the population was being assimilated.

Am I being unfair to these acts? Whether or not you liked their records, they sang and danced and were visually lively. This made them the same as TLC, against whom I would not hear a word. Aside from any tough-neighbourhood origins and hip hop credentials, they too had been put together by a management team to address a niche in the market. One of them was involved in the songwriting, something occasionally true of moulded moppets.

The telling factor was the gene pool each came from. The difference lay in being able to trace your lineage from *baby, baby; where did our love go?* as opposed tracing it from *you too can have a smile like mine if you buy this vacuum cleaner.* It was enough of a difference. There was no courting whatsoever of rock 'n' roll authenticity. It *was* cynically done. It *did* demonstrate how utterly undemanding mainstream audiences could be. The fact that so much of it was aimed at pre-pubescent kids was no excuse.

I did at the time consider S Club 7 and Westlife to be proof of the existence of Satan and of his impending triumph. You can dismiss that idea as melodramatic and bitter. I can do that, too. I often have, leaving me feeling mature and at peace with the world. But this idea about evil keeps creeping back. I can evidence its presence in 1999 from chart statistics. In my capacity as a Wise One, I had a duty to be alert. I was one of the guardians. Seeping poisons had to be resisted.

But there were nevertheless some wonderful moments. That May 1999 stranglehold on the number one position by Westlife, the Backstreet Boys and Boyzone was finally broken thanks to 'Sweet Like Chocolate' by Shanks & Bigfoot, washing away the dirge like a gentle tropical waterfall, feeling like a victorious cavalry charge of old. It was the kind of record we would hear increasingly: brisk, clicking rhythms; melodic vocals with an eye on pop posterity; strong urban infusions.

Among new classifications that would soon be familiar were garage - specifically UK garage - and 2-step. I was never sure which term applied where. But, once again, the only thing that really mattered was whether a record was any good or not, and 'Sweet Like Chocolate' - specifically the Metro 7" Remix on the CD single - was pure ear candy. It stayed at number one for two weeks, which was now beginning to seem worthy of a public monument.

But such episodes were rare in the last months of the decade, indeed of the century, indeed of the millennium. My urge to participate, coupled with my age, drove me to familiar territories. I could never have gone to a Shanks & Bigfoot gig, if indeed they ever did gigs, but I went to plenty by guitar bands. In 1998-9 I saw, among others, Ash, Rocket from the Crypt, Cast, Embrace, Rialto and Stereolab. Some of these London nights were fantastic.

Perhaps the best was Hole, who played a warm-up gig at Brixton Academy in advance of their 1999 Glastonbury appearance, with *Celebrity Skin* their current album. The girls in the audience simply adored Courtney Love and every so often she would fish one out of the mosh pit with the help of security so that they could sit at the back of the stage as the band played. By the end of the gig there were loads of them. One girl with down syndrome got up and threw her arms deliriously around the singer, who allowed her to remain wrapped around her waist for the rest of the song. And of course when they played 'Celebrity Skin' there was pandemonium. Back out in the night air, I had to march round the block twice before getting on the tube, just to burn off the energy.

So, Hole were off to Glastonbury. I wasn't. I would never go to Glastonbury. But, in order to participate, I did go to Reading again, as well as to a new festival, V. As in Virgin. It was a way of participating in a context away from the charts, among "my" people. *The Evening Session* on Radio 1 continued to be hosted by Steve Lamacq until 2002: essential things remained in place.

Some punters were probably half my age but didn't realise it. I was like some hip uncle. Or so I told myself. There were plenty of others my age anyway, in small groups; geezers with day tickets, standing slightly back from the throng, hugging pints, moving to the music from the neck up, commenting thoughtfully on performances.

V was at Chelmsford in Essex, over two days, each day's billing swapping with a sister venue in Staffordshire. V97 was the second one. I got town-centre digs at Chelmsford but at Reading I had to camp. This meant emptying my little dome tent completely each morning and putting everything into the car, parked a considerable trudge away, to stop it getting stolen. The car additionally acted as a makeshift washing facility and as somewhere to stash sandwiches, giving me the option of avoiding the abrasively-priced wares of the catering trailers.

At V97, I saw Echobelly, whose new album was more of the same but not quite as good and sank quietly. I also saw Foo Fighters, who were excellent, Kula Shaker, who were disappointingly lacklustre, and Mansun, who I saw by accident and who were the highlight of my whole weekend. Veruca Salt were also there. Among the headliners were the Prodigy, whose new album, *The Fat of the Land*, containing 'Firestarter', 'Breathe' and the controversial 'Smack My Bitch Up', was massive. They put on a circus-like performance which didn't work for me, but which pleased the crowd, including families with day tickets who hoisted their primary-age children onto their shoulders to excitedly wave their glow-stick whizzers at the twisted firestarter and sing along to 'Smack My Bitch Up'.

At V99, I saw two bands who personified how indie had been tamed and niced-up, both of whom were having an extremely successful year: Travis, who had one song I liked, 'Writing to Reach You'; and the Stereophonics, who had two, of which 'Pick a Part That's New' was the most recent. I also saw the Cardigans, an unorthodox bundle of tuneful fun from Sweden. There was also Supergrass, who were still having Top 20 hits, and headliners Suede, whose status remained undiminished. There was another act, memorable for its own distinct reasons, which I will come back to.

I then went to Reading three years on the trot. In 2000, I saw Super Furry Animals, who were brilliant; I saw Muse, a theatrical three-piece with a proggish veneer, who were quite splendid; I saw Slipknot, a theatrical nine-piece, whose masks and costumes evoked several of the most disturbing horror movies that may or may not have actually been made, and whose bottomless well of energy was invested in tight-formation headbanging and roaring, to the utter delight of some and amusement of everyone else.

The most memorable 2001 set came from Amen, a rock band from the same gene pool as Slipknot. They were flagged up by the *Evening Session* and also by the magazine *Kerrang!*, which was at the peak of its twenty-years-and-counting lifespan due to the popularity of various subterranean strands of rock. They had arrived the previous year with an extraordinary single called 'The Price of Reality', the sound of violently stroppy youth destroying stuff on the insistence of their hormones. It was from an album entitled *We Have Come for Your Parents*. Their lead singer was called Casey Chaos. I *had* to see them. In the Evening Session Tent, I determinedly held on to a supporting post for forty minutes while two thousand fifteen-year-old boys bounced and bellowed as a single organism, a heaving, writhing blanket of youth, as Casey and the boys soothed their zit-riddled brows with the sounds of Hell. How to cater for a target audience. It was a sight I will never forget.

It was while I was at this festival that news came through of a plane crash in the Bahamas in which Aaliyah had been killed. News of a tragedy is saddening whoever it involves, but for someone at a music festival still trying to participate, this was crushing. Aaliyah's best records, with Timbaland at the production helm, had been one of the few aspects of new music that had rendered the effort to participate truly worthwhile.

Her single the previous year, 'Try Again', was like a shop-front for how brilliant modern music was capable of being. It had been the first single to go to number one in the US Billboard chart on airplay alone. It was a stunning record. Here it got to number five, but was in the charts for three months. It had made you wonder what might lie in the future. There would be one more album, *Aaliyah*, yielding 'More Than a Woman', a quite exquisite piece of Timbaland/Aaliyah mastery that would be a posthumous UK number one the following year.

I heard the news while I was queuing in the morning drizzle for a bacon roll. It was to be my last festival weekend. I returned the following year, but on a day ticket only, choosing the Friday so that I could see genuine all-time indie heroes the Breeders. I only just lasted the day. It was exhausting. Okay, I had as usual been smoking and drinking, but no more than in the past. By four o'clock I could barely stand. Visitors may have been momentarily distracted by the sight of a thirty-eight-year-old man trudging around, wishing there was a nice comfy sofa to crash on. Somehow, I lasted and saw the Breeders; then made my way back to the train station in a state of relief. My festival days were, I felt, over.

But let's get back to that other act at V99. An item was added to the bill late, after all the listings had been published. Melanie C, a.k.a. Melanie Chisholm, Sporty Spice from the Spice Girls, was following Ginger Spice and going solo. She was, of course, a bit different to the others: a Liverpudlian, and a relatively anti-glam moulded moppet. So her management had seen a rock festival angle and here she now was, on the main stage on a V99 afternoon, bouncing around and attempting to elicit noise from an understandably hesitant crowd.

The mere fact of her being here was something. One of those wretched Spice Girls had seen the error of her ways - perhaps having been visited by three indie spirits during the night - and now wanted a piece of the real action, to be part of a proper crowd enjoying proper music. Many would have had open minds on this assumption. But then she spoilt it, launching into a version of the Sex Pistols' banner-raising 'Anarchy in the UK', which she began by adapting the opening line of the original, singing: *I am an Antichrist; I am a Sporty Spice!* No, this wasn't communion. It was a launch.

So the Sex Pistols had quite a summer in 1999, what with Melanie C and Jonathan Ross. Each of these incidents is riddled with ambiguity. You might conclude that one of the greatest displays of dissent and rebellion in music history had been reduced to the status of a silly hat, something to put on for a quick bit of role play, and if it didn't work you could just toss it into the corner and forget about it.

But you might conclude something different. If the beauty of having an original recording is that it goes about its business exactly as it did on its day of release, you have a piece of bottled power. The protagonists have aged and maybe evolved away, the world may indeed have changed all around it, but the record is the same as it was on day one. Melanie C manipulated a legacy. Jonathan Ross played an original recording.

The crowd standing in front of that stage at V99 had, in the end, allowed themselves to be entertained by the spectacle of a Spice Girl at a rock festival, although on precisely what level it had been impossible to tell. No doubt many were, like me, muttering expletives. But I had concerns about some of the others. The door was open and the threat was real. Nowadays, kids with glow-stick whizzers were being brought by their parents to see the Prodigy. In the mere six years that I had been attending festivals, their atmospheres had changed. Lots of atmospheres had changed.

I had once revelled in the dissent and defiance of football crowds. But professional football was now an increasingly corporate and gentrified world. Customers had already cheerfully accepted all-seater stadiums and sky-rocketing prices. Music was now being used to shepherd them further. When a team had a big win, as in a Wembley playoff final I happened to attend, some grinning schmuck with a microphone would appear during the lap of honour, urging the crowd to join in with 'Rockin' All Over the World' or 'Simply the Best' as it blasted out of the PA; and the fans were welcoming this without hesitation, bastions of obedience, straining to hit the notes, doing that *left right left right* sky-punching thing, perhaps with one of those fucking pointy-finger sponge hands on. Once upon a time, the schmuck would have been told to fuck off in glorious, bellowing unison. I was no longer a regular.

It was against this backdrop of willing conformity, of treating indie like a scruffy pet, of pre-Grade-1 practise pieces masquerading as dance music and the launch of solo careers by moulded moppets, that Jonathan Ross played 'Pretty Vacant' on a Saturday morning on Radio 2. How wild it sounded, when everything around us was so tame. What possibility it spoke of. What reminders it provided. And what a suggestion it made - that becoming a Radio 2 listener would not inevitably constitute surrender. Yes, I needed to be cautious - but past glories would not inevitably be shrunken, valuable old lessons would not inevitably be un-learned. I could, perhaps, now march forward into post-youth, donning my Wise One cloak with confidence.

This was all to the good, since many of the arenas catering for the aging music obsessive were already familiar to me. But also, the next half decade would witness a quite sensational high point in the history of the UK singles chart.

Ten

Wembley: the venue of legends. Today it would host the biggest record fair of the year. I wasn't sure whether I was more excited about the prospect of being surrounded by all that desirable vinyl, or the fact that I was going somewhere where I wouldn't have to be diffident about my age. I got up extra early, full of that Special Occasion feeling and, to enhance the mood, tuned in to Capital Gold.

Begotten of Capital Radio, Capital Gold was situated on the AM band rather than FM where these new-fangled stations were. It was an oldies schedule in an oldies place, replete with atmospheric interference, making the Mamas and the Papas, Amen Corner and Donovan sound all the more authentic. It was enormously popular, the background hum for a sizeable chunk of the population; a hum crowned by the ageing voices of vintage DJs who had once introduced many of these records as new releases.

You knew what you were getting with Capital Gold, but I had little real idea of what the rest of the day would bring. In the late 1990s, it was easy to suppose that music's days of legend were long over. Within a few years that would be rigorously challenged. For now, I was off to Wembley with excitement in the stomach and £40 in the wallet.

The queue shuffled along under a grey sky, down the side of the building for maybe a hundred yards, across drab paving with views opposite of windowless walls and plant-beds set in abrupt rectangles. I got chatting to an energetic guy with lank hair and gaps in his teeth. He was carrying a 45s box just like my old one. He told me he was into collecting old rock 'n' roll singles: "I sell them when I need the money; then I start collecting them again." I also got chatting to a mother and daughter wrapped in woolly cardigans, who giggled and said they wanted to see if there was any Boyzone stuff. I couldn't really reciprocate; I wasn't after anything in particular, just original UK pressings of singles I might not even realise I wanted until I was holding a copy with a clean label and a well-preserved cover.

I paid a small entrance fee and was given a bright yellow VIP Record Fairs bag containing a clutch of promotional flyers. Soon I was inside a huge, echoey hall, a space swirling with the competing sounds of countless music systems. Between the stalls, partition screens exhibited premium stock in pinned-up polythene: rare singles and first-edition classic albums – Beatles, Hendrix, Led Zeppelin, plus others you had heard of and some you hadn't - which any collector worth their salt would recognise, getting hot under the collar simply by being this close. Cards tucked inside the polythene displayed intimidating prices, perhaps with a small write-up justifying the valuation.

There were stalls specialising in picture discs. There were others specialising in Japanese issues, or Dutch ones, or ones from South America, each with their own distinctive visual characteristics. You like your 60s originals? Get them all again, but in brighter colours. Others offered merchandise - books, posters, collectable magazines, tour programmes, autographed photos, or rosettes and scarves from the 70s teenybop era alongside equivalent items from more recent years. Loathe Boyzone though I did, part of me hoped the mother and daughter from the queue would find something to excite them.

Some stalls were set up to exude character, with banners and signage in iconic styles from the era they served. But most were set out simply, with little if any decoration, just sparsely-labelled crates packed with records you had to flick through. I would soon recognise "crate digging" as the default approach for record collectors. I got my first grown-up dose of crate-digging that day.

Effective digging required steely resolve and the ruthless application of strategies for combatting fatigue. Stamina was essential. You also had to deal with intimidation. I would be bugged by new arrivals at the next crate, rudely jostling for elbow room. I would be unnerved by people putting *their* piles of records on top of ones in *my* crate that I had yet to flick through. One guy, rigidly flicking through a neighbouring crate, sniffed, turned to me, and with the air of a driving examiner said: "I hope you play your Lulu B-sides".

Once you had gathered a pile, the most painless way of disengaging from a busy stall was to catch the eye of the stallholder and thrust it out with a wordless and neutral expression. He would balance it on his stomach, flick through it, and then confirm the total, maybe rounding it down to the nearest tenner. You would thank him, pay it, and leave. Do anything else and you're laying yourself open. As I discovered at a well-attended stall near the entrance, where I decided to negotiate over two early-90s chart hits in good quality covers, each priced at three pounds. "Both for a fiver?" I enquired, putting on my best cheeky-but-harmless face.

"Fuck me," exclaimed a suddenly energised vendor, at a volume which made me jump even in that crowd. "What, have I got a sign up here saying *please haggle*?" He turned to the guy sharing his space. "You hear this? You fucking hear this? They see one price and they want to pay another. Fuck me!" He leant towards the items I had pulled out. "How much are they? Three pounds each? *Three pounds?* Is it really worth it to you, saving a quid? Is it? Fucking... go on then, have 'em both for a fucking fiver. Fuck me." He snatched the note and turned away, sighing and shaking his head. I decided not to ask for a bag.

I had a very different experience in a quieter part of the hall. Having suddenly remembered my ambition to own original copies of Russ Conway's number ones 'Roulette' and 'Side Saddle', I mentioned them to a stallholder with crates of 50s/early 60s material. He couldn't help me, but a middle-aged couple standing nearby overheard and said they had both records – they would send them to me if I provided an address, and wouldn't hear of taking any money for them. I was flabbergasted. I asked them to nominate a charity instead. They shrugged and told me to choose one. I assumed the records would never arrive, or would prove to be unplayable. But they did and they weren't.

In the next fifteen years or so I would attend other record fairs of this size; as well as ones in village halls, upstairs in pubs, downstairs in community centres, outside in covered markets and round the corner in scout huts. I would arrive with wants lists of records I needed to fill perceived gaps. They would include things I now felt I should've bought at the time, but also stuff I had discovered in the course of history study. In order to thus swot up, I watched TV documentaries, I rented videos and I read books. I had started doing these things years before out of curiosity, but now I was committed to self-improvement.

There were various routes a scholar could take in order to furnish themselves with an authoritative overview. The most recent music history series on TV had been *Dancing in the Street: A Rock and Roll History*, broadcast on the BBC in 1996. It began with 50s rock 'n' roll which for many, including me, was the cradle of the modern musical era. It would be followed in 2007 by *Seven Ages of Rock*, whose narrative began with Jimi Hendrix and covered well-trodden ground from new and thought-provoking angles. A stylistic contrast was provided by 90s series *Rock Family Trees*, also on the BBC and narrated by John Peel, which delivered its stories of personnel changes to key bands and genres in somewhat earthier tones. Just as entertaining was the Channel 4 series *Top 10*, broadcasting at the turn of the millennium, which light-heartedly counted down the leading acts in categories including punk, soul and - most memorably, in 2001 - prog rock.

Then there were the books. The importance of the *Guinness Book of British Hit Singles* I have already mentioned. By 2001, it was on its fourteenth edition. There was also the *Guinness Book of British Hit Albums* (by 2006 these were combined into one volume, with singles listed in black and albums in orange).

It was hard to imagine anything more exciting, but then something even more exciting happened. In the 90s there appeared the *Guinness Book of Top 40 Charts*, containing every Top 40 listing since 1960, one after the other. I took long holidays in its pages, tracing the rise and fall of favourites, wanting to know, among other things, whether that brilliant number two had ever outsold the accursed drone that had kept it from number one during the weeks in which they slid down the chart together (it rarely had). It remains the best book I have ever owned. Due to contractual arrangements with the Official Charts Company, Virgin would take over from Guinness for these publications in 2006.

Other important reads included Charlie Gillett's distinctive rock 'n' roll chronicle *The Sound of the City*, Nelson George's Motown history *Where Did Our Love Go?* and Gerri Hirshey's stash of soul profiles *Nowhere to Run*. There were plenty more, but, for now at least, few as good as these.

I was never really a magazine reader until 1993, when *Mojo* was launched, as a serious music journal, with half an eye on new releases but explicitly targeting the mature fan. It was classy and heavyweight and by the turn of the next decade I was a devoted reader, inhaling each issue from cover to cover and filling gaps in my overview.

However, it did reinforce the widely-held consensus on what was, and was not, worthy of reverence. With some exceptions to detail, music histories followed the basic trajectory of Elvis, Beatles, Rolling Stones, Hendrix, James Brown, Led Zeppelin, Bowie, Kraftwerk, punk, Bob Marley and hip hop. Not much to quibble about on the whole; but these hadn't always made the best records. Occasional space was given to producers who had broken new ground in the studio, such as the Jerry Lieber-Mike Stoller partnership, Phil Spector or the Holland-Dozier-Holland team: these guys got some recognition, but strangely, their net product, i.e., the records, often didn't.

Well it did in my world; and, having reached what would prove to be my peak of disposable income, I retrieved all my vinyl from my parents' place and set about creating a music room. Its walls were psychedelic green. It contained all my 7" singles, 12" singles, 12" EPs and albums, all my CD albums and CD singles, all my books, music papers, magazines and videos. A pair of Soundlab decks and a Citronic Pro-8 four-channel mixer, sourced with the help of a DJ-ing cousin, stood on a unit with shelves made of centimetre-thick glass. My world now included this room.

It also included pop quizzes. I loved pop quizzes. I joined pub quiz teams in order to be the one that the captain simply passed the pen to when the music round was announced. Since my 1992 Marvin Gaye moment there had been one significant quiz event. A company associated with ours hosted a music quiz organised by *Record Collector* magazine aboard the *HMS President* moored in the Thames. My department wasn't invited, but it was seen to at a high level that I would be involved. It was lavish. The quizmasters sat beneath giant screens for displaying images, playing video clips and updating scores across several engrossing rounds. Our two teams came first and third. First prize was a crate of Jack Daniels, which I was given custody of for the tube ride home. Seriously rock 'n' roll. And we won the raffle.

And I did my own quizzes for parties - often at gatherings I would have been invited to anyway, but sometimes not. Friends of friends would offer payment in various non-cash ways (which meant things I could drink or smoke, just to be clear). This, I felt, put me in a position to challenge, at least on a local level, that accepted trajectory. Liking Motown, for instance, was not greatly respected - if you liked 60s soul, you liked Aretha Franklin and Otis Redding, because that was *proper* music. If you liked the pre-punk 70s, you recognised David Bowie and T. Rex, rather than the likes of Mud and the Rubettes.

But at my quizzes, I would see to it that knowing about Mud and the Rubettes was every bit as important. This was a radical idea at the end of the 1990s. Then, and for years afterwards, people spoke about "guilty pleasures" - records you liked on the quiet, having to conceal your affection for them because they were not on the prescribed list. The big genres – rock, soul, reggae, punk, psychedelia, indie – were fine in their purest form, but anything that smacked of "pop" wasn't. Poppy soul wasn't as worthy as proper soul; hit reggae tunes were treated with suspicion; fame-hungry aspirants jumped on psychedelic, punk and indie bandwagons to have hits and were usually rumbled. If you happened to like one of their records therefore, hush it up; or publicly proclaim it a guilty pleasure, coming clean about the guilt and keeping quiet about the pleasure.

This would one day begin to change. The trigger would be the legacy of Abba. In 1992, I had been thrilled by the music press recommending their originals to its readers in the wake of Erasure's *Abba-esque* EP topping the singles chart; it had seemed a rare moment of enlightenment. The compilation *Gold: Greatest Hits* was then released, becoming a number one on the albums list and as common to British households as toothpaste.

It meant that I could think of Abba with a contented glow. I did so for several years. But then, in 1999, a West End stage production called *Mamma Mia* opened. It had a storyline based around a fantasy wedding on a Greek island. Actors performed Abba songs to illustrate the situation of their characters.

I was shocked and disgusted. Abba records were historical artefacts. On original release, they had painted their own pictures, conveyed their own meanings and had their own effects. Not only that, but they had my deep personal gratitude, for freeing us from 'Bohemian Rhapsody', for pushing back the threat that punk had posed to my thirteen-year-old perceptions, for simply being better than anything else in what was anyway a tremendous era, a blizzard of exhilarating disco, prog and new wave energies. Now, apparently, this was no longer enough.

"Yeh, but you can get to know the songs all over again", people said.

I can still remember them.

"It gives their songs new life", they went on.

I wasn't aware they needed it.

"It's just a bit of fun", they laughed.

Oh, for fuck's sake.

I had begun coming to terms with the uncheckable tides of the mainstream, trying to be tolerant and appreciative. But I wasn't yet good at it. It never took much to re-ignite my anger and with *Mamma Mia* came the feeling that something important was being undermined. Abba's records were not just a bit of fun. The best of them were miracles: real magic in the real world, resonating in my memory, starring in scenes alongside school commutes on vandalised trains, suppers dug out of the freezer and fistfights with bullies.

The scale on which they had succeeded justified all pop, their sheer quality overwhelming all other analytical considerations. *Mamma Mia* the musical was nothing to do with the real world – it was escapism. It was just-a-bit-of-fun. It was anti-truth.

It was also wildly successful. People bubbled about getting tickets, proclaiming it the highlight of their year. They squealed and raised trembling fists. Friends were pleased for them. And they all said it enhanced Abba's legacy, rather than shrivelling it. The production had the material support of Benny Anderson and Bjorn Ulvaeus - the architects of Abba were actively involved in their own embalming. As I write, *Mamma Mia* the musical is in its twentieth year, having run in 50 countries including a mega-long run on Broadway, and has spawned two insufferable and successful movies.

Abba of course occasionally featured in my quizzes, where I kept a good selection of oldies simmering away to test powers of recall and re-kindle buried affection. But there would always be newies, too. I had a special round of hits from recent months so they could get points for identifying the up-to-date. I liked these rounds. They made people nervous.

I managed them even in the parched, barren landscape of 1999, as the indie dream slurped from shrinking, muddy pools and moulded moppets smirked from high windows in air-conditioned towers. Yes, there were some terrific records – there always are – but the trend was towards the bland; it was all a bit fractured and, sometimes, dispiriting.

That year saw the career launch of white rapper Eminem, whose first single, 'My Name Is' got to number two in April. It was a nasty-arsed novelty, with references to his mum's tits and putting nails through eyelids making him sound like a kindred spirit of Beavis and Butt-Head on speed. He was supported by NWA member and producer Dr Dre, and his stated mission was to shock.

You could say that about Britney Spears, too. A child TV star in America, including via a stint on the *Mickey Mouse Club*, she was now launched into pop aged eighteen, and '...Baby One More Time', with its sung-yell vocal and grinding boot-crunch of a beat, spent two weeks at number one in March. In the video, she stomped, pranced and gyrated in a loosened school uniform in a high school setting, delivering the chorus refrain: "Hit me baby one more time". This can be interpreted in a number of ways and peddling fantasies about schoolgirls is only one of them. But the controversy certainly played its part in springboarding her into megastardom and it all landed on us like a ton of bricks.

Christina Aguilera had once been alongside her in the *Mickey Mouse Club* and she, too, was now launched into pop, enjoying her own two-week stay at number one in October with 'Genie in a Bottle'. She was kind of the same, but different, and this was a moderately likeable record; same beat, less worrying – you simply rolled your eyes at hearing lyrics stating that, as the genie in the bottle, she would need to be rubbed the right way.

The sense of exploitation was hard to ignore. Sex, obviously, has always been part of the deal in one way or another; but the music industry was now beginning to use sexual controversy to launch mainstream stars straight into the number one slot in defiance of all other considerations. This seemed to represent a fresh development.

Yes, I was getting old and hurrumphy. But it was manipulative, uncomfortable and disappointing. Barely half a decade ago I had been dreaming of guitar bands taking over the top of the charts with bright, melodious and damn-loud songs that pressed our buttons masterfully, making us sing until we were hoarse, making us bounce and groove until we dropped; a constant stream of unstoppable, head-swimming wonder. But indie had been flattened out by mainstream adulation, hijacked by corporate interests and the tabloid agenda, its promise of a different and better world steamrollered by the Spice Girls and Westlife. The bastards had won again. We were back on those old, cynical tracks, devoid of any real ambition. Gyrating schoolgirls and advice on genie-rubbing were merely the latest steps along the way.

But there would be an unexpected and glorious twist. The first years of the new millennium would be a time of dramatic change and, between 2002 and 2005, all-time great pop dripping in sparkles would after all take over the top of the charts and put moulded moppets firmly in their place. A golden age was about to arrive. And given that I had originally conceived the notion of sparkles as a child listening to mid-60s Motown, it was particularly gratifying that this new wave of magnificence would be rooted in R&B, fuelled by a fresh generation of producers; a list including Wyclef Jean of hip hop band the Fugees, Pharrell Williams of production outfit the Neptunes and of course, Timbaland - along with everybody influenced by them.

Its dawn was already breaking. Whitney Houston was the very embodiment of R&B conservatism, but by 1999, with Wyclef Jean at the production helm for 'It's Not Right but It's Okay' and 'My Love Is Your Love', she was making records with a stripped-down sound, full of crafted atmosphere; the vocal in the service of the record, not the other way round. This was no longer the Whitney of 'One Moment in Time'. Something was happening.

Jamaican dancehall was certainly happening. Over the previous decade and a half, the sounds of the big island had changed. Listen to the difference between Aswad's 1988 number one 'Don't Turn Around', which was conventional reggae, and their 1994 number five 'Shine', which was in the dancehall style, albeit that both were sweetened up for mainstream radio. Where reggae emphasised each off-beat - *dom-chang, dom-chang* – dancehall had introduced a more complex pattern of off-beats - *dom, da-dom-da; dom, da-dom-da*.

Reggae rhythms were often used in dancehall, but they sounded nothing like roots. And the distinctions were as much about attitude as about beats. Dancehall wasn't wailing about yesterday's freedom; it was yelling about tonight's party. 'Don't Turn Around' and 'Shine' give you a feel for the relative attitudes involved - one was for chilling and reflecting, one was for parading and bigging up yourself. White reggae fans were, in the main, less comfortable with the latter. I know, because I was one.

Dancehall vocals, whether male or female, covered everything from ragga-like growling to smooth crooning. Somewhere between sat an assertive masculinity, exemplified by stars like Beenie Man. I had heard girls in our office banging on about Beenie Man years ago, going into wide-eyed detail on his manly allure, in a patois which, given the gleam in their eyes, I was kind of glad I couldn't wholly decipher. When I heard his voice, I understood the fuss. But a dancehall vocal could just as easily be the tender serenade of a lover-boy (or girl). Dancehall rhythms could - and would - be used in the cause of sweet sounds.

As would the newest urban genre: garage, or 2-step, or UK garage – it was hard to know what to call it. Distinctions are apparently do with subtle variation in the drum patterns, but in the main, most people understood this urban garage stuff to be a stripped-down cousin of R&B; a hectic electronica with bits of jungle and various other American detail mixed in.

It was capable of producing conventional pop songs, although it used all kinds of structures; sometimes with successions of samples instead of verses and choruses; sometimes with that *gloop-wom* bass sound, but always with a distinctive, quick-tick-clickety beat whipping it along. It was raw, unnerving and promising. 'Sweet Like Chocolate' by Shanks & Bigfoot was garage. It was also characteristically British, hence the term UK garage. I'm going to call it UK garage and if you want to call it something else you go ahead.

What R&B, dancehall and UK garage had in common was fresh dynamism and the pre-eminence of youth. To an extent, this served the prevailing orthodoxy in the market served by Radio 1, because the prevailing orthodoxy was dance. It was rare now for any chart hit not to have the production values of a dance record, even if it wasn't at a conventional dance tempo. The airwaves were rammed-full of the big, compressed, reverberating noise that dance insisted on.

Coincidentally, the year 2000 saw dance music giving a generally-improved account of itself. The dull fug of 1999's offerings, epitomised by the aforementioned 'Better Off Alone', as well as ATB's energy-sapping number one '9pm (Till I Come)', was in large part cleared the following year by Top 10 hits like 'Pitchin' (In Every Direction)' by Hi-Gate, 'Blow Ya Mind' by Lock 'n' Load and 'Time to Burn' by Storm – records of character and verve. And dance hits weren't the only things getting better. 2000 saw plenty more, but it took a while to get going.

The first new chart of the year was horrific. Its Top 10 contained Westlife, S Club 7, Vengaboys, Steps and Alice Deejay. It also had Cliff Richard, for the meanwhile still considered as integral to Christmas as mince pies, with 'The Millennium Prayer' - the Lord's Prayer performed to the tune of 'Auld Lang Syne', the only possible upside being that it was one of just three 1999 singles to *climb* to number one. Also in that Top 10 was 'Mr Hankey the Christmas Poo' by Mr Hankey, from adult-oriented TV animation *South Park*. 'Cognoscenti vs Intelligentsia' by Cuban Boys was also there, a novelty dance record featuring a speeded-up vocal from Disney's *Robin Hood* on a loop, that had originally accompanied a dancing hamster somewhere on a newly-popular phenomenon known as the internet. In with all this, was a re-release of 'Imagine' by John Lennon.

But that doesn't quite make ten. The other single - which had gone in at number two, had then dropped, but was now at number five and climbing steadily - was a big UK garage hit: 'Re-Rewind the Crowd

Say Bo Selecta' by Artful Dodger. It was odd, a bit puzzling; its chorus consisted of the title being spoken amid broken-glass sound effects; but the rhythms defaulted to that quick-tick-clickety beat. It featured vocals from Craig David, who would go on to enjoy major chart success in his own right. His was a voice clearly capable of good old-fashioned warbling, the fleeting *yeh-eh-ehs* told us that: but it was also clean and meticulously controlled. Listeners with old-school tastes could get as much from it as new garage fans.

UK garage records had many jarring, uncompromising moments, but they could also be effortless crowd-pleasers. On one of those inebriated South London nights where I might have ended up anywhere, I re-surfaced in a club where these sounds, sprinkled with sweet melodies and delectable vocals, were being smoothly grooved to. I too grooved, calm and contented, surrounded by beautifully turned-out black youngsters, who didn't have me thrown out but nevertheless maintained a subtle distance. I may, the next day, have tried switching between pirate stations hoping to access these tunes. I don't remember being successful.

These sounds were beginning to assail the Top 40. They gave a new flavour to those months. But something else gave that period at least as much. It has already been suggested that number ones have a special ability to set the tone, and 2000 saw a distinct improvement in the records getting there. Given that there were forty-one number ones that year, this was only ever going to constitute a minority, but it did represent a discernible shift, one that felt like a kind of fightback; one that, with hindsight, seems almost to have been laying the ground for the golden age that was on the way. Let's start with Oasis.

They had a new album, *Standing on the Shoulder of Giants*, and its lead single, 'Go Let It Out', went to the top spot in mid-February. For one week, obviously. Beatles-influenced title, Beatles-influenced keyboard effects, a beat half-way between baggy shuffle and military march - pure, winning Oasis; and much closer to 'Supersonic' than to 'Don't Look Back in Anger'. Its replacement at number one was 'Pure Shores' by All Saints. William Orbit added his woozy swirls and out-there gravitas to the group's now-trademark vocal sound and it resulted in something powerfully wonderful, spending two weeks at the top.

In early spring there came a chart-topping duet between Lisa 'Left-Eye' Lopes of TLC and Melanie C of the Spice Girls, 'Never Be the Same Again', which may or may not have been a gay love song, but *was* excellent, incorporating the legacy of TLC, but not necessarily that of the Spice Girls. It went on the Melanie C solo album.

Among the many facets of UK garage was a gangsta attitude, one which fit a springtime soundtrack flavoured to a large degree by the number six hit 'Still D.R.E' by Dr Dre featuring Snoop Dogg, both of whom had longstanding gangsta credentials, the latter occupying a niche where ugly pimps flourished among complicit, gyrating bitches. 'Still D.R.E' was dragged from the gutter by its *plink plink plink* piano riff and by Snoop Dogg's role in its memorable chorus. It's hard to think of that spring without it tinkling away in the background. But gangsta flavours didn't have to be that sleazy. 'Bound 4 Da Reload (Casualty)' by Oxide and Neutrino wasn't sleazy, but it was just as street-tough - and it became a second UK garage number one.

It had been less than two years since the release of Brit movie *Lock, Stock and Two Smoking Barrels*, a cheerful take on London's violent criminal underworld. Its "Can everyone stop getting shot?" dialogue clip was used as a sample on 'Bound 4 Da Reload (Casualty)'. The record had a distincly rough-house edge, but UK garage had the knack of encasing even the most jarring elements in sleekness and it did so here. Its lyric name-checked the So Solid Crew, the collective to which Oxide and Neutrino belonged. We would be hearing more from them.

Another big UK garage hit, 'Flowers' by Sweet Female Attitude, was slipping down the same Top 10 having gone in at number two. It had a lovey-dovey lyric, but its sleek casing did the job of toughening it up to the same level as any other UK garage record, providing a strong contrast with the sugared urban love songs we were used to getting elsewhere.

'It Feels So Good' by Sonique was another kind of contrast. It was unusual, with various characteristics of the dance genre but not a full-on dance beat. What it did have was a chorus delivering instant intoxication – just plug in and go. Those who were annoyed by it were way out-numbered by those who sent it to the top of the chart for a thumping great three weeks in June.

Uplifting stuff like this was going down a treat. To keep the mood going, what we perhaps needed next was a number one evoking classic disco. In July, we got it.

Which brings us back to Kylie. 'Spinning Around' was billed as a Kylie return to what Kylie does best, a party-time disco tune in a spangly costume. Kylie's costumes had, in the past, drawn attention to her anatomy in various ways; but Tabloid Land was now properly fixated with her bottom, and that, more than the song, is what 'Spinning Around' is remembered for.

The next bid for the disco diva crown would come from an unlikely source. Teenager Sophie Ellis-Bextor had appeared at the end of 1997 fronting darkly-brooding indie band Theaudience, a role which the oven-warmed-sandpaper tones of her voice seemed made for. But she now sang guest vocals on out-and-out dance track 'Groovejet (If This Ain't Love)' by Spiller, which proved an equally good fit. It was number one for a week at the end of August, knocked off by another one-weeker, the new one by Madonna. 'Music' was produced by the latest of her discoveries, Mirwais Ahmadzaï. I loyally bought it, unimpressed by early radio plays, but once I had listened to it at home on headphones – oh boy. I hadn't been so loyal as to get her version of 'American Pie' which had been number one early in the year, one of the most pointless cover versions in history. But 'Music' is an electronic masterpiece.

In October, her old mucker William Orbit produced a second number one of the year for All Saints, 'Black Coffee', with an awesomely lovely chorus. A week later, following the examples of Oasis and Kylie, there came even-older-old-timers U2, who left their reputation for pomposity and pretentiousness behind for good with 'Beautiful Day', a record proving that awesomely lovely had many forms. From now on, U2 would be cool. They would even get William Orbit to produce them.

Next: Eminem. He had spent the last year establishing himself as a flash-arsed threat to society, but he now released 'Stan'; a single sounding like a play-for-radio with musical accompaniment. It had a haunting atmosphere; its plot tracking the progress of an obsessed fan into madness and murder. It lacked the cheap swagger of his other records. It was stunning.

Masterful though it was, and welcome though it was, we needed an antidote to such bleakness. It came from 'Can We Fix It?' by Bob the Builder, the eponymous hero of a kids' TV animation, a character with an unshakably sunny outlook and construction appliances for friends. The record was a fully-realised mix of the main title theme and came out just in time for Christmas – as were Bob the Builder toys, Bob the Builder books and Bob the Builder videos. Bob the Builder was *it*. Even more so than William Orbit. 'Can We Fix It?' went to number one in the fourth chart of December.

The new Westlife single, 'What Makes a Man', was due for release the following week, in time to become the coveted Christmas Day number one. In our house, we were expecting a first child, but not until February. Officially, I had nobody to buy 'Can We Fix It?' for. But I'm sure I wasn't the only non-parent going out and buying it in that second week. Indeed, I wonder how many existing parents were asked, as the last of the Christmas shopping was being done, whether Mummy's little soldier had the Bob the Builder single - and who lied and said no. The chance to get one over on Westlife is certain to have focused many an able mind. And it had the desired effect. Bob stayed at number one and, following seven chart-toppers out of seven releases, 'What Makes a Man' became the first Westlife single to fail to get there. Joy to the world.

So the number ones in 2000 were a rising tide of advancement. And there were other things bubbling up. Destiny's Child were an R&B girl group from America. In late autumn, following eight UK hits, they had their first number one, with 'Independent Women Part 1'. Their lead singer was called Beyoncé. Most of us already called her "Bouncy". It was going to be a Beyoncé-rich future. Sugababes were a girl group from Britain. They got to number six in September with the intriguing and rather good 'Overload'. They were not like other girl groups. They were very young and very cool. It was going to be a Sugababes-rich future, too.

Both acts would grace this golden age from end to end. Both had some say in their own direction, including via songwriting credits. They were rigorously managed, having their visual style and line-ups adjusted according to the needs of the business. But they made great records;

and that was the point of the years from 2002-2005. There were more genuinely worthwhile records per hundred yards than almost anybody under the age of twenty could remember. I refer to this period as The Golden Age of the CD Single.

Which, without doubt, is a rather grand title. You would think that it involved a healthy swell in sales. But far from it. Indeed, in late spring 2003, the industry and media were wailing and wringing their hands over the fact that 'Loneliness' by German DJ Tomcraft had made it to number one on a week's sales of only 30,000. This was indeed shocking and it triggered a crisis. Singles sales had halved since 1999; in the following year they would contract further. So in calling it a Golden Age we're not talking about till receipts. We're talking about the quality of what was in the charts regardless of the number of copies being sold.

Well then, you might ask: if it was so great, why were more copies *not* being sold? A good question. As we have seen, the intrinsic quality of records is only one factor in music biz success, and people have long been in the habit of buying records with or without it. Me included. But quality does get recognised. That point was made amidst all the despair over Tomcraft. And there are different ways of recognising quality. At the turn of the century, one of them was going to the record shop to buy the CD. But another was getting it free of charge from that new-fangled thingy known as the internet.

I was an internet user. I had a dial-up connection, which called the web over a phone line and, in making contact, performed a cacophony of oscillated squawks with a backline of static, until finally connecting so that you could watch a web page load up at lava lamp pace. I mean it was, without doubt, massively exciting, but it was so slow that it often wasn't worth it.

I once tried to download a web-exclusive song by Hole. It took fucking ages. Entire belief systems grew old and died while I was watching that line of little rectangles turn green. The process seemed to complete, but then it all disappeared. I was not yet possessed of the initiative necessary for finding "downloads" files. Downloading music seemed crap.

But others were not so challenged. Younger people. With more

274

insight. And initiative. And something called broadband, a form of internet connection miles better than dial-up; fast and ever-present. And they probably also a non-UK address - it would take until 2009 for as much as 50% of UK users to have broadband. These were the ones getting their music free over the web.

The format for this kind of music access was the MP3, a digital file type within which music tracks could be compressed for fast download and efficient storage without loss of quality. Unsigned artists could present their own music on the internet using the MP3, which was fantastic, but you could also rip tracks from a CD you had bought in Woolworth's and put them into MP3 files online for others to access, and this caused real trouble. One CD album with twelve tracks could become twelve discrete MP3 files. In 1999, the website Napster was launched as a hub for this kind of peer-to-peer file sharing.

Napster was a harbinger of revolution. It caused an avalanche of litigation. It caused artists to quarrel with other artists. It caused artists to quarrel with their record companies. It caused artists to quarrel with their own fans. These fans, meanwhile, carried on happily getting their music from Napster and elsewhere without paying.

The furore had two main parts. First, there was the copyright part. Many artists and their record companies aggressively asserted their right to control the distribution of their product so that anyone wanting to own their music would have to pay for it. There was talk of prosecuting Napster, talk of prosecuting individual users, talk of raiding the homes of file sharers and confiscating their hard drives.

Secondly, there was the changing times part. The internet was clearly here to stay and to play an increasing role in our lives; especially, it was assumed, in sharing stuff. Some artists thought that file sharing simply spread the word, questioning whether it would have much impact on physical sales, since real fans would buy the CDs anyway. For many of the loudest voices, the Napster controversy provided a pretext for attacking the major labels, the control they exerted and their obstruction of anything alternative. It was a genie that could not be put back in the bottle. Napster use was widespread. At the very least, a compromise would have to be made.

I was no computer whizz-kid. One of my late-90s bosses had labelled me a "desktop dunce". I would improve, but for now, I was calling the support people a lot. Clearly, therefore, I was nowhere near Napster. In any case, I had an in-built conservatism when it came to formats and had adopted CDs relatively late. I didn't want a world without physical formats. But I liked the idea of this challenge to the majors. I was going to have to compromise too.

From the industry's point of view, there was the attendant piracy issue. Piracy had always existed, but raiding market stalls for scrappy cassettes with badly photocopied covers was going to be a walk in the park beside policing the internet. Still, that was their problem.

The bigger problem was that choosing individual tracks online was a very real threat to the majors' cash cow: the album. Album sales had overtaken singles sales in 1968 and the ratio was now more than six to one, despite the postcard sets, fold-out posters and embedded videos being offered with singles. Albums were where the industry action was - $16 in the States, £11 in the UK. Getting individual tracks from Napster was an alternative to having to get a whole collection in order to own the ones you liked. In other words, on Napster, you could just get the good tracks. On Napster, everything was a single.

An *NME* cover story of June 2000 addressing the Napster phenomenon speculated about future online services where, for a monthly subscription, fans could freely access a broad range of music, licenced and legal, with a potential increase in overall revenue to the industry. This would indeed be a reasonable compromise. And it would give fans an option. Different people wanted their music in different ways. Having a physical single and the artwork that went with it, to own, store and treasure, was only one niche. Why have all the boxes and the artwork? Was it not after all the case that music conjured its own images in the listener's head? Was this not the very reason that people like me grumbled about videos? For many, the MP3 was enough.

Some wanted even less. There would soon be talk of a ringtone chart, a hit parade of looped two-bar clips that rang out every time someone called you on your mobile phone; a list of the catchy bits – perhaps the only bits that really mattered. Billboard would launch a US Hot Ringtones Top 40 in 2004. You could stop buying whole songs altogether. You might get into a discussion about what a "whole song" actually is. Demands varied. And most people didn't want the bother of storing physical records if it could be avoided.

Throughout the Golden Age of the CD Single then, it's possible that most fans, able to access the best of its tunes elsewhere, avoided the CD single. It's possible that each classic record of that short succession of years was owned by several times the number of physical sales it took for Tomcraft and his contemporaries to get to the top of the charts, representing a scale of participation that never registered anywhere.

So let's agree that the CD single had a lifespan and that this was the best part of it, since so many of the records cramming the Top 40 represented the freshness of their time and happened to be brilliant. I go back to the mid-90s for indie and various other scraps; I go back to the late 90s for very little; I got back to 2002-2005 for almost anything it wants to shove at me. So now let's get back to the important stuff.

2001 had been skipping along nicely, often to the tune of the latest UK garage hit. In February there had been Genius Cru with 'Boom Selection' at number twelve; in April, Architects took 'Show Me the Money' into the Top 20; Oxide & Neutrino reached the Top 10 in May with 'Up Middle Finger'. Then, in June, DJ Pied Piper and the Masters of Ceremonies took 'Do You Really Like It' all the way to number one, with its irresistible cry of "We're lovin it, lovin' it, lovin it!" and its reference to Ayia Napa, a Cypriot resort fast becoming a Mecca for garage-loving clubbers in the same way that Ibiza shone like a beacon for *dom-tiss dom-tiss* merchants.

But the real action began in high summer. In July, Napster was forced by the courts to shut down. Other websites sprang up to take its place. Then, in August, '21 Seconds' by So Solid Crew was released. Namechecked and alluded to for months, they had finally put their heads above the mainstream parapet, with Oxide and Neutrino and others included in a line-up that we suddenly felt we were expected to know. On the record, each member was given 21 seconds to present themselves in rap and/or song. The backing was sparse – a tinny keyboard riff, an electronic kid's voice, inflammations of gloopy bass, quick-tick-clickety beats. Black London was sounding honed and sophisticated. It was real, refusing to dodge the nasty stuff, reflecting modern realities. Like punk once had.

For months I thought this was the future. When the album *They Don't Know* was released, I wondered whether it might be this generation's *Never Mind the Bollocks*. It was the sound of more than a scene, more than a mere moment in time; rather, a mega-genre into which all kinds of song structures might be made to work. *They Don't Know* went on too long, but among its tracks were three more singles, two of which went Top 10, all of which were bloody great.

It needed another bridge to be fully mainstream and conquer the world. At the end of the year it seemed to arrive, in the form of 'Gotta Get Thru This' by Daniel Bedingfield, a quite brilliant pop record, a UK garage record, outstandingly arranged and produced, a song depicting a desperate struggle with heartbreak – breathless, passionate, absolutely sensational; a number one truly worthy of the position. It hit the top for two weeks in December, then got ousted for Christmas, then went back to number one in January. Daniel Bedingfield was white. I thought he might become the UK garage equivalent of Elvis. The prospect inherent in all of this was mouth-watering.

But it would be a huge let-down. UK garage quickly went back underground, sending occasional missives high into the chart, but not dominating, not making that or any other era its own. UK garage compilations subsequently appearing on CD and online were wonderful. But future So Solid Crew releases would not be, and Daniel Bedingfield went on to record toe-curling love songs, apparently for the consumption of primetime television audiences, to the extent that he was widely referred to as "Daniel Bedwettingfield". His list of credits would include two further number ones - each a cultural obscenity. So we didn't get to witness the primacy of UK garage. But the rising sense of excitement that autumn was impossible to miss. The continuing improvement to the general soundtrack was undeniable.

Which brings us back to Kylie. Rarely has a single been so fanfared, so prepared for, so lauded as an all-time-great number one before even being released, as 'Can't Get You Out of My Head'. Meticulously engineered while sounding effortless, it stayed at the top for four weeks, its *la-la-la* vocal hook sending murmurs down bus stop queues and through surgery waiting-rooms for day after day, with little evidence of complaint from anywhere.

Slightly more divisive was the number one that replaced it, 'Because I Got High' by Afroman; a kind of *Rake's Progress* for a modern dope smoker, the open appreciation of which by the record-buying public seemed shocking, even those of us regularly smoking dope ourselves. There was also the burly, irresistible guitar noise of 'Bohemian Like You' by the Dandy Warhols, peaking at number five and with a long shelf-life ahead. At number sixteen was the 'The Block Party' by Lisa 'Left Eye' Lopez, perhaps too strange and quirky to do better, but pleasingly experimental. As was 'I'm a Slave 4 U' by Britney Spears, to which aforementioned production crew the Neptunes delivered sloping effects, melodic dis-harmonies and echoes of Prince, to forge a Britney Spears record that didn't make you feel exploited. It got to number four.

Over Christmas and the new year, the soundtrack got better still. There was the atmospherically dancy 'Who Do You Love Now (Stringer)?' by Riva feat Dannii Minogue (sister of Kylie), the disco-dancy 'Crying at the Discoteque' by Alcazar, the unhinged-shouty dancy of 'Where's Your Head At?' by Basement Jaxx, as well as the parent-approved dancy of 'Murder on the Dancefloor' by Sophie Ellis-Bextor. 'Gotta Get Thru This' was at its peak. The latest So Solid Crew single 'Haterz' was doing its riveting stuff. Then there was 'Addicted to Bass' by Puretone, a playful celebration of Drum & Bass, which, thanks to its chorus, made everyone go *a-wow, wuh-ow* several times a day. There was also 'Point of View' by DB Boulevard, a piece of thoughtfully charming electronica that might have been made by a professor.

All of these were Top 10. But the star turn of this soundtrack was the posthumous number one by Aaliyah, 'More Than a Woman', hypnotic swirls of overlapping studio parchment that was number one for just one week and was out of the Top 10 two weeks later. A sign of the times. But still, it remains in place alongside 'Are You That Somebody?' and 'Try Again' as a three-starred monument to an important artist who should have been with us for much longer.

There were other good records. Very good records. Plenty of them. This was an intensely varied and attention-sharpening soundtrack and it just kept on and on coming. It covered all kinds of genres, and yet talking about genres is riddled with imprecision because things were crossing over everywhere, as they do in times of heightened creativity.

In effect, there was one big new genre towering above everything else – a popular R&B built on experimental, innovative production, influenced by Timbaland and epitomised by the Neptunes but owned by nobody. It used soul, funk, rap, sampling, dancehall, electronica and catchy pop as a pick-and-mix, arranging them in whatever balance it saw fit, for records devoid of complacency and that'll-do-ness; brandishing it all with joyful mastery. If the point of pop is to lift, transport, delight and energise, this was indeed a Golden Age.

Really it deserves its own book, one with the trauma of 9/11, the Iraq War and a retrogressive sexist culture as its backdrop. So many of its number ones are all-time greats: 'Freak Like Me' by Sugababes, 'Beautiful' by Christina Aguilera and 'Crazy in Love' by Beyoncé, just for starters. You might want to include 'Ignition' by R Kelly in that list, perhaps 'Toxic' by Britney Spears, or possibly 'These Words' by Natasha Bedingfield, sister of Daniel. If you're feeling mischievous, 'Cha Cha Slide' By DJ Casper; if you're in the mood for elated clubbing, 'Lola's Theme' by Shapeshifters; if you want Britain's greatest kitchen-sink melodrama, 'Dry Your Eyes' by the Streets; if you want trouble, 'Don't Cha' by the Pussycat Dolls.

Reams of its non-number ones shone likewise, as charismatic in their time as the best of any other era: 'What About Us?' by Brandy; 'Turn Me On' by Kevin Lyttle; 'Hey Ya' by Outkast; 'Milkshake' by Kelis; 'Dip It Low' by Christina Milian; 'Superstar' by Jamelia; 'Lose My Breath' by Destiny's Child; '1 Thing' by Amerie; 'Lay Your Hands' by Simon Webbe; 'Gold Digger' by Kanye West - all of these were out in that period, and in the Top 10. Gangsta rap hit fresh heights – listen to the mighty 'In da Club' by 50 Cent. UK garage could still occasionally do the business – check out the stupendous 'True' by Jaimeson featuring Angel Blu.

All this excellence numbed us to the fact that Westlife carried on unaffected, right to the end of the era: like cockroaches in a post-nuclear environment, they survived conditions generally hostile to their kind. Most other moulded moppets needed special protection. They found it in the form of the TV talent show, now re-imagined, updated and freshly energised. This new breed of TV talent show had conventional structure and conventional modes of expression. To get through to the next round you had to meet narrow criteria; to sing like Whitney Houston or Luther Vandross, to formation-dance like Take That or Steps. It was a world where vast audiences tuned in, expecting to swoon and holler as emotional contestants performed cover versions with aching sincerity and proper-singing faces. It was a world stripped of innovation, where conformity was polished up and set marching down thoroughly-worn paths with its head held high.

But in the Golden Age of the CD Single, even this back-lit Hades produced Girls Aloud, whose records were always at least interesting - often surprising - which was precisely why they saw the era out. Will Young emerged from it. So too did Leona Lewis. Look, I'm being fair. Coincidentally, Black Eyed Peas began their own long stretch of Top 10 successes in this same era – a modern R&B collective with acres of credibility. One of them would one day be a judge on a TV talent show.

There was so much, of everything, for month after month, even in those months where the top spot was colonised by dross. This was an era where exotic sounds evoking North Africa and the Near East were in high fashion. Records used samples, riffs, or sometimes entire arrangements, that could have come from anywhere between Morocco and Sri Lanka. Let's call it Morlankan.

'Kiss Kiss' by Holly Valance was a thoroughly Morlankan number one, based on a Turkish song and sounding like something Tom and Jerry might perform around a Saharan campfire while trying to kill each other. 'Toxic' by Britney Spears was Morlankan from top to tail. There were Hindi samples in 'Addictive' by Faith Hurts and 'React' by Eric Sermon, which gave each of those records their special buzz.

In a further contrast with the turn of the decade, this was also an era of long-reigning number ones. In 2002-2005, in addition to those already mentioned, there were twenty-seven that stayed in the top spot for three weeks or more. 'Sound of the Underground' by Girls Aloud, 'All the Things She Said' by t.A.T.u. and 'Bring Me to Life' by Evanessence were among those at number one for four weeks; 'You're Beautiful' by James Blunt and 'Call on Me' by Eric Prydz were there for five; 'Where Is the Love?' by Black Eyed Peas was there for six; but '(Is This the Way To) Amarillo' by Tony Christie featuring Peter Kay

- a revival of a 1971 under-achiever released for charity - was up top for seven.

There was still room in amongst all this for excellent straight pop. 'The Ketchup Song (Aserejé)' by Las Ketchup was mad and partly in Spanish and number one. Sugababes went properly pop with their number ones 'Round Round', 'Hole in the Head' and 'Push the Button', as well as with other Top 10 successes including the excellent 'Stronger'. Former busker KT Tunstall became a solo sensation towards the end of the period and her single 'Suddenly I See' was a primal, shamanistic drum and acoustic-guitar rumble that drugged you up and left you in a heap. We were as hungry as ever for enigmatic female soloists.

Which brings us back to Kylie. Two of the era's finest records were hers – the 2003 number one 'Slow' and the 2004 number two 'I Believe in You'. And deep in the autumn of 2005, Madonna was number one for three weeks with perhaps her best single ever, 'Hung Up'. Like other great Madonna records, it took a while to get used to - this one since its chorus was made from a distinctive Abba sample; but it quickly stopped being an Abba sample and became part of 'Hung Up', with its massive energy, pounding rhythms of distorted bass, euphoric chorus and damn-near-perfect sequencing – it even faded out at exactly the right moment. The end of the Golden Age crowned by the best single ever from the Golden Girl.

The end of 2005 is a good place to draw the line for two reasons. Firstly, despite some excellent releases in new popular R&B, it all started thinning out and feeling a little tired. Secondly, the spring of 2006 would see the death-knell for the CD single; when, after chart rules changed to include MP3 purchases online, 'Crazy' by Gnarls Barkley became the first record to get to number one on downloads alone, one week before its release on CD.

It seemed extraordinary that, at this point and at this age, I was into the Top 40 and flying from delight to delight, from joy to joy, from new love to new love, with a rapidity that I hadn't known even when I was a kid. It might be explained as simply as I have told it: that more people were indeed making better records in this short span of years than at any point since I had started following the charts in the early 70s.

That of course needs challenging. My post-youth automatically places me under suspicion. You might imagine that my gathering age left me more determined to enjoy what was there, either to prove I could still hack it with the kids, or that in my Wise One role I could demonstrate the ultimate understanding of this pop lark with judgements of mature clarity delivered from beneath a bench wig.

And yet the very fact that I am worrying about this suggests that, back then, I was just loving the music. I was concerned about how this looked for a forty-year-old, but I never claimed that a dull or offensive record was a worthwhile one, any more than I did in that earlier golden era of 1978-83, the one which had seen the all-time peak in singles sales and that richly innovative post-punk period, the one that had occurred while I had been slap-bang in the middle of the age that pop music is designed for. Then, as now, I had occasionally wanted to like a record more than I was able to. That was as bad as my self-deception ever got. Then, as now, a good record was a good record, regardless of who had made it. Things might have been rather different nowadays – but they weren't that different.

Except my age. Who was I sharing this with now? As teenager, I knew who I was sharing Abba, the Jam and the Specials with - I spent my days with them; music was a core reference point and automatic fall-back position. But now? I was beginning to make excuses to young counter staff in Virgin stores. "I've decided it's time I stopped pretending I don't like this" I said, with a nervous smile, when handing over 'I'm With You' by Avril Lavigne, a cute nineteen-year-old who made records that I *did* like; which was okay, except that she was a cute nineteen-year-old. I didn't tell any of my forty-year-old mates that I thought Avril Lavigne was good (but I'm telling you now: in addition to 'I'm With You', check out 'My Happy Ending').

My work commitments meant I was in an office three days a week and working from home for two. And I was no longer in London, so there was no short trot to a gig. Our nearest big town didn't get big new acts. The closest I came was getting ready to go to see an all-girl rock band called Twist; when I rang the club to check the stage times, I was told they had split up in the bus on the way down.

Youngsters in the office were into cool, sampled product like that of Avalanches, whose hit 'Since I Met You' was the sound of carrying a jug of iced sangria out to the patio. They liked the electronica of Röyksopp from Norway, and of Lemon Jelly from London. They talked about other current acts, too, ones I knew things about. But they talked past me and around me. Some of them were fifteen years younger than I was.

To add to these problems, my Wise One persona sometimes made talking to people my own age difficult. Nobody enjoys having their tastes judged. Being a self-appointed authority leads you to judge things and I was quite genuinely enjoying the Golden Age for its youthful energy.

The LSM, meanwhile, was innocently enjoying the new album from Scottish guitar band Texas, whose youthful energy, assuming they had any, was routinely checked in at the studio door. Still, Texas were a big deal and Radio 2 mainstays. When he mentioned them, I must have had an involuntary look on my face, because he immediately paused, worried, and said: "What? Is that a bit *old?*"

How dare I do that to someone? Let alone my longest-standing mate. I was immediately remorseful; and we quickly found common ground in the excellent 'Pass It On' by Liverpool guitar band the Coral, the CD single of which was upright beside the portable CD player in his kitchen. That seemed to be the problem - still appreciating the best of the Top 40 because of being a Wise One, while my peers shied away from it; perhaps, sensibly, because of all the exposed tummies and increasingly alien slang that came as part of the package.

The LSM's first child had been born within two months of mine. This was why I too had a portable CD player in the kitchen, with a stack of latest singles beside it. That's where I did my day-to-day music now. I could make a reasonable fist of DJ-ing in the kitchen, but circumstances might scupper this – if the fish fingers became ready just as the lead song was about to finish, I had to serve the fish fingers rather than the next single. Helpfully, there were additional tracks on a CD that I could let it run on to; with any luck, ones that didn't involve anything inappropriate for the ears of a toddler in a high chair. The exposed tummies and increasingly alien slang of the Top 40 had no real place in my domestic settlement. From at least one angle, this Wise One was a sad and tragic figure.

It was during the Golden Age that my immediate peer group turned forty. So there were parties. I had a joint celebration with a school friend and it was brilliant. We danced to loads of 80s soul plus the Beatles and the Supremes. Another friend's 40th took place while 'Hung Up' was number one and it went on at least three times, making us all bop around like kids. At another 40th, however, when 'One Step Beyond' by Madness came on, I learned that my knees were no longer capable of sustaining the nutty train for longer than a minute. None of the guests at any of these gatherings had exposed tummies and I understood everything they said.

It was of course okay for people our age to like guitar bands – hence Texas and their various Radio 2 comrades; hence the Coral, hence loads of others. There had been big guitar hits during the Golden Age, for example 'American Idiot' by a resurgent Green Day, and 'Vertigo', another deserved number one from U2. Foo Fighters were keeping it up, notably with the spectacular 'All My Life'. There were the "nu-metal" bands – like Slipknot and Amen. There were the primeval, guitar-and-drums shouty-thrashy bands, like John Peel-endorsed duo the White Stripes, from Detroit, and the Yeah Yeah Yeahs, from New York.

Less wonderful was the phenomenon of suburban US punk, or at least it was called punk, with bands like Blink 182, who wore sort-of punky clothes and had sort-of punky hair and sort-of punky scowls; but who were clean and neat - and dull, for all their noise and leaping about. Their songs had over-tidy cadences which couldn't have sounded less punk.

In the UK, teenybop guitar bands Busted and McFly did what on the surface appeared to be a similar job; but really, they were just the latest stage in moulded moppet evolution. First, the moulded moppet authorities had heard everyone saying "the songs are all boring" so out came Girls Aloud; then they heard "none of them play instruments", so now we had Busted and McFly. They had eight number one singles between them in the Golden Age.

There was still an indie scene. The *Evening Session* kept going until 2002. There were still endless gigs whose bills were decanted into the running order for the Reading/Leeds Festival and elsewhere every summer. It sometimes dented the Top 40. Its ranks now included Elbow and Badly Drawn Boy, sincere and thoughtful acts with stylish flourishes and excitement allergies; Gomez, a bunch of normal-looking people occasionally producing something distractingly odd; and the Vines, whose affected vocals and growly guitar noise suggested mere role-play.

This lot were of interest to the gently, under-statedly trendy - those who liked the notion of indie, or who had once been one of the starry-eyed indie faithful, and who now, out of loyalty to an idea, latched into anything half decent that made the right shapes. They revered the Mercury Music Prize, a high-profile award for new music, given to one album per annum and now in its eleventh year. Past winners included Suede, Pulp and, in 1998, Gomez. In 2001, *The Hour of Bewliderbeast* by Badly Drawn Boy won it. When celebrities were asked about music, it was safe to say they liked Badly Drawn Boy. The new alternative was in mature, cafetière-familiar hands.

Meanwhile, Oasis had kept going, adding three more number ones to their tally. 'The Hindu Times' was a classic Oasis groove-rocker with a Morlankan guitar riff; 'Lyla' was less electric but catchier; 'The Importance of Being Idle' was a good old-fashioned pub singalong. Despite what some might say, Oasis still had something of an edge to them. They didn't sit comfortably alongside any cafetière.

Neither, certainly, did the White Stripes or the Yeah Yeah Yeahs; nor a Nashville band called Be Your Own PET (capitals intentional). Their Rough Trade single 'Fire Department' ticked a whole line of boxes on my musical lovemap. New Zealander Zane Lowe was now delivering alternative sounds on Radio 1 in the slot vacated by the defunct *Evening Session* and I heard that from him. He also introduced me to the Go! Team, from Brighton, who sounded like the cast and crew of *Sesame Street* having a wild party after the kids had gone; as well as to M.I.A., a female Sri Lankan rapper whose *Arular* album was, for three months in 2005, the only thing I was interested in listening to. It was nominated for the Mercury Prize. It didn't win, its brilliance being beyond the comprehension of people who gave prizes to Badly Drawn Boy. Neither *Arular*, nor anything from it, made the slightest dent in any bit of the chart.

Maybe she should have promoted herself online in the lead-up to its release. Maybe she did and it didn't work. It was getting this right that led to Sheffield guitar band Arctic Monkeys having their debut single 'I Bet You Look Good on the Dancefloor' go straight in at number one in October 2005. They seemed to come from nowhere, but their fans had been steadily gathering on the internet, and the internet was where young people now resided.

In Alex Turner, they had a frontman spouting sharp lyrics on neighbourhood drama and everyday seediness, delivered with utter clarity and incorporating astute references ranging from Sting's Police lyrics to 70s sitcom favourite Frank Spencer. It was all recognisable and agreeable - you were in safe hands with Alex, whatever your age. They were not, at least to begin with, a groovy bunch; they used choppy, jerky, fast-pumping rhythms of the kind popularised by recent groups like Franz Ferdinand.

All this made them a stand-out act, primed to impress. Their second single, 'When the Sun Goes Down', became a second number one the following January. Then their LP *Whatever People Say I Am, That's What I'm Not* became the fastest-selling debut album of all time in the UK. Success on this scale for a guitar band seemed incredible in the era of Sugababes and Black Eyed Peas. But that was the internet for you. This was becoming a very different world.

I was nervous about this different world and how I was going to fit into it. I spoke to the youngsters in the office about the prospect of having to buy music online in future. They reassured me that any downloaded track came with artwork that popped up on the screen of your laptop or MP3 player (assuming you could afford an MP3 player that had a screen). That sounded okay. Kind of. I remained unnerved. I kept buying CD singles but the world was closing in.

After 2005, the stars of the Golden Age matured off in different directions. Beyoncé kept making good records. Pharrell Williams continued to hone his craft, going on to make some of the most widely-loved sounds in the world. Timbaland had number ones under his own name. Sugababes didn't have their final number one until 2007. There was lots of other good stuff. There always is. But there was less of a convergence, less *congestion*.

Arctic Monkeys would remain successful for years, although not quite on the scale of that initial burst. There were other guitar successes, but ones that relied on well-trodden paths and niche crowd-pleasing. It didn't matter; they could make a living. The kids of the post-punk era and those of the 90s indie boom proved a reliable fanbase, turning up at gigs with their greying hair and bald patches and nodding to the beat - one hand holding a beer and the other knuckle-deep in a jeans pocket.

Almost everyone around them would be the same. They would listen to the same radio stations, ones whose audiences consisted of their niche and little beyond. They would read the same handful of magazines, visit the same handful of websites. They might go to the same festivals; but instead of camping in fields, they might be going to a holiday camp, their accommodation consisting of cosy chalets with en-suite facilities.

This was a glimpse of the future that suited me better. Festivals in holiday camps were going to be more genteel than record fairs usually were.

"No I haven't got any Marvelettes" said the stall-holder, with sharp impatience, as I stood before three long crates of Motown originals, towards which he now flew a hand. "You can see what I've got".

I had hoped for a smile and a "No, sorry, haven't seen one recently; can I take your phone number in case I do?" But no. So I stopped digging through his crates and he began stroppily reorganising the one I had last touched, even though I had been careful to leave it in good order.

Other vendors I encountered were more pleasant. Down a trendy side-street in our nearest big town was a guy who sold movie memorabilia and vinyl. He had fresh seven-inch stock coming in all the time. It was well-sourced, well-stored and affordable; no visit was ever entirely wasted.

It was here, in the Golden Age of the CD Single, that I found an original copy of 'Bridge over Troubled Water' by Simon & Garfunkel, a 1970 number one of massive status; the title track from an album which, when I was a kid, every home I visited seemed to have. People chatted and edged past me in the shop as I stared down at it, mesmerised. This was a thing of immeasurable power - greater than kings, more terrible than armies, overwhelming like nature - and it was now in my hands, on that handsome blood-orange CBS label, a pristine copy. A piece of vinyl, of which there were any number of copies in circulation; worth £2-£5, depending on how much you felt like paying. But I had never had one. My hands shook. My throat was dry.

Silly, you might think. Perhaps even ridiculous. But, also, a justification for this entire book. And the one before it.

Eleven

The poor little CD single. It was never really loved. People enjoyed taking swipes at it. They gleefully pointed out that a CD was a CD, with an 80-minute capacity whether it was a single or not. This raised all sorts of questions about value for money, leading to suspicions about industry skulduggery, and ultimately to justifications for online file-sharing. There was also the storage issue. MP3s meant an entire lifetime's worth of music on a device no bigger than a hardback. Displays of neatly-stacked vinyl have always had a special aesthetic appeal, but CDs meant walls of plastic.

Few spoke up for its impressive range of packaging or for all the additional bonus tracks, embedded videos, foldout posters and alluring sets of colour postcards it had provided down the years. Ironically, during the Golden Age, it was largely shorn of these gimmicky extras, aping the vinyl 45 by offering a standardised two tracks at the fixed, lower price of £2: a red sticker the size of a postage stamp proclaiming this fad from the front of the pearl case. There was something pleasingly retro about this Throughout the noughties, while the public was getting used to finding and purchasing music online, I was still faithfully queuing up at HMV and Virgin to buy CD singles.

And suddenly, HMV and Virgin were the only ones supplying them. WH Smith stopped selling singles in mid-decade. I was told by a sniffy assistant: "...because if people like the song, they tend to buy the album". Oh, really? Well that was exactly the kind of baloney that was undermining the physical format. Online, you could pick and choose the good tracks and didn't have to pay for the dross. While we had CD singles, I felt we had an equivalent option.

The last single I remember buying in Woolworth's was 'Love Song' by Sara Bareilles, a quality mainstream bounce which reached number four in 2008. I had already made my first MP3 purchases by then and Woolworth's itself ceased trading a year later. The old world was pulling its wagons into a circle.

Woolworth's owned Zavvi, the retail chain that had taken over the Virgin megastores. With Woolworth's demise, they too went out of business. So now the megastores were also gone. There was no longer an HMV in my area either, although by the end of the decade my one reliable source of CD singles was HMV Online, which sent them in the post.

Not all chart hits were available in the physical format now, anyway. There were some that I had to get online if I needed them. And I did need them, so I was now a customer of iTunes, the Apple Inc. online MP3 store and library facility. I had an account and an app on my laptop. I paid between 59p and 99p for individual tracks which I downloaded and organised.

At first, I played them on the computer and burned them onto CD for use elsewhere. But in 2009 I bought an iPod nano, a slick piece of tech kit that was cute, smaller than my hand, on which I could store and play hundreds upon hundreds of tunes. I loved it, even given the difficulty in preventing those stupid little bud headphone things falling out of my ears. The iTunes store and the nano became my default music facility and the CD Walkman was recycled. I bought my last CD single in 2011.

I got a Sony CD recorder for my 40th birthday. It meant I could make good quality compilations and quiz resources. It also meant I could record my old vinyl onto CD and upload it to iTunes, thereby retaining that authentic vinyl crackle. Importantly, it also meant I didn't have to re-purchase anything. But getting it all recorded and uploaded took months. The task was, without doubt, a demanding one. I rolled my eyes to friends but I wasn't fooling anybody. "It's a labour of love," I was smilingly told. "You're having a great time."

As promised by the youngsters at work, when you bought a new release from iTunes, it came with a little artwork file that popped up on the laptop or other device when it played; whereas with your own uploads it was just a dull square displaying the greyed-out iTunes logo. But that dull grey square soon began to look like a badge of honour.

There have always been loud voices banging on about the superior sound of vinyl, occasionally including mine, but the subject is riddled with bullshit. Any format can deliver good sound or bad sound. Furthermore, any recording can be affected in its reproduction by different speakers, mixers or headphones. Once you digitise a piece of vinyl it behaves digitally and, assuming the sound was good to start with, it will carry on being good. There are problems with digital versions of records that first appeared on vinyl, but that's to do with shoddy work on the part of those mastering it. It's not the fault of the technology.

Speaking of which, I now had new turntables. My Soundlab ones had burned out and I began eyeing up Technics 1210s, the hardcore DJ's turntable of choice. Our nearest big town had just the outlet; a dusty, slightly damp space, with bare floorboards, a three-bar electric fire, racks of dishevelled vinyl, and towering piles of second hand hi-fi equipment everywhere.

I happened to discover it at the exact point when the sale of MP3 players like the iPod nano and the smaller iPod touch were reaching their peak, leaving the demand for turntables and CD decks at an all-time low. I got a pair of 1210s for a total of £400, when they would have been around £2.5k brand new. Or so he told me, anyway.

So now I was happier than Larry and the proverbial shit-covered pig combined. Not only could I mix between vinyl and CDs, but I was now doing so on some of the best kit ever. A record collection, I haughtily declared, was not something to merely own, but to be used; and it was on this principle that I exerted my right to have regular headphone parties. Not ten minutes here or half an hour there, but hours at a time.

I would stay up until two, three and four o'clock on Saturday nights, working my way through piles of vinyl oldies, CD single oldies and

MP3 newies on CD. This was my communion - a rotating diet of eras, all planned and prepared in advance. With the aid of a few glasses of dry white and maybe one or two other things to help me along, this was my me-time for several years; wallowing in DJ fantasies, riding on waves of euphoria, experiencing moments of spiritual clarity. Then, a matter of hours later, I was having to weed the path and clean the bathroom. Usually with a hangover.

Of course, this wasn't the only time that the vinyl came out. Visiting friends were keen to play with it, especially following a good meal and a bottle or two. Pulling out the oldies was reliably convivial and always rewarding, but it could lead to anxiety. They often wondered how precious I was being about sharing them. I often wondered how cavalier they were being about handling them. To further enhance their storage, I began buying protective plastic sleeves to slip them into. Within a year, I had done the lot. One guest, on lifting the lid off a box and being suddenly faced with a battery of meticulously-filed and plastic-protected specimens, recoiled with a yelp.

But I never doubted the correctness of being meticulous. When you see an old 7" cover that looks like it once went several rounds with Joe Bugner, you can't help imagining the needless abuse it must have suffered. Some will smile warmly and say "Well, it *is* getting on for forty years old". No, I'm sorry; damage is not inevitable.

I had one near disaster when moving house: I was carrying a load down a staircase in a collapsible crate, when collapse it did - the bottom fell out, sending a big chunk of the early 80s crashing, tumbling and spilling down the steps. It took days of distressed checking before I realised that the damage was, actually, minimal. I had kept and protected my records for decades. Normal people would look at damaged and blemished sleeves and say they're in great nick. But I have no desire to be normal.

The condition of those sleeves, whether picture covers or not, is the biggest issue when collecting 7" vinyl. They can be battered and torn and bent and faded and stained. Yes, *stained.* Many of those that I spent my mid-70s pocket money on, singles on Bell and RAK for instance, were sold in plain white covers with a distinctively dipped lip. These are now as hard to find in good condition as many of the company bags, especially since, being white, any staining is horribly conspicuous.

After that crate incident, I switched my 7" storage to purpose-designed cardboard boxes, supplied by a company I saw advertising in *Record Collector* magazine. Soon afterwards, I found a different company supplying replica company bags and I ordered several designs, with the intention of replacing specific covers and making my collection look the absolute business.

Matching specific covers to specific singles is a can of particularly wriggly worms. It's important to know your dates. Company bag designs can alter radically from era to era, changing their colours, visual concepts and even their logos. Mercury is an example of a company whose sleeves looked strikingly different at various points between 1960 and 1972. Parlophone, by contrast, changed their distinctive green bag little and often – perhaps with the logo in a different place, perhaps with different ads on the back. Yes, *ads*. When I was a late-70s teenager, the only ads you saw on sleeves were for the act's albums, occasionally their tour dates. But in the 60s, they advertised all sorts of things; not only albums by other artists on the same label, but record tokens, music magazines, shampoo and even hairdryers. If you wanted it to look as if you had bought 'All You Need Is Love' in July 1967 and kept it in the same bag since, you had to do your research.

This replicas supplier was an exciting find and rescued me from all sorts of wrong and horrible things I had been storing records in. But the paper that they were made from was very different to that of the originals – thicker, more fibrous. Also, the colour was often not quite matched. You could tell the difference. Buying a replica was only a fix of sorts. I was committed to finding an original.

That word mattered to me. I had never been the type of collector who wanted something just because it was rare – I wanted it because it was brilliant, or important, or was shit but something I loved anyway. And I had to have the original release version. With albums, this is riven with anxiety. It's not simply a matter of: *Is it the original or a re-issue?* There's also: *Is it a first release original or subsequent original?* Whole layers of chronology are involved. Albums have something called matrices which, apparently, give important clues. Dealers take close-up photographs of run-out grooves to help you scrutinise a matrix. Here, even I draw the line. All I want is a copy carrying the label design that was current on the first release date. So, for example, with early Beatles albums, it's the Parlophone label with the yellow logo, rather than the boxed-up black and silver one - unless of course we're talking about the original black and gold design of the *Please Please Me* LP, but that would require a whole chapter I haven't got room for.

My early-noughties weakness for collecting original albums was mainly a result of Channel 4's outstanding *Top 10 Prog Rock* programme. Its compère was Bill Bailey, a comedian whose musical virtuosity was central to his stand-up routines. He was a regular on BBC2's celebrity music quiz *Never Mind the Buzzcocks*, which was - then - eagerly-anticipated weekly viewing.

There was also a narrator: Mark Radcliffe, a Radio 1 presenter a little more worldly and alternative than most of his station colleagues. He had formed a partnership with Marc Riley, or "The Boy Lard", as he was apparently happy to be called. For a while they hosted the coveted *Breakfast Show* together, as well as the Sunday Top 40 countdown.

Radcliffe was a piss-taker, perfect for the job of spotlighting prog rock, one of the most ridiculed of all genres, while Bailey was a genuine prog aficionado who framed the subject as a cross between Hammer Horror and slapstick panto. It worked a treat. Bands including Rush, King Crimson, Camel and Yes began to look worthy of fresh investigation.

So I started investigating. If I was going to buy a 70s prog masterpiece, it had to be the original, which made progress slow, or expensive, or both. But I now have a whole section of prog albums, some of which, including *A Farewell to Kings* by Rush and *Fragile* by Yes, have become close friends.

Like albums, singles also get re-issued: you have to be wary of ones that look like originals but aren't. They, too, can cost a bomb. The most I ever paid was £92, for a pristine, as-if-bought-yesterday, copy of the Motown release 'Every Little Bit Hurts' by Brenda Holloway, on Stateside, without the slightest blemish to either disc or cover.

Many of my favourite Motown releases hadn't made a dent in the UK charts, so their press-run was limited and original UK releases can therefore now cost £30 or more. Sometimes I got lucky. That same grumpy-arsed, Marvelettes-lite dealer at the record fair had a jovial friend in a smart blazer hanging around his stall. At my mentioning of 'When the Lovelight Starts Shining Thru His Eyes', an early Supremes belter, also on Stateside and also hard to find, he casually said he had one at home, in the same way he might have said he had a sock drawer. He told me I could have it for £40. One postal exchange later and I did. £40, when I had been outbid at over £50 on eBay. Ah, eBay. I discovered eBay in 2005. It is thanks largely to eBay that I now own almost every bit of vinyl I have ever dreamed of having. I don't need to tell you about eBay. I do need to stress how thrilling it was to discover it.

But this originals thing was beginning to get out of hand. There was a point where I would refuse to listen to a record unless I had the original vinyl in good condition. It ate up time and money - I was the king of deferred pleasure and, I thought, perhaps a little unwell. So I weaned myself off it. When, soon afterwards, I began investigating rock stoners Hawkwind and acid soul freaks Funkadelic, I got their albums on CD, for less than a tenner a go. Making this change wasn't easy. I felt like a traitor to something. But after a brief, Gollum-esque struggle, a new me emerged, liberated and happy to own old music in new formats. Now: is that freedom? Or is it retirement? You decide.

As well as oldies, I continued buying new music; still on CD at first - while concerned friends were demanding "please tell me you're not still buying singles" - but then from iTunes. And I found that, despite being forty-five, new hits could still do extraordinary things to me. I was the fool leaning dangerously over the counter of a busy kebab shop one evening, straining to hear the radio announcer name 'Hello' by Martin Solveig & Dragonette because I just had to know what it was - all that the other customers saw was an older man scrambling up a partition. I was the nutter on the busy commuter bus one morning, letting out an involuntary groan of pleasure listening to 'Like a G6' by Far East Movement on the nano - all that the other passengers heard was an older man making a funny noise.

Both of these superb tunes were hits on the official chart as - still - revealed weekly by Radio 1. But within a few years I would be paying little attention to anything on that station. I had been having serious doubts about mainstream radio for over a decade by the time Chris

Moyles took over the Radio 1 *Breakfast Show*, slap bang in the middle of the Golden Age of the CD Single in 2004. He had been working his way round the Radio 1 schedules while the *Breakfast Show* was suffering a decline in ratings, one that neither Marc & Lard nor Zoe Ball - 90s ladette icon and spouse of Fatboy Slim - had been able to reverse. But this self-styled "Saviour of Radio 1" succeeded, adding a million listeners in his first year and winning accolades.

Sadly, this appeared to have little to do with his treatment of music. He had a crowd in the studio with him, a gang of mates with vaguely-defined roles, with whom he interacted in a way that made you think you were eavesdropping on a conversation in a bar between appalling smart-arses. This variation on the "zoo format", used by Chris Evans in his *enfant terrible* Radio 1 days and endlessly re-fashioned by Steve Wright on Radio 2, was given a new flavour; one of sneering pseudo-boredom, through which opinions on musical acts, TV personalities and movie stars were expressed, mainly for the sake of taking them down a peg or two – usually a good crowd-pleaser – or saying how "fit" they were, or weren't. No wonder he was awarded DJ of the Year by *The Sun*. So, in the midst of this most inspiring of chart music periods, did the flagship programme of the nation's youth music station champion and celebrate it? Did it bollocks.

I may have been unlucky. They certainly did talk about music. But the programme annoyed me almost every time I tuned in. Some of his studio gang wandered off to other parts of the Radio 1 schedule and were just as aggravating there.

In addition to all this, there was also the baffling regularity of the show's two favourite oldies. One was 'Rock DJ' by Robbie Williams, a skin-hiving, single-week number one from 2000, which they carried on playing even after he had released six further singles including two more number ones. The other was an okay-ish cover of Talk Talk's 'It's My Life' by No Doubt, which, in two chart runs between December 2003 and May 2004, got no higher than number seventeen, and yet was treated like some kind of all-time classic. It remained on the playlist months after it had dropped out of the chart. Here we were, surrounded by all-time urban pop greats, and what did we get? 'Rock DJ' and 'It's My Life', a flap of the showbiz hand and an also-ran.

Of course, I wasn't part of the target audience for the Chris Moyles *Breakfast Show*. Because I was old. And, because I was old, I was, very possibly, judging a station's ability to celebrate outstanding new music on the extent to which its key presenters sounded like Tony Blackburn. I tuned in anyway, because Radio 2 wasn't playing Beyoncé or the Streets or Sugababes.

But Radio 2 did have a Saturday evening programme called *The Critical List*, hosted by Stuart Maconie, a seasoned music journalist with a lengthening track record in broadcasting. His style of delivery and store of knowledge convinced you that he (a) knew what he was talking about and (b) understood how you wanted to hear it. He is credited with coining the term "Britpop". He had chaired BBC Radio's crisis debate on the future of chart music triggered by Tomcraft. *The Critical List* featured tracks linked by association to a classic album. It was always interesting.

Radio 1 still had a few goodies to offer. Zane Lowe was on in the evenings and I have already mentioned some of the great things he was capable of introducing. But I had my ups and downs with his style. By the end of the decade there was also Annie Mac on Friday nights, whose varied and well-pitched show was the only dance-specific programme I found myself able to enjoy. Here, I was an official visitor, under no pressure to fit in, which made it a little easier to block out the annoying bits. There had been annoying bits on dance shows for over a decade. But there were annoying bits everywhere. Sometimes I felt a bit Radio 1, sometimes I felt a bit Radio 2, sometimes I felt neither. I was still in limbo.

Until April 2007. Because it was then that Radio 2 began broadcasting *Radcliffe and Maconie* for two hours, three nights per week; and I immediately began finding more things to do in the kitchen where the radio lived. Mark Radcliffe and Stuart Maconie. Together. This was the right programme at the right time, a gift for every Wise One in the country. Listening to Zane Lowe had represented an increasingly desperate effort to keep up, but here was somewhere I could flop onto cushions and relax. Here, at last, was something for which I was the right age and the right type. Its approach was alternative and its taste impeccable. I understood its points of reference. It honoured the classic, showcased the new and eulogised the under-appreciated. It was ludicrously silly as well as deadly serious. It was like attending music university three times a week and wanting to be first in the queue outside the lecture hall.

I was still buying the Top 40, but I felt increasingly like an imposter, unless it was something whose appeal was universally recognised and not age-specific, like the cheerful modern cynicism of the Kaiser Chiefs from Leeds and of Lily Allen from London; or the continuing succession of terrific singles by Beyoncé that made her the biggest star of the period and absolutely okay to like.

But there were loads of things that irritated me deeply; for one, the unstoppable rise of a skinny white boy from the *Mickey Mouse Club* called Justin Timberlake. I just could not understand the scale of his success, nor the robotic, unhesitating reverence shown to him by the R&B community - it stank of mob influence. I wouldn't have minded if his records had been more than average.

Of course, his near-namesake Timbaland was someone for whom I had great reverence. But the latter's recent move to stage-front felt little better. Hits such as the number one 'The Way I Are' were well-appointed, but clumpy and pedestrian. Plus, he was dabbling in moulded moppets, launching US boyband OneRepublic in his name. He was also instrumental in one of the most questionable make-overs in music history. Nelly Furtado was a neighbourhood swot in a woolly hat whose urban tendencies were confined to artwork and remixes of her mainstream, cafetière-familiar hits. But then Timbaland transformed her into a sultry, street corner hip-thruster in leather gloves by producing the single 'Maneater' and it looked ridiculous. I shook my head at the nonsense of it. Then it went to number one for three weeks and annoyed me even more.

And there was Girls Aloud. Their continued success was a steady source of vexation, like a buzzing fly that spoils your afternoon nap. I have already been more than reasonable about them. Records as good as 'Call the Shots' in 2007 and 'The Promise' in 2008 did not obscure the fact that they were rank showbiz; a bunch of dancers who'd simply been in the right place at the right time. When people spoke about them, they never actually mentioned the records, they just mentioned *them*. And no vocal group really needed five members anyway, it was taking up extra space for the sake of it. It looked for a while as if line-up numbers were going to be an issue. The Pussycat Dolls, launched in 2005 as sexy girls (yawn) with a sexy song ('Don't Cha'), had six members. *Six*. It was like an amplifier going up to eleven.

Both these acts and others typified the onward march of gratuitous sexualisation. I was beginning to realise the extent of the pressure it puts on girls. Young men find young women perfectly riveting without it. Smouldering pouts, hip-tilting posture and bared flesh was just plain boring.

On top of that, there was now twerking: that dance move where women get into a half-squat with their arses sticking out, wobbling their buttocks in a prolonged, deliberate tremble. Suddenly, twerking seemed to be the big craze. Few things I'd ever known were as laughable as twerking. Girls have wiggled their bottoms since the dawn of time, but never before had it looked like they were trying to shit over the side of a boat.

Anyway, we were talking about Girls Aloud. Their most photographed member, Cheryl Tweedy, married an international footballer and became Cheryl Cole; then, in 2009, with energy-draining predictability, she launched a solo career. Her first release was 'Fight for This Love' and I confidently got a bucket ready. But then I heard it and my shoulders slumped. 'Fight for This Love' was superb - twinkling, tense and delicious - a record that did the number one position full justice. This was now a baffling and frustrating world.

The UK launch of Lady Gaga increased my unease. Her career trajectory came straight from dystopian fiction. A fully-formed and refined proposition on initial appearance, with a scorching album *The Fame*, from which came two number one singles. For her second album, she re-released the first one with new tracks, called it *The Fame Monster*, and bagged a third number one. The fourth would be a collaboration with Beyoncé.

Lady Gaga changed costumes and personas a lot. She had highly sexualised lyrics. She outraged the Catholic church with one of her videos. Remind you of anyone? Just as Madonna's candle was burning down (she had needed to duet with Justin Timberlake in order to make it to number one the previous year) here was a ready replacement, whose timeline was foreshortened in some Einsteinian distortion, such that, by 2011, she was duetting with veteran crooner Tony Bennett. From chart debut to supper club in two years.

In amongst all this, Take That reformed, at first without Robbie Williams, but *with* the unforeseen ingredient of genuinely good songs, proof that composer Gary Barlow was a significant talent who had matured well. Singles like 'Patience' and 'Shine' were all the better on the palate for the group's dreadful past. Fans were easily re-mobilised, with girls all over the country hastily organising babysitters and crowding together into vehicles with crisps and sweets to drive for hours to see them in concert, congealing into one giant, metaphorical hoist of the pointy finger sponge hand.

All of this took place as use of digital radio was becoming standard. In the main, digital radio was brilliant because it solved the problem of getting good reception. You pressed a button and went straight to the station it was programmed for with instant clarity; no more painstaking knob-twiddling. Digital sets were groovy. Most had a display ticker, running a looped text across a little screen, telling you what station you were listening to, who the presenter was and what track was playing.

I am certain that this led directly to the infuriating phenomenon of DJs playing a record without telling you what it was. Once upon a time, a responsible presenter would say, as a record finished: *There it is, the sensational sound of Diana Ross with 'Touch Me in the Morning'.* Now, instead, presenters said: *It's a big shout out to Squizz and Phlegm on the M6, heading up to Carlisle to pardaaaay!* or *Don't forget; later we've got Kate Winslet and Christopher Biggins in the studio!* Or they'd go straight into another tune and not tell you the name of that one, either. I imagined they simply didn't care.

And another thing: shows playing great oldies but giving us the album edit, rather than the 7" version we had fallen in love with all those years ago. And yes, it does matter; make it genuine, for fuck's sake. This sometimes even happens on Radio 2's otherwise-irreproachable *Pick of the Pops*, whose presenters should, you would think, know what they're doing. You could be driving around, happily singing along, when up jumps a verse you've never heard before, or the instrumental break goes on four bars longer than it should and, suddenly, nothing can be trusted. They sometimes even use remixes. Yes, *remixes*. Someone says: *We need 'Ever So Lonely' by Monsoon*; so some junior minion does a search and clicks on whatever comes up with the right title. Three minutes later, we're yelling at the radio; and they're thinking *blimey - no wonder this doesn't get played much*. And there's never even a whiff of an apology.

Yet, despite the grumbles, this new digital world was capable of being astonishing. I was awestruck when I first visited a friend with broadband. I still had a squawky dial-up internet connection which loaded still pictures at snail's pace. But my friend could watch YouTube. I had never seen YouTube before. Suddenly I could watch clips of music performances that it had been beyond my wildest dreams to access. I could do a search for 'Wig Wam Bam' and, a matter of seconds later, find myself in front of the Sweet on *Top of the Pops* in 1972. Mind-blowing doesn't come close. Our under-considered region got broadband in 2012.

Soon, a modest digital revolution had taken place in our house - we finally had broadband; we finally had a digital radio. I was listening to Radio 2 with clarity; plus, I now had access to the BBC's digital-only, serious music station 6 Music. I was buying music online, checking out new tracks via thirty-second preview clips. If I liked one, I bought it on the spot. I had occasionally known record shops with listening posts, but this was even better. So I didn't actually have to listen to the radio at all.

There's a mate up the road who's into his music and his music gadgets. We occasionally meet for a beer in town and swap notes. One of our regular haunts used to put bands on in the upstairs room. We were there one Friday night in the summer of 2013, watching four guys in leather waistcoats and big hair doing rock covers. Fewer than ten people came in and not many of them stayed for more than a few minutes. We sat down and gave them a bit of support. They did things like 'All Right Now' and 'Feel Like Makin' Love'. They enjoyed themselves.

During the interval the front-man came over to chat. It turned out they were semi-pro and usually played in front of decent crowds. We talked about other songs from that classic rock period. It was during this conversation that he used the phrase "heritage music".

I hadn't heard it before. The implications seemed obvious, but the casual use of it felt shocking. It brought certain things into sudden, sharp relief. The music of that classic era - the vinyl era, if you like, *my era* – had been assigned to a historical period. It was part of the past, just as much as any Spitfire, penny-farthing, or suit of armour. Of course, I knew this deep down. I saw evidence everywhere but until now it had gone unsaid. Not only was it now said, but it was understood. This guy's band had been formed for the specific purpose of dishing it up.

I now began hearing echoes of this everywhere. It was pointed out on TV by Danny Baker that all the classic rock albums incorporating Jimi Hendrix, Led Zeppelin, Black Sabbath, Pink Floyd and a wealth of others, from *Are You Experienced?* to *Dark Side of the Moon*, as well as the all-time great soul LPs by Stevie Wonder, Marvin Gaye, Curtis Mayfield and Sly & the Family Stone to name but a few, came out in a period of just seven extraordinary years to 1973. Just seven.

That was forty years ago now. The time between now and then was the same as that between 1973 and 1933, when George V was king, Winston Churchill was warning people about German rearmament, and Elvis Presley hadn't even been conceived.

It was said that music was no longer a platform for protest and rebellion, no longer a conductor for social change, but something subsumed into the commercial landscape: a set of separate, manageable products driven by market forces. We were told that nobody even spoke about the charts anymore. *Top of the Pops* had stopped broadcasting seven years previously because of plummeting viewing figures and despite a succession of re-vamps; *Melody Maker*, *Sounds* and *Record Mirror* had long since folded, and the *NME* was still chugging along only because of revenue streams in areas other than print.

Punk, heavy metal, mod and even new romantic, had become respectable everyday fashion lines. You could adopt any of these looks, picking components off the peg in the high street without offending anybody. A friend's son adopted a punk look a few years ago, with studded wristbands and a tall, spiky, bright blue Mohican. None of it prevented him getting work on a supermarket checkout or serving in a well-known coffee house chain. It's all heritage. As threatening as a *Blue Peter* badge.

A year earlier, London had hosted the Olympic Games. The opening ceremony showcased Britain's cultural wealth, with popular music an integral component along with literature, entertainment, industrial innovation and technology. Its soundtrack comprised pop hits spanning almost half a century, from the explosive 1963 number two 'My Boy Lollipop' by Millie to the wonderful 2010 number one 'Pass Out' by Tinie Tempah. It also included 'Pretty Vacant' by the Sex Pistols. The night ended with Paul McCartney leading a worldwide singalong to 'Hey Jude'.

The closing ceremony was nothing less than a music party in costume, with various expressions of Britishness accompanied by a torrent of pop and of pop stars, including performances by the Spice Girls, Fatboy Slim and Madness. A troupe of mods rode through the stadium on scooters.

This was the stuff of national identity that counted now. Shakespeare, Newton and Brunel were taking a back seat to the Duran Duran, Queen and the Who. Cool Britannia indeed. There had been a lot of negativity in the build-up to the Games, much of it justified; but that was almost entirely swept away. And here were most of the originators of that heritage - still with us, still performing, still making the world see the union jack and smile.

'Pass Out' by Tinie Tempah was a rap record, but a demonstratively British one, characterful, humorous and self-deprecating - in 2010 it had been delightfully fresh. Its inclusion inferred that pop was very much an ongoing story. But for most onlookers, this was no more than a gesture. Few had heard anything new recently that they genuinely liked. Not many even knew what was in the charts nowadays. New music didn't matter enough. New musical personalities didn't matter enough. Once, music people had been the barometers of social change; their opinions had been sought on everything because theirs were the opinions that counted. Now it was more likely to be the stars of soap operas and reality TV that got asked. When it came to music, the past was where the action was.

And it wasn't even action in its own right. It was often a mere component in the action of others. TV programmes were now using carefully-chosen oldies with the vocals removed so that, as you watched the glazed pork being triumphantly produced from the oven, your reaction was enhanced by the sound of something that felt great and was somehow familiar. Music we loved was being chopped up and re-styled to match somebody's design idea; no longer a standalone piece of work, but an adornment.

I have seen favourite after favourite denigrated in this way; used as the soundtrack for a smug corporate TV ad ('Crockett's Theme' by Jan Hammer), or to accompany the slapstick finale in an animated movie ('I'm a Believer' by the Monkees), or as the signature for a comedy character in a sketch show ('Moonlight Shadow' by Mike Oldfield). Steve Lamacq has been using 'Red River Rock' by Johnny and the Hurricanes as incidental music - *incidental music* - on his teatime 6 Music programme. And he's not the only offender in this category, not even on 6 Music. Some records now require detoxifying before you can enjoy them again.

My feathers have been equally ruffled by the business of "re-evaluating a band's legacy". Of course, we all change our minds about things and it is standard practise for an artist to be dismissed for decades before becoming properly appreciated – just look at Van Gogh. But do me a favour: when someone mentions a band we all remember being slagged off for years and says "perhaps it's time to re-evaluate their legacy" - even if they're being a bit tongue-in-cheek - always be suspicious. It's often no more than a pretext for the next lot of magazine articles, TV documentaries, podcasts, immersion-boxset reissues and reunion tours - as well for a surge in demand for original copies. There's only so much rock and pop history to go around, and nobody's really interested in anything new, so let's choose some old bollocks and re-launch it. It's like hitting on the latest inner-city area to be gentrified – who would have thought it would be *that* postcode?

I hope I live long enough to see the re-evaluation of the Outhere Brothers and Snoop Dogg. At least they shook things up a bit and put people's noses out of joint. Now that rock 'n' roll has become part of the establishment it seems impossible to find anything that will perform that rebellious role. Everything has a niche, and within its niche nothing is out of place or shocking. It's all contained.

That doesn't mean I never get excited. Even past the age of forty, I found new records to properly obsess about: 'Too Little Too Late' by Jojo in 2007, 'Bang Bang Bang' by Mark Ronson and the Business Intl. in 2010, 'Starships' by Nicki Minaj in 2012, 'The Mother We Share' by Chvrches in 2013; and so on, right up to 'He's 31' by Geowulf in 2019. When these things landed on me, it was (almost) like being fifteen again. Couldn't get enough of them.

Yet my annoyance keeps simmering away. I promised I'd come back to guest rappers, didn't I? The moment has come. How many perfectly good records have been sullied by some bloke butting in to tell you how great he is when they could easily have had another verse instead? Why don't they piss off and make their own records? Listen to 'Dark Horse' by Katy Perry for a prime example. Juicy J (rapper names – let's not even go there) turns up to tarnish what is actually one of Ms Perry's better efforts, starting with the announcement: "It's Katy Perry". Yeh, we know that, son - we clicked on a Katy Perry track. There are loads of others. How does Kanye West improve 'Talk About Our Love' by Brandy? What on earth do Bun B and Slim Thug bring to 'Check on It' by Beyoncé? Thank God there's a "no rap" version on the CD single.

Then there's the way that the advent of the MP3 has sent the price of headphones rocketing. In my day, a set of headphones to fit your stack system cost £20 - and that was when you wanted to splash out. Now, of course, everyone listens to their music in a personalised bubble, and so headphones have replaced amps and speakers as the premium accessory. They want £70 just for something basic and with half-arsed sound quality. My kids scoff at the very thought of a set of headphones costing less than £150. Are they mad? That's about eighteen months' worth of prescription charges.

One day, my nano stopped interfacing properly with iTunes. Having made two long calls to Apple support, I decided to visit the cathedralic Apple store in our nearest big town to ask for help. A huge white guy with trailing dreadlocks and an air of spiritual exhaustion responded to my smile as if it was the least interesting thing he'd had to do all day. I told him what I wanted to do, with which devices and in what way. His response: *Nobody uses that anymore; that's no longer being updated; that doesn't really exist these days; no one listens to music that way now.* I left the store with my head bowed. Within weeks we had a family membership of streaming service Spotify. And despite my fears, it turned out that all those MP3s I had created by digitising my vinyl and uploading CDs didn't go to waste - they showed up in Spotify as "local files", ready to be used. So on top of everything else, I could play songs through Spotify that Spotify didn't have.

Both of my kids are teenagers now, and their entire entertainment world is online. They both scroll down lists, clicking on whatever looks interesting - just like I do. My daughter, who is older, uses "recommended" lists, following suggestions based on what she has selected recently, which is something I rail against, keeping you as it does in a narrow channel of experience. Say what you like about Mike Read, but on the Radio 1 *Breakfast Show* back in the day he played me Adam and the Ants followed by Stevie Wonder followed by Talking Heads. People who liked one of these sometimes liked all of them.

I asked her how, in that case, she would ever get into different music. I was told that between them platforms push various music types. TikTok is a website for video clips taken on phones, into which music is edited, providing a buffet of new sounds with (apparently) no copyright issues because the clips are so short. She looks at TikTok a lot and, if a tune catches her ear, she investigates. If her ear is similarly caught while she's out shopping, she uses the Shazam app.

Shazam is one of the wonders of the modern world. Fire it up on your phone, point it towards where the music is playing, and it tells you what the track is. Once, I was in town and having to wait in a ladies' underwear department when this fantastic song started coming out of the speakers in the ceiling. Whenever this had happened before, I had gone bounding up to an assistant in the belief they could identify it for me. But this had never worked out. Either they genuinely didn't know, or they were so disturbed by a middle-aged man bounding up and asking about pop music that all they could think about was making it stop.

So instead, stuck in the underwear department with no one to turn to, my only course of action seemed to be to slip my phone out, fire up the camera, and start to film the floor, hoping to get the song into the mic. Middle-aged men take a big risk when they choose to video busy underwear departments, but such was the allure of the track that I held my nerve. Back home, with the help of Shazam, my daughter managed to identify the trigger for this behaviour as 'Lost Lions' by Priest, a song that our family now identifies with cherished holiday memories. And one day I downloaded Shazam to my own phone.

KSI is a rapper who used to be a YouTuber. My son looks out for news about him, mainly on YouTube. He uses Shazam when he's out. He spends ages scrolling down new music playlists on Spotify to find other stuff. Spotify provides new music alerts and presents various lists of fresh and current releases. This seems to prove something I have said ever since I first heard someone declare that the chart no longer matters: if the singles chart didn't exist, it would have to be invented. He asks his sister about things he hears coming from her room. One of these recently was 'The Runner' by the Three Degrees, from 1979, which she heard me play on vinyl one night and pointed Shazam at. He thinks 'The Runner' is a lit bop.

Which makes me instrumental in their music world, although, I suppose, not essential. Music has always been more important to some kids than others. Some enjoy a wider range of music than others. Some stay largely within a scene that serves to define them. And they nearly all look at charts, their judgements influenced by the relative position of songs therein. So things haven't changed that much.

Both of our kids can use the turntables and the mixer. They can pick through my vinyl and form opinions on what they hear, although, surprisingly, a lot of it they already know. I am constantly amazed at the familiarity of youngsters with relatively minor hits from back in the mists, because they've been used in an advert, in a movie, or in the overture to a video game and they pointed Shazam at it. As a result of a computer game my son is now into the Sweet - the heavier stuff, he's yet to be convinced about 'Co-Co'. And yet both kids have successfully maintained a united front in slagging off whatever I happen to be playing when they enter the room.

This, however, works both ways. I've swapped notes with my peer group on this and there does seem to come a point when you listen to a chart run-down, often with a fully-engaged youngster sitting close by in the car, and, with an air of superiority, think: *This all sounds the same.* It happened to me around 2014. I continued to enjoy various chart hits thereafter, but new popular music seemed to have developed a feature-lite uniformity whose synthetic coating made me struggle to respect any positive appreciation of it.

There are nevertheless some pleasing elements, including the fact that the rhythms of the chart are now a lot closer to something that I as a teenager would have recognised. The migration from physical sales to downloads, and then from downloads to streaming, have enabled new releases to give an account of themselves that reflects the actual rise and fall of their popularity. And of course the numbers are therefore huge, and have been since it all moved online, proving how important new music remains to young people. And putting the Tomcraft crisis firmly into perspective.

To add to which, vinyl is cool again. Youngsters are buying turntables and enjoying the physical experience of playing records. Those HMV stores that continue to trade have large vinyl sections, with new releases as well as all-time classics on their shelves. Collectors' shops have New Vinyl sections, with latest missives from the coolest and trendiest in delightfully sturdy and heavy packaging. Even some fashion retailers have a little corner offering LPs by Billie Eilish or Dua Lipa in exciting coloured vinyl.

In a period of time equivalent to that between 'Like a Virgin' and 'Like a Prayer', I will be in my sixties. It doesn't bother me unduly. We are all capable of accepting the changes that come with ageing. But we also want to go on nourishing the things that gave our younger selves the most pleasure, excitement and belonging - to continue experiencing echoes of the thrill. This is harder to achieve.

There's pressure at work, which may include having a job that will still be there next year; providing for children, which may include being able to have them in the first place; the decline and death of your parents, relationship break-ups, illness, environmental concerns and a vision of the future which may sometimes seem nothing but bleak and defeat-ridden - all these things become harder to balance out with a brilliant new song. There have been a few times when listening to music at all has felt, well, *inappropriate*.

But there are more subtle corrosions at work. When you have finally decided what you want to do, where you want to do it and with whom, there's a layer of energy that seeps away. Being settled and contented removes the drama - good and bad. Pop doesn't sound quite the same then. For me, this draining of intensity is mirrored in the changes to the language I have used over the years when raving about records. This once went from "neat", to "fucking brilliant", and from there on to "wicked". Then I became settled and contented. I now refer to lit bops as "well-executed and worthwhile".

When I was a schoolboy, South London was a landscape of dilapidated Victorian housing, badly maintained 60s estates and poorly secured bomb sites, all demarcated with rusting wire fences and corrugated iron. When I set off for the record shop, this is what I passed.

It wasn't Hell; it was home, it was what I knew. I had to be alert; dog shit was everywhere, piles of fly-tipped furniture and fridges colonised clumps of pavement, muggings and kickings could burst on you out of the blue. But the record shop was at the other end of the journey; that single that I'd not been able to get off my mind since I heard it days ago was waiting for me there. There was romance in getting through all that ugliness for something beautiful. Now when I hear a new tune I like, I tap my phone three times and it's in my library.

Everything's so clean and tame. The coolest thing you can get is if the gig sponsors are guys with hipster beards who used locally-sourced ingredients to make the beer. That's if you make it to a gig. Now I'm this age, this is never straightforward. Because music is available so cheaply online, live appearances are ever more vital in helping an act to make a living. I feel guilty about not going to more gigs.

A few years ago, I tried to see a blary guitar act called Honeyblood, who came to our nearest big town in support of their terrific album *Babes Never Die*. I had to drive there and needed to be in work at 7.30 the next morning. I tried repeatedly to get the stage times – but the internet wouldn't yield them and nobody would pick up the phone anywhere. So I arrived at 7pm, not wanting to miss anything. I was then told Honeyblood weren't on until 9.45. I went to the bar and had the one pint I was going to allow myself. An hour later, I had finished it. I had watched everything on YouTube I could stand via my phone. I was bored and nodding off. So I went home.

But I'm sure there'll be more gigs. One day. Perhaps we'll get a chalet at one of those comfy festivals. Then I can have a nap in the afternoon if I need one, and be able to last to the end of Echobelly or the Primitives in the evening. Maybe Honeyblood will be there. In the meanwhile, Radcliffe and Maconie are doing the weekend breakfast shows on 6 Music and I'm on a B-sides odyssey, finding treasure on the shamefully high percentage of flips I've never played.

All this convenience suits pop fans of our vintage – the comfy festivals, the tailored media, the range of hats available for concealing our bald patches when we venture out, the continuing facilitation of vinyl running alongside access to all the heritage music we could want on streaming services. I could go on exploring that rich 1967-73 period without ever exhausting it. There's loads of stuff from other periods that I've yet to listen to properly.

We can have all this while continuing to compare ourselves to the younger generation, realising, if we're honest, that things change, but don't change that much. One day they'll be like us (although don't for heaven's sake tell them that). They too will find that the things they know most about, that they have the strongest emotional attachment to, that energises them the most and makes them feel most fully themselves, is that which comes through the time machine.

Because the time machine can still work. Its potency may be threatened by the over-exposure of golden hits, by the corruption of their context in the cause of corporate advertising and television mood-setting, not to mention by the relentless scramble for things to talk about and link on social media. But a record can still whisk you back through time and space. When it wants to. You might hear a special oldie four, five times and it does nothing; but then the next time, all at once, *bang* - like a magic-eye picture suddenly slipping into focus. I can get the original tingles, the anticipation, the thrill; with no use for it all now because I'm this number of years on. But I get it. I have those associations. My memory is organised into parades of records. I can think back to any moment in my young life and have a pile of images and sounds come tumbling instantly into my head.

I can *see* the autumn of 1974. It's 'All of Me Loves All of You' by the Bay City Rollers and I'm sitting by the water fountains with the nicest girl in the primary school; she's smiling at me and I haven't a clue what to do next. I can *feel* the early summer of 1984. It's 'Automatic' by the Pointer Sisters and I'm waiting outside the exam hall; I know I've done enough revision but there are two subjects I am praying not to see on that paper. I can *smell* the spring of 1990. It's 'De-Luxe' by Lush and I'm in a car on the Fulham Palace Road with the windows down and the song blasting, and knowing for a fact that nobody in the world is better off than I am right now.

Acknowledgements

The author wishes to recognise the writers of the lyrics used in this book and the relevant copyright holders.

The songs, in order of appearance, are: '(Hey You) The Rock Steady Crew' written by Stephen Hague/Ruza Blue/Budd Dixon, © Charisma Music Publishing Co Ltd; 'This Charming Man' written by Steven Morrissey/Johnny Marr, © Warner Chappell Music, Inc, Universal Music Publishing Group; 'Michael Caine' written by Cathal Smyth / Christopher Foreman /Daniel Woodgate /Graham McPherson /Lee Thompson /Mark Bedford /Michael Barson, © Sony/ATV Music Publishing LLC; 'Relax' written by P. Gill/H. Johnson/M. O'Toole, © Sony/ATV Harmony. Perfect Songs Ltd., C-Water Publishing Inc., Perfect Songs Ltd; 'The Ballad of Chris and Judith' written by Alexei Sayle, © Alexei Sayle; 'Ghostbusters' written by Ray Parker Jr., © Sony/ATV Music Publishing LLC, Songtrust Ave, Ray Parker Jr Dba Raydiola Music; 'The Power of Love' written by Brian Philip Nash/ Holly Johnson/Mark William O'Toole/Peter Gill/Rudy Perez, © Universal Music Publishing Group, BMG Rights Management; 'Do They Know It's Christmas' written by Bob Geldof/Midge Ure, © Warner Chappell Music, Inc; 'Like a Virgin' written by Billy Steinberg /Tom Kelly, © Sony/ATV Music Publishing LLC; 'One Vision' written by Brian May/Freddie Mercury/John Deacon/Roger Taylor,

The author additionally recognises the writer(s) of the song that may or may not have been called 'Frontloader', as performed on the fringe Crap Stage at the 1994 Reading Festival.

317

The author also recognises that Crater Critters are an original set of popular toys produced by the Rosenhain and Lipman (R&L) company of Melbourne, Australia.

Thanks

I am once again indebted to Kerstin Muggeridge for giving me an imprint to use. Thanks is also due to Ashford's of Exeter for their legal advice and to SW1 of Wellington for their production knowhow. Finally, I am grateful to my partner Sarah for her editorial expertise, her determination with technology and her patience.